Massachusetts's Criminal Justice System

Carolina Academic Press

State-Specific Criminal Justice Series

Criminal Justice Basics and Concerns

William G. Doerner, ed.

Alabama's Criminal Justice System

Vicki Lindsay and Jeffrey P. Rush, eds.

Arkansas's Criminal Justice System

Edward Powers and Janet K. Wilson

California's Criminal Justice System

Third Edition

Christine L. Gardiner and Georgia Spiropoulos, eds.

Florida's Criminal Justice System

Second Edition

William G. Doerner

Georgia's Criminal Justice System

Deborah Mitchell Robinson

Illinois's Criminal Justice System

Jill Joline Myers and Todd Lough, eds.

Maryland's Criminal Justice System

Debra L. Stanley, ed.

Massachusetts's Criminal Justice System
Lorenzo M. Boyd and Francesca Spina

Minnesota's Criminal Justice System
Jeff Bumgarner, Susan Hilal, and James Densley

Missouri's Criminal Justice System
Frances P. Reddington, ed.

New York's Criminal Justice System
Robert Costello

North Carolina's Criminal Justice System
Second Edition
Paul E. Knepper and Mark Jones

Ohio's Criminal Justice System
Joshua B. Hill, Nancy E. Marion, Kevin M. Cashen, R. James Orr, III, and Kendra J. Kec

Pennsylvania's Criminal Justice System
Mary P. Brewster and Harry R. Dammer, eds.

Texas's Criminal Justice System
Durant Frantzen and Marshall Lloyd

West Virginia's Criminal Justice System
Second Edition
Kimberly A. DeTardo-Bora, Dhruba J. Bora, and Wendy Perkins

Massachusetts's Criminal Justice System

Lorenzo M. Boyd
Associate Professor and Director of the
Center of Advanced Policing
Henry C. Lee College of Criminal Justice and
Forensic Sciences, University of New Haven

Francesca Spina
Assistant Professor and Chair
Department of Social Sciences, Springfield College

With contributions by
James Forrest

Carolina Academic Press
Durham, North Carolina

See catalog.loc.gov for Library of Congress Cataloging-in-Publication Data

ISBN: 978-1-61163-657-4
eISBN: 978-1-5310-0352-4

Carolina Academic Press, LLC
700 Kent Street
Durham, North Carolina 27701
Telephone (919) 489-7486
Fax (919) 493-5668
www.cap-press.com

Printed in the United States of America

Contents

Series Note

Carolina Academic Press's state-specific criminal justice series fills a gap in the field of criminal justice education. One drawback with many current introduction to criminal justice texts is that they pertain to the essentially non-existent "American" criminal justice system and ignore the local landscape. Each state has its unique legislature, executive branch, law enforcement system, court and appellate review system, state supreme court, correctional system, and juvenile justice apparatus. Since many criminal justice students embark upon careers in their home states, they are better served by being exposed to their own states' criminal justice systems. Texts in this series are designed to be used as primary texts or as supplements to more general introductory criminal justice texts.

Preface

Context is important when exploring the criminal justice (CJ) system. It provides a historic lens through which students can explore its many complexities. Context is particularly important when studying the criminal justice system in a state as steeped in history and nuance as the Commonwealth of Massachusetts. So it's from this historic perspective that this book is written with the hope of putting events, developments, and the formation of agencies into a context that will give a big picture view of *Massachusetts's Criminal Justice System.*

The *Massachusetts's Criminal Justice System* takes a historic look at crime, justice, and society's response to crime. British common law, a fugitive slave trial, the origins of probation, high profile executions, and the first-in-the-nation policing are covered. The historic context helps the reader understand the development of each area of criminal justice and how this all guides what is now policy and practice in the criminal justice system in Massachusetts.

As we highlight the historic content of the criminal justice system, we do so with an eye toward emerging issues and the future. With the Boston Marathon bombing as the backdrop, we partnered with our friend and former colleague, James J. F. Forest, PhD, to give an overview of the issue, threat, and response to terrorism in Massachusetts. Dr. Forest is the director of the Security Studies graduate degree program and the Center for Terrorism and Security Studies at UMass Lowell. He is also a senior fellow with the Joint Special Operations University, where he conducts research on emerging terrorist threats, insurgencies, transnational criminal networks, and U.S. Special Forces training.

The purpose of this book is to introduce the reader to the complexities of the criminal justice system in the Commonwealth of Massachusetts in a way that they can relate to. Because nothing happens in a vacuum, understanding how we got to where we are in the system is important. History often sets the stage for future rulings and actions.

Chapter 1 is an overview of the entire book and sets up the reader with information on the evolution of the criminal justice system. How did we get here from there? The book explains the basic foundations of criminal justice, starting with the evolution of the CJ system and crime trends in Massachusetts. A special added feature is profiles of prominent practitioners and their views of the commonwealth's criminal justice system.

Chapter 2 allows students to become critical consumers of information, as the overview of crime trends, crime data, and responses to crime are explained. This chapter looks at the UCR and NCVS data with national trends and trends in Massachusetts. The book looks at various index crimes and explores crime trends in major cities in the commonwealth.

Chapter 3 introduces students to the beginnings of policing and how it has developed into the multi-jurisdictional agencies that we see today. The chapter starts with the difference between policing and law enforcement and moves into the formation of modern day policing. A distinction is drawn between local, state, and transit police and the county sheriff's departments. This chapter also examines the merger of several state police agencies and ways to join the force.

Chapter 4 begins where Chapter 2 ends, with the explanation of index crimes but with a deeper explanation. This chapter illustrates the local, state, and federal laws that are all in play in Massachusetts. We also look at how laws are created and the distinctions between criminal and civil laws as well as procedural versus substantive laws. This chapter also covers the biggest fugitive slave trial in the state—the 1854 case of escaped slave Anthony Burns.

Chapter 5 walks students through the many complex levels of the court system. This chapter will allow students to become familiar with the structure of the courts, the actors in the courts, and the events that occur before, during, and after a trial in Massachusetts. In addition, students will also learn about the role of specialty courts in Massachusetts and a special ruling from the High Court about people of color fleeing the police.

Chapter 6 includes all of the institutions and methods used to punish, control, and change the behavior of convicted offenders. These institutions and methods include jails, houses of corrections, prisons, probation, parole, and intermediate sanctions. We will discuss the purposes of sentencing and why we punish offenders. We will explore the historic prisons in Massachusetts including the Charlestown State Prison whose more notable inmates included Sacco and Vanzetti and Malcolm X. This chapter also notes the last execution in the Commonwealth of Massachusetts.

Chapter 7 explains how the juvenile justice system differs from the adult criminal justice system. Specifically, it covers the evolution of the juvenile justice system, delinquency, juvenile crime rates, juvenile court processing, and juvenile corrections throughout the Commonwealth of Massachusetts. This chapter will also cover juvenile waivers to adult court and diversion programs.

Chapter 8 shines a spotlight on the often overlooked victims and how they play a large role in the criminal justice system. Many crimes involve an individual who has been victimized by an offender. However, until the 1970s, the criminal justice system did not pay much attention to the rights of victims. We will discuss how legislation has impacted victims, and this chapter will also cover victim compensation and various services the criminal justice system provides to victims throughout the commonwealth.

Chapter 9 seems to be ripped from the front pages of current news. With the Boston Marathon bombing as a backdrop, this chapter examines the broad spectrum of terrorist threats related to the Commonwealth of Massachusetts. We define terrorism and terrorist ideologies and then review the contemporary nature of "do it yourself" terrorist attacks. This chapter examines the kinds of targets modern terrorists might be interested in and how Massachusetts is responding to the threat of terrorism. The chapter concludes with recommendations for collaborations for effectively reducing the likelihood of terrorist attacks in Massachusetts.

Chapter 10 describes employment trends and the future of criminal justice in Massachusetts. Employment in criminal justice offers stable growth opportunities to work in law enforcement, the courts, or corrections. Throughout this chapter, you will learn about some opportunities to work in the criminal justice system within the Commonwealth of Massachusetts. This book will help students become critical consumers of information as they map out their future as change agents in the criminal justice system.

Chapter 11 describes the ever-changing evolution of the criminal justice system. Societal, political, economic, and technological changes create new types of crime, and members of the criminal justice system must adapt accordingly. In this chapter, we will focus on several of the challenges that are shaping the future of our criminal justice system—cybercrimes, forensic evidence, environmental justice, and the legalization of marijuana.

We hope this book will give readers a more complete understanding of Massachusetts's criminal justice system—how it began, how the different components fit together, and how it may evolve from here.

Lorenzo M. Boyd
Francesca Spina
July 30, 2018

Figures and Tables

Massachusetts's Criminal Justice System

Chapter 1

Introduction to the Massachusetts Criminal Justice System

Learning Objectives

- Familiarize yourself with the primary components of the criminal justice system.
- Learn about the evolution of the criminal justice system.
- Understand the role of federalism within the criminal justice system.
- Learn about the formal and informal criminal process.
- Compare the crime control model with the due process model.
- Familiarize yourself with the structure of this book.

Introduction

Welcome to *Massachusetts's Criminal Justice System.* This text is part of the series of state-specific criminal justice books published by Carolina Academic Press. It provides a comprehensive overview of the Massachusetts criminal justice system. Intended for both undergraduate students and the general public, this book teaches about the history, purpose, structure, procedures, and possible future of the criminal justice system in the Commonwealth of Massachusetts. Each chapter of the book focuses on a different element of the criminal justice system and the aspects that make the criminal justice system in Massachusetts different from other states. In addition to the core elements of law enforcement, courts, and corrections, the book also describes criminal laws unique to the Commonwealth of Massachusetts. These topics include the juvenile justice system, victims' rights, the threat of terrorism, employment trends, and a conclusion that includes a discussion on cybercrime, emergency management, and environmental justice.

It is important for all criminal justice students to be familiar with the criminal justice system and how it operates. The ***criminal justice system*** is the set of agencies and processes that the government establishes to control crime and penalize people who have violated the law (The National Center for Victims of Crime, 2008). This set of agencies is responsible for protecting the public, maintaining order, enforcing the law, trying defendants in court, and correcting criminal behavior. Note that the criminal justice system is not just one system, but rather it is composed of many individual systems depending on its ***jurisdiction***, or power to govern an area. Consequently, the criminal justice system can operate at the local, county, state, or federal level. Each jurisdiction has its own set of laws, agencies, and procedures. The purpose of this book is for you to learn about the criminal laws, agencies, and procedures that are specific to Massachusetts.

The majority of Introduction to Criminal Justice courses discuss the different components of the criminal justice system, including law enforcement, the courts, corrections, and the juvenile justice system. However, most introductory courses do not adequately address how local and state criminal justice systems operate. Therefore, this text is designed to fill in those gaps and help students and the public learn about the criminal justice system and how it operates within the boundaries of the Commonwealth of Massachusetts. In this chapter, we provide an overview of some of the topics you will be learning about throughout the book, including the structure of the criminal justice system, the criminal justice process, and crime trends in Massachusetts.

The Evolution of the Criminal Justice System

Crime and violence have existed in the United States for over 200 years. For example, our nation has experienced the Revolutionary War and the Civil War, and we have a long history of gun violence. In addition, the early 20th century was controlled by Depression-era outlaws who paved the way for organized crime families. These crime families spread throughout urban areas across the nation, including New York City, Philadelphia, and Chicago (Siegel, 2011).

The increase in crime families and criminal gangs gave rise to the beginning of the formal criminal justice system. The London Metropolitan Police was the first professional police department (PD) in the world, and it was established in 1829. Our nation's metropolitan areas began modeling their police departments after London's, starting with Boston in 1838. Also, the first penitentiary in the United States, the Eastern State Penitentiary, opened its doors in Philadelphia in 1829 (Eastern State Penitentiary, n.d.). The purpose of the penitentiary was to provide correctional treatment for convicted offenders. Shortly after, penitentiaries began opening across the nation, and they paved the way for modern day prisons.

Our nation's criminal justice system has continued to evolve since the first half of the 20th century. It is now considered a means of ***social control***, and it plays a pivotal role in regulating individual and group behavior through both informal and formal means. Specifically, agencies in the criminal justice system try to prevent or control illegal behavior by arresting, adjudicating, and sanctioning individuals who break the law.

The contemporary criminal justice system is comprised of three main components—law enforcement, the courts, and corrections. Law enforcement investigates crimes and apprehends suspects, the courts oversee trials and determine sentences, and correctional institutions supervise and rehabilitate convicted offenders. These agencies will be discussed in further detail in Chapter 3 (policing), 5 (courts), and 6 (corrections), but we will give you an overview of the three components in the section below.

The Structure of the Criminal Justice System

The criminal justice system operates under the concept of ***federalism***, whereby government powers are shared by the federal government and the state governments. The framers of the U.S. Constitution decided to use the idea of federalism as the basis of the laws in our nation so that the federal government would not become too powerful. The U.S. Constitution gave our federal government certain powers, such as coining money, regulating interstate commerce, and raising an army (U.S. Const. art. I, §8). However, the Tenth Amendment to the U.S. Constitution states that all powers not delegated to the federal government are reserved for the states (U.S. Const. amend. X). Thus, the states can enact laws related to the health, safety, and welfare of their citizens.

Police

The concept of federalism is seen in local, state, and federal law enforcement agencies. At the local level, police are responsible for investigating crime, deterring crime, keeping the peace, and providing social services within their particular jurisdiction (e.g., Boston Police Department, Lowell PD, or Springfield PD). At the state level, police have the authority to conduct criminal investigations and other law enforcement activities throughout the state (e.g., Massachusetts State Police, Connecticut State Police, or New York State Police). Finally, federal law enforcement agencies operate and have jurisdiction throughout the entire nation (e.g., Federal Bureau of Investigation, Department of Homeland Security, or Drug Enforcement Administration). Federal agencies often work with state or local agencies to help solve regional crimes.

Courts

In the United States, we have a ***dual court system*** with two administratively separate systems—one at the federal level and one at the state level. Thus, there are 52 separate court systems, including the federal system, one for each of the 50 states and one for the District of Columbia (Gaines & Miller, 2016). Usually, defendants who have violated federal criminal laws are tried in federal court, while defendants who have violated state criminal laws are tried in a state court within the state they are accused. We will discuss the court system that is unique to Massachusetts in Chapter 5.

Corrections

After the court system has sentenced an offender, he or she is then under the supervision of the correctional system. Individuals convicted in federal court will be under the supervision of the federal correctional system, while those convicted in a state court will be under the supervision of the state in which they were convicted.

Based on the severity of the crime and individual factors, a person who is convicted of a crime can receive a variety of ***sanctions***, including probation, jail, or prison. ***Probation*** is the most common sanction, whereby the offender remains in the community under the supervision of a probation officer. The offender has certain conditions that he must adhere to while on probation, and if he fails to abide by these rules, he may face incarceration.

Other offenders are sentenced to incarceration in jail or a prison. ***Jails*** typically operate at the county level, and they hold people who are awaiting trial or offenders convicted of misdemeanors or less serious offenses. On the other hand, individuals convicted of more serious crimes will be housed in ***prison***. In Chapter 6, you will learn more about the correctional system within Massachusetts.

Figure 1.1 Overview of the Criminal Process

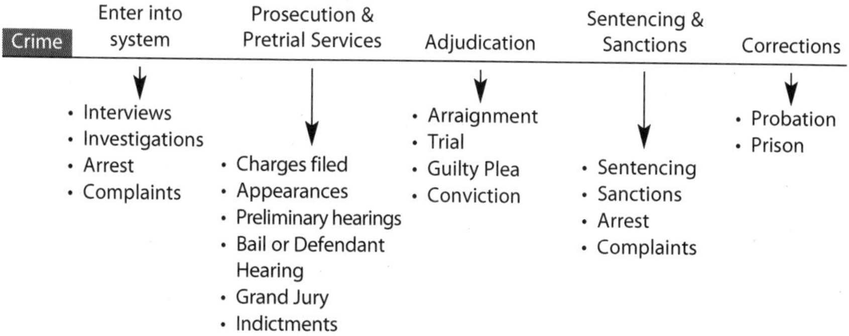

Source: "A brief description of the federal criminal justice system" by Federal Bureau of Investigation, n.d. Retrieved from https://www.fbi.gov/resources/victim-assistance/a-brief-description-of-the-federal-criminal-justice-process.

The Criminal Justice Process

In this book, you will not only learn about the agencies that are involved in the criminal justice system but also the criminal process. Throughout this process, members of the criminal justice system determine if an offender should remain in the system or be dismissed without further action. The formal process begins with a crime taking place and, if taken to the end of the process, finishes with an offender completing his sentence and returning to society (see Figure 1.1). You will be learning about this process in further depth throughout the remainder of the book.

It is important to note that very few cases are administered through the entirety of the formal process due to a lack of resources. For example, there are not enough police officers to give a speeding ticket to everyone who speeds, and there is not sufficient time for every case to go to trial. Consequently, the criminal process is influenced by individual ***discretion***, or the authority of criminal justice practitioners to choose what should be done in a particular situation. Altogether, these discretionary decisions made by members of the criminal justice system create an informal criminal justice process.

For instance, sometimes cases are dropped at the early stages of the process because there is insufficient evidence to identify a suspect, or a ***victim*** may decide not to press charges against the alleged offender. Other times, suspects are released before trial due to insufficient evidence or procedural errors. In addition, many cases result in a ***plea bargain***, or an agreement between the prosecutor and defendant, whereby the defendant agrees to plead guilty to a charge in return for a concession from the prosecutor—usually a lesser sentence or charge. In fact, over 90% of defendants plead guilty instead of going to trial (U.S. Courts, n.d.).

Although this informal process can be beneficial in regards to resources, it has some drawbacks. Most notably, individual discretion can be influenced by personal bias, resulting in an unfair system. Unfortunately, discretionary decisions have the potential to be biased regarding race, ethnicity, gender, age, class, sexuality, or other extralegal factors.

Criminal Justice Perspectives

When considering the purpose and goals of the criminal justice system, two models are often in competition with one another—the ***crime control model*** and the ***due process model***. The crime control model focuses primarily on the right of society to be protected from crime and criminals. This model considers the purpose of the criminal justice system to punish criminals and to deter criminal behavior through the fear of punishment. According to this model, law enforcement should have limited restrictions and be able to exercise discretion when apprehending criminals.

The due process model, on the other hand, focuses on the rights of individuals to be protected from government and to provide fair treatment in the criminal process to individuals accused of a crime. This model protects the rights of the accused by restraining the power of law enforcement, the courts, and corrections. For example, everyone is entitled to their constitutional rights, including impartial hearings and competent legal counsel. According to this model, it is more important to protect people's rights than to punish people. Keeping these two models in mind throughout this book is important. Sometimes they complement each other, while other times they compete.

Crime Trends in Massachusetts

In Chapter 2, you will learn about the nature and extent of crime across the nation and in Massachusetts. In this chapter, we will examine how official crime statistics are determined and discuss the importance of these statistics. We will also examine crime trends in Massachusetts and see how they compare to the national average. Finally, we will determine if crime rates are uniform across Massachusetts or if some cities exhibit more crime than others across the commonwealth.

Juvenile Justice

In Chapter 7, you will learn about the juvenile justice system and how it differs from the adult criminal justice system in Massachusetts. You will learn about the evolution of the juvenile justice system, juvenile delinquency, juvenile crime rates, juvenile court processing, and juvenile corrections throughout the Commonwealth of Massachusetts.

Victims

Over the past several decades, the criminal justice system has been giving victims a voice in the criminal process. Although they are often overlooked, victims play a large role in the criminal justice system because most crimes involve an individual who has been harmed physically, emotionally, or financially by an offender. In Chapter 8, we will be examining some of the legislative efforts and advocacy for crime victims that has taken place in Massachusetts over the years.

Terrorism

After 9/11, there has been more attention on terrorism in Western countries, including the United States. Consequently, this book would not be complete without discussing how this topic relates to Massachusetts. In Chapter 9, you will learn about terrorism, terrorist ideologies, the targets modern terrorists might be interested in, and how Massachusetts is responding to the threat of terrorism. The chapter concludes with some recommendations for how authorities and communities can work together more effectively to reduce the likelihood of terrorist attacks in Massachusetts.

Employment Trends

In Chapter 10, you will learn about employment trends for criminal justice-related jobs in Massachusetts. Specifically, we will be discussing the prospects for a variety of careers in law enforcement, the courts, and corrections. Because you are reading this book, it is likely you will be entering the criminal justice field, so this chapter will be helpful as you begin your job search.

Key Terms

Crime Control Model: Criminal justice model that emphasizes the right of society to be protected from crime and criminals.

Criminal Justice System: Set of agencies and processes that the government establishes to control crime and penalize people who have violated the law.

Discretion: Ability of people in the criminal justice system to make decisions based on personal judgment instead of formal rules.

Dual Court System: Administratively separate court systems in the United States, consisting of the federal courts and the state courts.

Due Process Model: Criminal justice model that emphasizes the right of the individual to be protected from the power of the government.

Federalism: Division of power between federal and regional governments.

Jail: Facility operated at the county level, used to hold people awaiting trial or those who have been found guilty of misdemeanors.

Jurisdiction: Power to govern an area.

Plea Bargain: Agreement in a criminal case between the prosecutor and defendant in which the defendant agrees to plead guilty to a charge in return for a concession from the prosecutor.

Prison: Place of confinement for people convicted of serious crimes.

Probation: Type of sanction in which a convict remains in the community rather than be imprisoned.

Social Control: Enforcement of conformity by society upon its members, by law, or social pressure.

Victim: An individual who suffers physical, emotional, or financial harm as the result of a crime.

Related Websites

Mass.gov
    http://www.mass.gov/portal/
Massachusetts Court System
    http://www.mass.gov/courts/
Massachusetts Department of Correction
    https://www.mass.gov/orgs/massachusetts-department-of-correction
Massachusetts State Police
    http://www.mass.gov/eopss/agencies/msp/#.V17xMbsrLIU

Office of the Commissioner of Probation
https://www.mass.gov/info-details/learn-about-the-office-of-the-commissioner-of-probation

Review Questions

1. What are the three components of the criminal justice system? Briefly explain each of them.
2. Explain the concept of federalism and how it relates to the criminal justice system.
3. Describe how the formal and informal criminal justice systems differ.
4. What is the difference between the crime control model and the due process model?

References

Eastern State Penitentiary. (n.d.). *Timeline.* Retrieved from http://www.easternstate.org/learn/timeline.

Federal Bureau of Investigation. (n.d.). *A brief description of the federal criminal justice system.* Retrieved from https://www.fbi.gov/resources/victim-assistance/a-brief-description-of-the-federal-criminal-justice-process.

Gaines, L., & Miller, R. (2016). *Criminal justice in action: The core.* (8th ed.). Boston, MA: Cengage Learning.

Siegel, L. (2011). *Essentials of criminal justice.* (7th ed.). Boston, MA: Cengage Learning.

The National Center for Victims of Crime. (2008). *The criminal justice system.* Retrieved from https://victimsofcrime.org/help-for-crime-victims/get-help-bulletins-for-crime-victims/the-criminal-justice-system.

U.S. Courts. (n.d.). *Criminal cases.* Retrieved from http://www.uscourts.gov/about-federal-courts/types-cases/criminal-cases.

U.S. Const. amend. X

U.S. Const. art. I, §8

Chapter 2

Crime Trends in Massachusetts

Learning Objectives

- Learn about the Uniform Crime Reporting (UCR) Program.
- Recognize the importance of crime rates.
- Compare crime trends in Massachusetts to the national average for violent crimes.
- Compare crime trends in Massachusetts to the national average for property crimes.
- Examine crime trends across cities in Massachusetts.

Introduction

If you had to take a guess, would you think that crime in the nation was increasing or decreasing compared to last year? What about compared to 10 years ago? If you are like most Americans, you probably guessed that crime has been increasing in the United States. According to one study, 63% of Americans believe there is more crime than there was a year ago, while 21% think there is less crime (McCarthy, 2014). Why do people continue to think that crime is increasing when government statistics indicate that crime has been decreasing for over 20 years? It is likely that the media plays a large role in people's perceptions of crimes.

However, after reading this chapter, you will be more informed about the nature and extent of crime both across the nation and in Massachusetts. We are going to examine how official crime statistics are determined as well as how these statistics benefit criminologists and members of the criminal justice system. In addition, you will learn about the importance of crime rates versus crime counts. We are also going to examine crime trends in Massachusetts and how they compare to the national average over time. Finally, we will determine if crime rates are uniform across Massachusetts or if some cities exhibit more crime than others across the commonwealth.

Uniform Crime Reporting Program

To know how much crime we have in the nation, we have a system in place that measures crime. In the United States, the ***Uniform Crime Reporting (UCR) Program*** is one of the most well-known systems used to keep track of crimes reported to the police. The UCR is the most widely cited source of aggregate criminal justice data in the country. This system was created in 1929 by the International Association of Chiefs of Police (IACP) so that our nation would have reliable and standardized crime data. Beginning in 1930, the Federal Bureau of Investigations (FBI) began collecting and publishing these data, which are reported from police departments across the nation. Today, over 18,000 local, college, state, tribal, and federal law enforcement agencies voluntarily participate in the UCR reporting program, and the data is published annually (FBI, n.d.). This information can then be used by researchers, policy makers, and criminal justice agencies to analyze different crimes by geographic location and from year to year.

Note that the UCR does not collect and publish data on all crimes. Rather, it only tracks data on the ***Part I index crimes***. The Part I index crimes include four violent crimes (murder/nonnegligent manslaughter, rape, robbery, and aggravated assault) and four property crimes (burglary, larceny-theft, motor vehicle theft, and arson[1]). ***Violent crimes*** involve force or the threat of force, while ***property crimes*** do not. We will be examining the eight Part I index crimes in depth throughout this chapter.

Even though the UCR program is one of the most common methods of tracking crime, it does have some limitations. Most importantly, it only provides data on information that is reported to police. It does not capture what is known as the ***dark figure of crime***, or crimes that are not reported to the police. In other words, if a crime is not reported, it is as if it never happened. Research has found that over half (52%) of violent victimizations are not reported to the police (Bureau of Justice Statistics, 2012). People do not report their victimizations for a number of reasons, including fearing retaliation from the

1. Arson is not reported in this chapter because the UCR does not provide publicly available data for this crime.

offender, fearing the offender may get in trouble, believing the police would not help, or feeling their victimization was not important enough to report. Although we are not covering the National Crime Victimization Survey (NCVS) in this chapter, it is important to note that this is a survey used as a complement to the UCR to capture victimizations that go unreported to the police.

Another limitation of the UCR is that it adheres to the ***hierarchy rule***, which requires counting only the most serious offense occurring at a criminal event; everything else is referred to as a lesser included crime. For example, if an offender were committing a rape during an armed home invasion but ended up killing the victim, only the murder would be counted because it is the more serious of the listed offenses. Consequently, many offenses are not counted in the UCR because of the hierarchy rule.

Crime in Massachusetts

Now that you have a background on the UCR, let's take a look at the amount of crime in Massachusetts in 2014,[2] according to UCR data. Table 2.1 indicates that there were 151,666 Part I index crimes reported to the police in 2014. Approximately 17% of these crimes involved violent crimes, while the other 83% involved property crimes. As you would expect, murders only comprised 0.1% of the total crimes in Massachusetts in 2014, whereas larceny-thefts accounted for approximately 61% of the total crimes in the commonwealth.

Aside from considering the amount of crime, it is even more important to examine the ***crime rate***. The crime rate takes into consideration the number of crimes out of a standardized population, such as 100,000 people. For example, if you were told that both City A and City B had 200 rapes in 2014, you would not have all of the information you need. If City A has 10 million people and City B only has 50,000 people, you could conclude that City B has a much larger problem with rape. To determine the crime rate, we divide the number of crimes in a specified time frame by the population of a particular geographic area and multiply that number by a standardized measure, often 100,000. Continuing with this example, the rates of rape for each of these cities in 2014 would look like the following:

City A: (200/10,000,000) * 100,000 = 2
City B: (200/50,000) * 100,000 = 400

2. The year 2014 is the most up-to-date data made publicly available by the UCR at this time.

Table 2.1 Number, Percentage, and Rate for Crimes in MA in 2014

Crimes	Number	Percentage	Rate (per 100,000)
Total	151,666	100.0	2,248.5
Violent	26,399	17.4	391.4
Murder	132	0.1	2.0
Rape	2,180	1.4	32.3
Robbery	6,036	4.0	89.5
Aggravated Assault	18,051	11.9	267.6
Property	125,267	82.6	1,857.1
Burglary	24,964	16.5	370.1
Motor Vehicle Theft	8,260	5.4	122.5
Larceny-Theft	92,043	60.7	1,364.5

Source: FBI's UCR Data Tool. Retrieved from http://bjs.gov/ucrdata (compiled by authors).

By determining the crime rate, we can get a more accurate picture of the nature and extent of crime in an area. Looking again at Table 2.1, the Part I index crimes in Massachusetts in 2014 were committed at a rate of approximately 2,250 crimes per 100,000 people. Throughout the remainder of this chapter, we will be referring to crime rates rather than crime counts.

Comparison of Massachusetts Crime Trends vs. National Crime Trends

In the following sections, we will take a more in-depth look at the Part I index crimes (violent and then property crimes). Specifically, we will look at crime trends in Massachusetts compared to national averages. After reading the following sections, you will be able to tell how crime rates in Massachusetts have changed over time and how they compare to crime rates nationwide.

Murder/Nonnegligent Manslaughter

First, let's examine murder and nonnegligent manslaughter, which is the most serious Part I index crime. The UCR defines ***murder*** and ***nonnegligent manslaughter*** as "the willful (nonnegligent) killing of one human being by another" (FBI, 2014e). Figure 2.1 shows the annual murder rates in Massachusetts and the national average from 1960 to 2014. Although murder rates in Massachusetts have been consistently lower than the national average, the trends

Figure 2.1 Murder Rates (per 100,000) in Massachusetts Compared to the National Average, 1960–2014

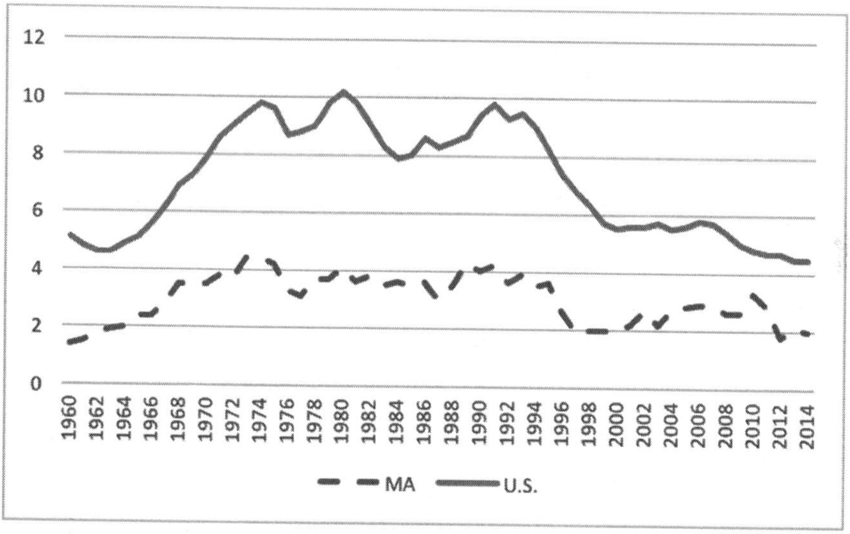

Source: FBI's UCR Data Tool. Retrieved from http://bjs.gov/ucrdata (compiled by authors).

demonstrate similar patterns. In general, murder rates increased from 1960 to the mid-1970s, exhibited several peaks and valleys from the mid-1970s to the early 1990s, and have decreased since the early 1990s. However, from 2000 to 2010, murder rates in Massachusetts appear to have slightly increased, but then down again in 2012, and have since remained stable.

The Supplementary Homicide Report (SHR) provides additional details about murders and nonnegligent manslaughters. Details include demographic information on victims and offenders, victim-offender relationships, and weapons used (Lynch & Addington, 2007). Table 2.2 provides us with demographic characteristics about the victims of murder in Massachusetts in 2014. Of the 132 murders, the victims were disproportionately male. Males accounted for almost 82% of the murder victims but just over 48% of the population in Massachusetts (U.S. Census Bureau, 2015).

In 2014, approximately 44% of the murder victims in Massachusetts were Caucasian, 50% were African American, 1.5% were Asian, and 4.5% were of unknown race/ethnicity. These statistics indicate that African Americans were disproportionately the victims of murder in Massachusetts in 2014. African Americans comprise approximately 6% of the population in Massachusetts, compared to half of the murder victims (U.S. Census Bureau, 2015). There

Table 2.2 Demographic Characteristics of Murder Victims in Massachusetts in 2014

Characteristics of Victims	Number of Victims	Percentage of Total Victims
Total	132	100%
Gender		
Male	108	81.8
Female	24	18.2
Race		
White	58	44.0
Black	66	50.0
Asian	2	1.5
Unknown	6	4.5
Age		
Under 18	6	4.5
18–24	35	26.5
25–49	72	54.5
50 and over	17	12.9
Unknown	2	1.6

Source: "Easy Access to the FBI's Supplementary Homicide Reports: 1980–2015" by C. Puzzanchera, G. Chamberlin, and W. Kang, 2015. Retrieved from https://www.ojjdp.gov/ojstatbb/ezashr/asp/vic_selection.asp (compiled by authors).

are also disproportionately more people 18 to 49 years old who were the victims of murder in Massachusetts in 2013. People 18 to 24 years old comprised only 10% of the population (U.S. Census Bureau, 2013) but 26.5% of the murder victims. Similarly, people 25 to 49 years old comprised approximately 34% of the population (U.S. Census Bureau, 2010) but 54.5% of murder victims.

Table 2.3 shows the relationship between the victim and offender in the murders committed in Massachusetts in 2014. Although the relationship was unknown in nearly 66% of the cases, only 4.5% of the murders were reported to be committed by strangers. Finally, Table 2.4 provides data on the weapons used in murders in Massachusetts in 2014. Approximately 62% involved a firearm, 26% a knife, and the remaining 12% involved another weapon or the weapon was unknown.

Forcible Rape

The next crime we will discuss is ***forcible rape***. *Forcible rape* is defined by the FBI as "penetration, no matter how slight, of the vagina or anus with any

Table 2.3 Victim-Offender Relationship for Murders in Massachusetts in 2014

Victim-Offender Relationship	Number	Percentage
Total	132	100%
Family	9	6.8
Acquaintance	30	22.8
Stranger	6	4.5
Unknown	87	65.9

Source: "Easy Access to the FBI's Supplementary Homicide Reports: 1980–2015" by C. Puzzanchera, G. Chamberlin, and W. Kang, 2015. Retrieved from https://www.ojjdp.gov/ojstatbb/ezashr/asp/vic_selection.asp (compiled by authors).

Table 2.4 Murders According to Weapon Type in Massachusetts in 2014

Weapon	Number	Percent
Total	132	100%
Firearm	82	62.1
Knife	34	25.8
Blunt Object	4	3.0
Personal	3	2.3
Other/Unknown	9	6.8

Source: "Easy Access to the FBI's Supplementary Homicide Reports: 1980–2015" by C. Puzzanchera, G. Chamberlin, and W. Kang, 2015. Retrieved from https://www.ojjdp.gov/ojstatbb/ezashr/asp/vic_selection.asp (compiled by authors).

body part or object, or oral penetration by a sex organ of another person, without the consent of the victim" (FBI, 2014f). Figure 2.2 provides rates of rape in Massachusetts compared to the national average from 1960 to 2014. Similar to murder, Massachusetts consistently exhibits lower rates of rape compared to the national average. In addition, the trends in this crime are similar in Massachusetts compared to the national average. Rates of rape increased from 1960 until they peaked in the early 1990s, at which point they began to decrease.

It is important to note that prior to 2013, the definition of rape was "the carnal knowledge of a female forcibly and against her will" (FBI, 2014f). Consequently, it appears as though rates of rate increased in 2013 and 2014; however, it is because the revised definition of rape is more inclusive. It now recognizes

Figure 2.2 Rape Rates (per 100,000) in Massachusetts Compared to the National Average, 1960–2014

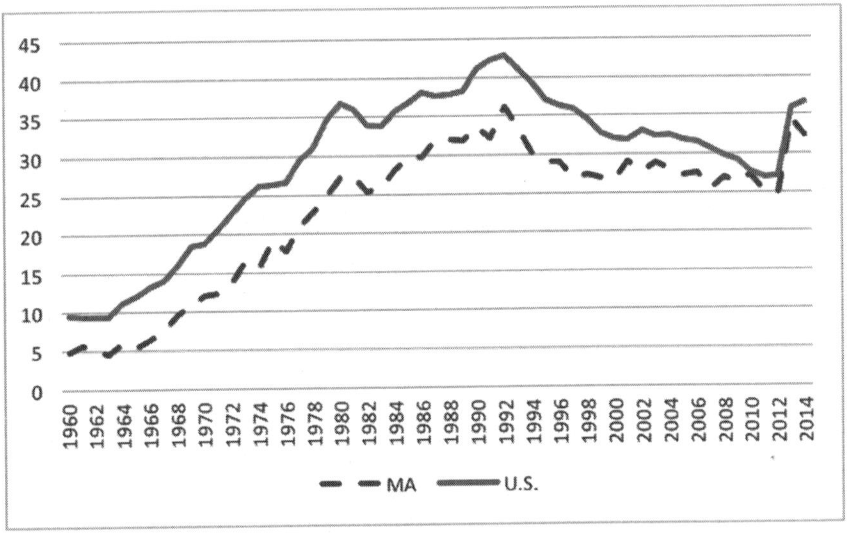

Source: FBI's UCR Data Tool. Retrieved from http://bjs.gov/ucrdata (compiled by authors).

that both genders can be victims of rape. It also recognizes that any unwanted sexual act (no longer only vaginal intercourse) can constitute rape. As a result of these changes, rape rates were expected to increase.

Statutory Rape

It is important to note that the crime of forcible rape is distinguishable from the crime of ***statutory rape***. Statutory rape (commonly known as rape and abuse of child) is defined as when a person "unlawfully has sexual intercourse or unnatural sexual intercourse, and abuses a child under 16 years of age, shall be punished by imprisonment in the state prison for life or for any term of years or, except as otherwise provided, for any term in a jail or house of correction. A prosecution commenced under this section shall neither be continued without a finding nor placed on file" (MGL c.265 §23).

Robbery

The UCR's definition of ***robbery*** is "the taking or attempting to take anything of value from the care, custody, or control of a person or persons by force or

Figure 2.3 Robbery Rates (per 100,000) in Massachusetts Compared to the National Average, 1960–2014

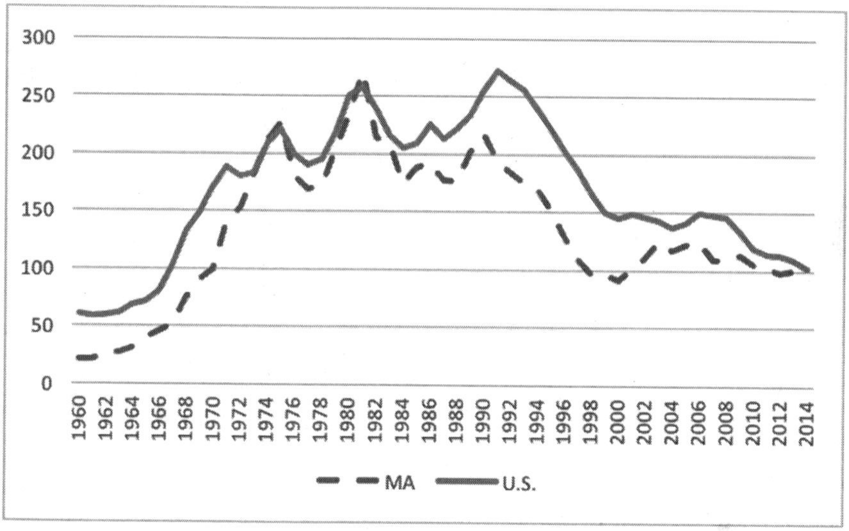

Source: FBI's UCR Data Tool. Retrieved from http://bjs.gov/ucrdata (compiled by authors).

threat of force or violence and/or by putting the victim in fear" (FBI, 2014g). Note that robbery is more serious than larceny-theft, which we will discuss shortly, because it involves the offender using force or threatening to use force, in addition to taking property.

Figure 2.3 provides robbery rates over time in Massachusetts compared to that of the nation. Except a couple of years in the mid-1970s and early 1980s, robbery rates in Massachusetts have been lower than the national average. However, robbery trends in Massachusetts are similar to robbery trends nationwide during this period. They increased steadily from 1960 until the early 1970s; from the early 1970s to early 1990s, they exhibited several peaks and valleys, and they have been declining since the early 1990s.

Aggravated Assault

The last of the violent Part I index crimes is ***aggravated assault***, which the FBI defines as "an unlawful attack by one person upon another for the purpose of inflicting severe or aggravated bodily injury" (FBI, 2014a). Furthermore, this type of assault is often accompanied by the use of a weapon, including a firearm, knife, personal weapon (i.e., hand, fist, or foot), or another object.

Although the use of a weapon does not always elevate an assault to aggravated assault, weapons often produce severe bodily injury. Therefore, it is the level of injury that differentiates an aggravated assault from a simple assault.

Figure 2.4 provides rates of aggravated assaults over time in Massachusetts compared to the national average. Unlike the other crimes, Massachusetts shows higher rates of aggravated assaults than the national average for nearly every year beginning in the late 1970s. Overall, the trends are similar in Massachusetts and for the nation as a whole. Rates of aggravated assault increased from 1960 until 1993, when they peaked, and they have been decreasing since then.

Burglary

The next three crimes we will discuss are the property Part I index crimes. The first of which is ***burglary***, which the FBI defines as "the unlawful entry of a structure to commit felony or theft" (FBI, 2014b). A structure can include a house, apartment, barn, house trailer, houseboat, office, railroad car, stable, or vessel.

Except the early 1970s to early 1980s, rates of burglary have been lower in Massachusetts compared to the national average (see Figure 2.5). Rates of burglary both in Massachusetts and nationwide increased from 1960 to the early 1980s. They peaked in 1981 and have been gradually decreasing. The current rates of burglary have not been as low since the mid-1960s.

Motor Vehicle Theft

The FBI defines ***motor vehicle theft*** as "the theft or attempted theft of a motor vehicle" (FBI, 2014d). The FBI considers motor vehicles to be self-propelled vehicles running on land, not rails. Motor vehicle can include automobiles, trucks, buses, motorcycles, all-terrain vehicles, and snowmobiles.

Figure 2.6 provides us with trends in motor vehicle theft rates in Massachusetts compared to the national average. Trends for motor vehicle theft are interesting both for the commonwealth and for the nation as a whole. First, Massachusetts has considerably higher rates of motor vehicle theft than the rest of the country from 1960 until the mid-1990s. Since then, they have continued to be lower than national rates. In Massachusetts, motor vehicle theft rates increased from 1960 until they peaked in 1975, and they have been decreasing since their peak. In 1975, there were 1,571 motor vehicle thefts per 100,000 people in Massachusetts. Conversely, in 2014, there were only 123 motor vehicle thefts per 100,000 people. Trends in motor vehicle thefts have not been as drastic when considering the national average. They gradually increased from 1960 until they reached their peak in 1991 (659 per 100,000 people), and they have been gradually declining.

Figure 2.4 Aggravated Assault Rates (per 100,000) in MA Compared to the National Average, 1960–2014

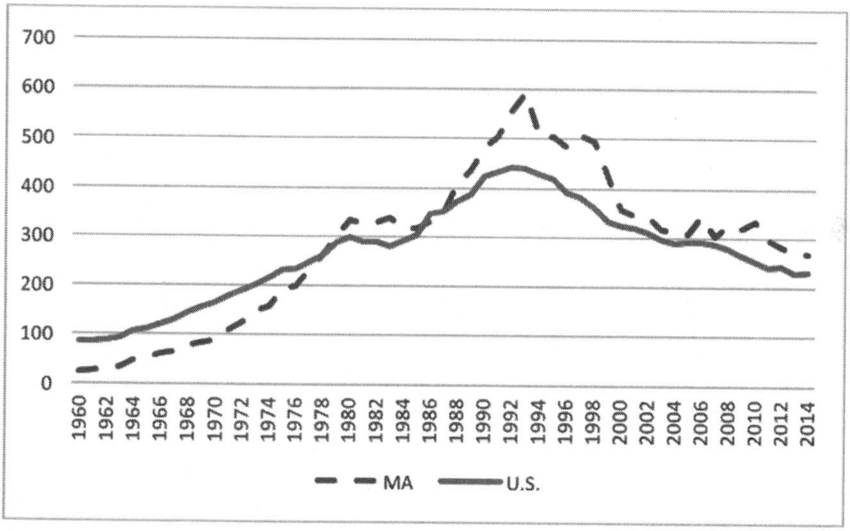

Source: FBI's UCR Data Tool. Retrieved from http://bjs.gov/ucrdata (compiled by authors).

Figure 2.5 Burglary Rates (per 100,000) in Massachusetts Compared to the National Average, 1960–2014

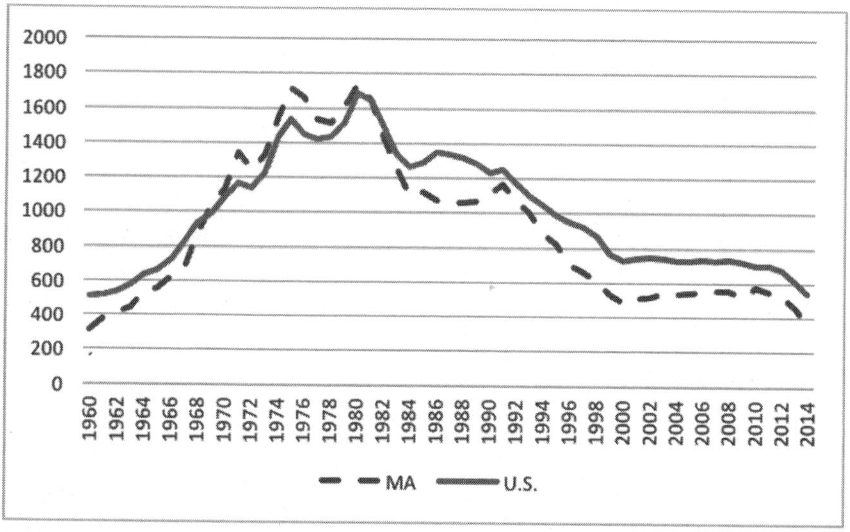

Source: FBI's UCR Data Tool. Retrieved from http://bjs.gov/ucrdata (compiled by authors).

Figure 2.6 Motor Vehicle Theft Rates (per 100,000) in MA Compared to the National Average, 1960–2014

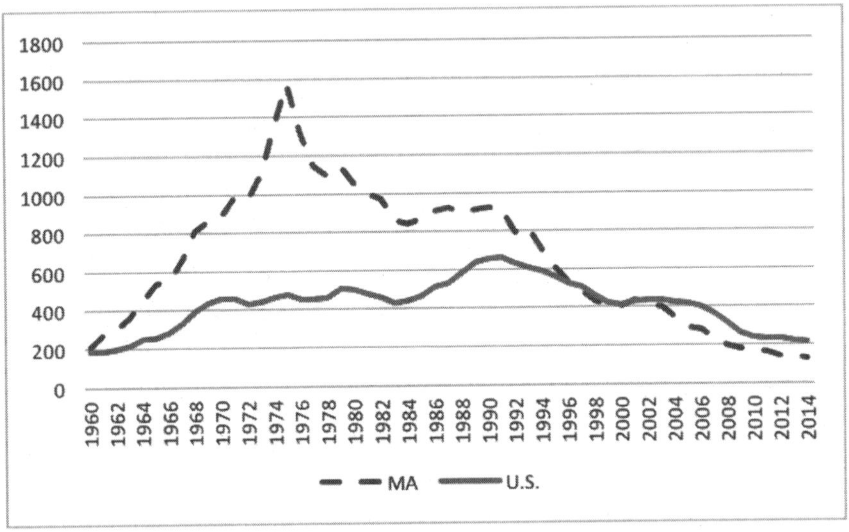

Source: FBI's UCR Data Tool. Retrieved from http://bjs.gov/ucrdata (compiled by authors).

Larceny-Theft

The last Part I index crime we will examine is ***larceny-theft***, which the FBI defines as "the unlawful taking, carrying, leading, or riding away of property from the possession or constructive possession of another" (FBI, 2014c). This crime includes the theft of bicycles, shoplifting, or stealing property without the use of force or violence. Furthermore, it also includes attempted larcenies. However, it does not include embezzlement or forgery in which the property was entrusted to someone before being misappropriated.

While the rates of larceny-theft are consistently lower in Massachusetts than the national average, the trends nearly mirror each other (see Figure 2.7). Rates of larceny-theft increased from 1960 until the mid-1970s; from the mid-1970s until the early 1990s, they exhibited several peaks and valleys, and they have since been decreasing.

Figure 2.7 Larceny-Theft Rates (per 100,000) in MA Compared to the National Average, 1960–2014

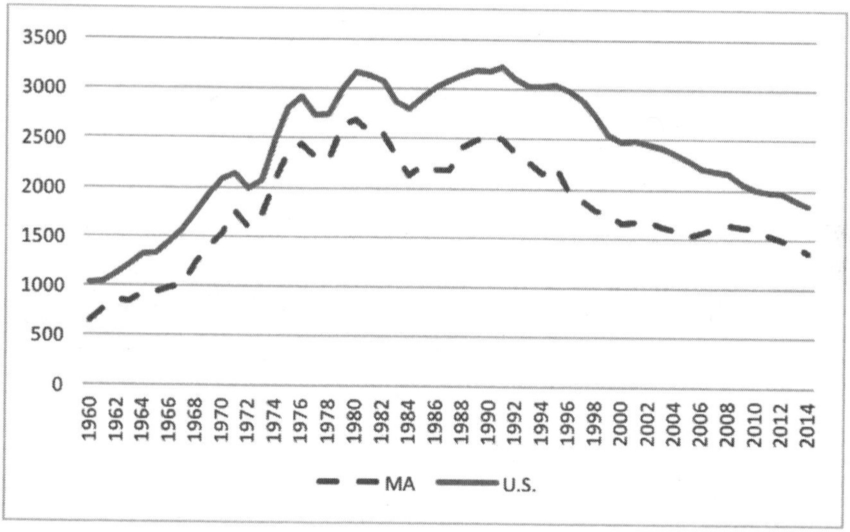

Source: FBI's UCR Data Tool. Retrieved from http://bjs.gov/ucrdata (compiled by authors).

Crime Trends in Major Cities in Massachusetts

So far, we have compared crime trends in Massachusetts with national averages. Does this mean that crime rates are uniform throughout Massachusetts, or do you think there is variation among the cities in Massachusetts? In the following sections, we will examine violent crime rates and property crime rates in cities in Massachusetts with populations greater than 100,000 from 1993 to 2014.[3] The cities include Boston, Worcester, Springfield, Lowell, and Cambridge.

As you can tell from Figure 2.8, there is variation in violent crime rates across the different cities. Overall, violent crime rates have been decreasing over time. When considering the different cities, Springfield has had considerably higher rates of violent crime than the other cities in the commonwealth, especially from 1996 to 2005. Reaching a peak in 1997, Springfield exhibited 3,076 violent

3. The first year that all of the major cities had publicly available data through the BJS was in 1993.

Figure 2.8 Violent Crime Rates (per 100,000) in Major Cities in MA, 1993–2014

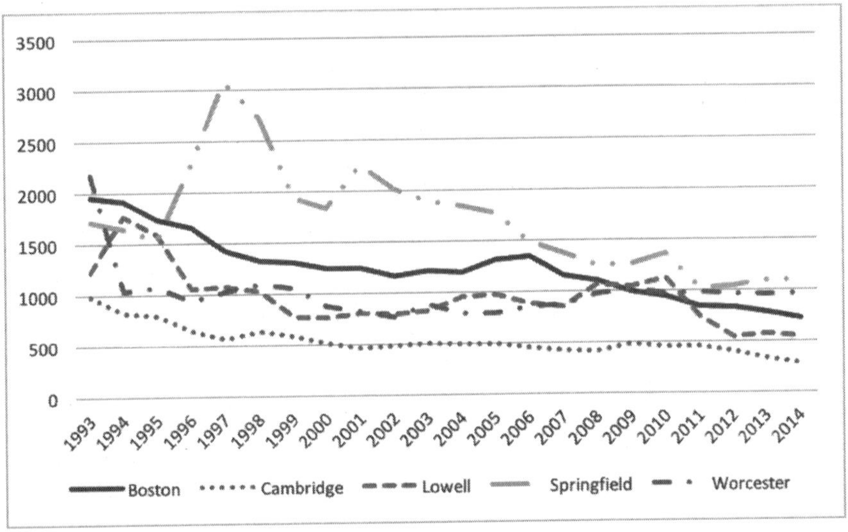

Source: FBI's UCR Data Tool. Retrieved from http://bjs.gov/ucrdata (compiled by authors).

crimes per 100,000 people. Boston has had the second highest rates, followed by Worcester and Lowell, which are similar. Finally, Cambridge has historically had the lowest violent crime rates of the major cities in Massachusetts.

Figure 2.9 provides property crime rates for the major cities in Massachusetts from 1993 to 2014. Overall, property crime rates have been decreasing over time. Similar to rates of violent crime, Springfield is also the city in Massachusetts with the highest rates of property crime. During this period, Springfield peaked in 2003 with 7,650 property crimes per 100,000 people. Boston had the second largest rates of property crimes, followed by Worcester, Cambridge, and Lowell.

A Closer Look at Springfield

In comparison to cities across the commonwealth, Springfield has historically exhibited significantly higher rates of both violent and property crimes than the national average. According to the Bureau of Justice Statistics, violent crime rates (per 100,000 people) in 2014 were 376 in the United States, but there were an astounding 1,091 in Springfield. Similarly, property crime rates were 2,596 for the nation as a whole but 3,842 in Springfield for the same year. See Figures 2.10 and 2.11 to see how the rate of violent and property crimes in Springfield compare to national trends.

Figure 2.9 Property Crime Rates (per 100,000) in Major Cities in MA, 1993–2014

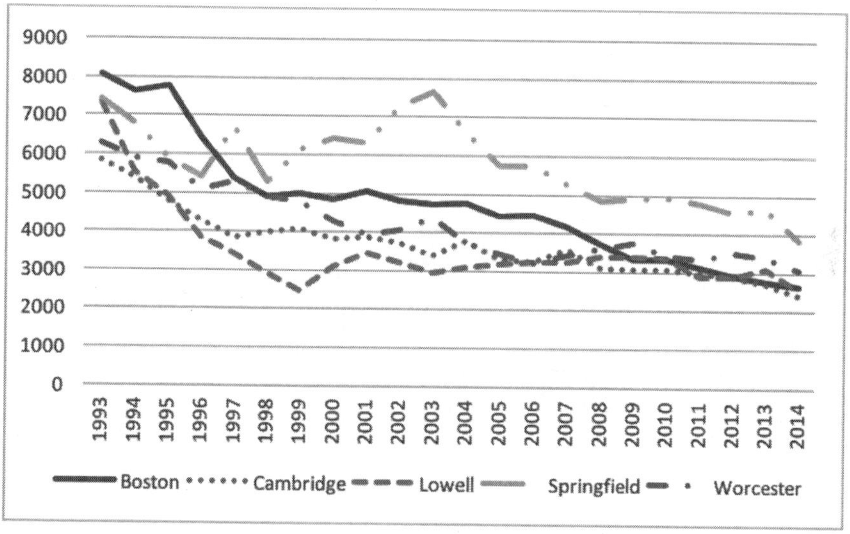

Source: FBI's UCR Data Tool. Retrieved from http://bjs.gov/ucrdata (compiled by authors).

Figure 2.10 Violent Crime Rates (per 100,000) in Springfield Compared to the National Average, 1985–2014

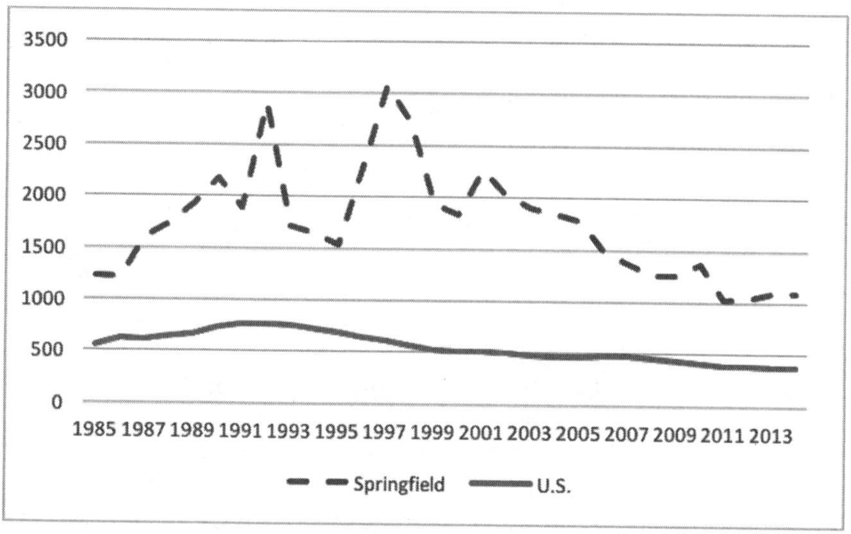

Source: FBI's UCR Data Tool. Retrieved from http://bjs.gov/ucrdata (compiled by authors).

Figure 2.11 Property Crime Rates (per 100,000) in Springfield Compared to the National Average, 1985–2014

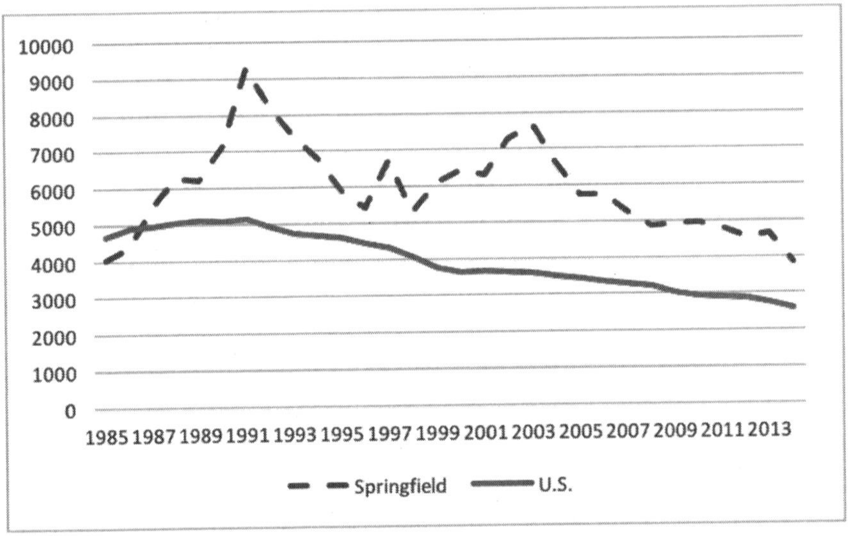

Source: FBI's UCR Data Tool. Retrieved from http://bjs.gov/ucrdata (compiled by authors).

Springfield also had 18 homicides in 2015 (Glaun, 2015). Given these high crime rates, we should look into some reasons why the crime rates in Springfield are so high. The U.S. Census Bureau estimates that nearly 15% of people in the United States were living below the poverty level in 2014, while 30% of the population of Springfield were living in poverty. Furthermore, some neighborhoods in Springfield, including Old Hill and Six Corners, have over half of their residents living below the poverty level.

Additionally, Springfield Public Schools is a vast and diverse school district, serving over 25,000 students throughout nearly 60 schools. This district is comprised of students from diverse backgrounds, including Hispanic (65%), African American (19%), Caucasian (12%), and Asian (3%). Disturbingly, 87% of the Springfield Public Schools district is classified as low income, and 67% of students are considered economically disadvantaged (Massachusetts Department of Elementary and Secondary Education, 2016). Additionally, 62% of all children in Springfield live in single-parent families (Massachusetts Family Institute, 2014).

According to Tcherni (2011), there are three primary structural determinants of homicide—poverty/low education, the disruption of family structure, and diverse racial composition. These three factors affect violence in general but have the greatest impact on homicides. Consequently, people who live in these communities are exposed to higher incidents of violence and homicide, and they are more likely to become the offenders or victims of crime. Furthermore, with the lack of job opportunities, a percentage of residents in these areas are also more susceptible to be involved in illicit activity, perpetuating the cycle of violence. Additionally, at the individual level, there can be a lack of supervision of youth in impoverished families. This lack of supervision makes juveniles more likely to associate with deviant peers and engage in delinquent activity.

Furthermore, the city has historically had a high percentage of African American residents, and in recent years, it has had a rising increase in the Hispanic population. While race and ethnicity do not cause crime, race can be used as a proxy (Tcherni, 2011) for the compounded disadvantages and adversities minorities face. Racial and ethnic minorities often live in high-poverty, high-crime, and highly segregated areas. Also, they often experience a lower quality of education and high unemployment, and they are disproportionately involved in the criminal justice system. As noted earlier, Springfield exhibits all of these structural characteristics—high levels of poverty, racial and ethnic diversity, and a large percentage of its children living in single-family households.

Conclusion

After reading this chapter, you should be familiar with the UCR and why it is important to examine official standardized crime statistics. With the exception of aggravated assault and motor vehicle theft, you can see that Massachusetts historically has had lower crime rates than the national average. However, in spite of lower crime rates, crime trends in Massachusetts follow similar patterns to the national average. Finally, you can also see that within Massachusetts there is variation in the amount of crime exhibited in its major cities. These crime statistics are important when deciding criminal justice policies and when assigning funding and resource allocation.

Key Terms

Aggravated Assault: Unlawful attack by one person upon another for the purpose of inflicting severe or aggravated bodily injury.

Burglary: Unlawful entry of a structure to commit a felony or theft.

Crime Rate: Ratio of crimes in an area to the population of that area, often expressed per 1,000 or 100,000 persons.

Crime Trend: Change in the nature of selected crime types within a specified geographical area and time period.

Dark Figure of Crime: Crimes that are not reported to police.

Forcible Rape: Penetration of the vagina or anus with any body part or object, or oral penetration by a sex organ of another person, without the consent of the victim.

Hierarchy Rule: The UCR requires counting only the highest offense and ignoring the others.

Larceny-Theft: Unlawful taking of property from the possession of another person.

Motor Vehicle Theft: Theft or attempted theft of a motor vehicle.

Murder/Nonnegligent Manslaughter: Willful killing of one human being by another.

Part I Index Crimes: Eight crimes (murder/nonnegligent homicide, rape, robbery, aggravated assault, burglary, motor vehicle theft, larceny-theft, and arson) that are reported to the UCR program.

Property Crimes: In the UCR, property crimes include burglary, larceny-theft, motor vehicle theft, and arson. The object of these offenses is taking money or property, but there is no threat of force against the victims.

Robbery: Taking or attempting to take anything of value from another person with the use of force or the threat of force and putting the victim in fear.

Statutory Rape: The unlawful sexual intercourse or unnatural sexual intercourse and abuse of a child under 16 years of age.

Uniform Crime Report (UCR): Official data on crime, published by the FBI.

Violent Crimes: The FBI's UCR considers four offenses to be violent crimes—murder/nonnegligent manslaughter, rape, robbery, and aggravated assault. Violent crimes involve force or the threat of force.

Related Websites

Federal Bureau of Investigation's Uniform Crime Reports
https://www.fbi.gov/about-us/cjis/ucr/ucr

Massachusetts Office of Grants and Research
http://www.mass.gov/eopss/law-enforce-and-cj/crime-stats-rsrch/

UCR Data Tool
http://www.ucrdatatool.gov/

Review Questions

1. Describe the Uniform Crime Reporting Program.
2. What are some limitations of the UCR?
3. Why is it important to examine crime rates rather than crime counts?
4. How do violent crime rates in Massachusetts compare to the national average?
5. What trends are there in Massachusetts and national violent crime rates?
6. How do property crime rates in Massachusetts compare to the national average?
7. What trends are there in Massachusetts and national property crime rates?
8. Compare violent crime trends for the major cities in Massachusetts.
9. Compare property crime trends for the major cities in Massachusetts.
10. How do crime trends in Springfield, Massachusetts compare to the national average?
11. What are some factors contributing to high violent crime rates in Springfield?

References

Bureau of Justice Statistics. (2012). *Victimizations not reported to the police, 2006–2010.* Retrieved from http://www.bjs.gov/content/pub/pdf/vnrp0610.pdf.

FBI. (n.d.). *Uniform Crime reports.* Retrieved from http://www.ucrdatatool.gov/.

FBI. (2014a). *Aggravated assault.* Retrieved from https://www.fbi.gov/about-us/cjis/ucr/crime-in-the-u.s/2013/crime-in-the-u.s.-2013/violent-crime/aggravated-assault-topic-page.

FBI. (2014b). *Burglary.* Retrieved from https://ucr.fbi.gov/crime-in-the-u.s/2014/crime-in-the-u.s.-2014/offenses-known-to-law-enforcement/burglary.

FBI. (2014c). *Larceny-theft.* Retrieved from https://www.fbi.gov/about-us/cjis/ucr/crime-in-the-u.s/2013/crime-in-the-u.s.-2013/property-crime/larceny-theft-topic-page.

FBI. (2014d). *Motor vehicle theft.* Retrieved from https://www.fbi.gov/about-us/cjis/ucr/crime-in-the-u.s/2013/crime-in-the-u.s.-2013/property-crime/motor-vehicle-theft-topic-page.

FBI. (2014e). *Murder*. Retrieved from https://www.fbi.gov/about-us/cjis/ucr/crime-in-the-u.s/2013/crime-in-the-u.s.-2013/violent-crime/murder-topic-page/murdermain_final.

FBI. (2014f). *Rape*. Retrieved from https://www.fbi.gov/about-us/cjis/ucr/crime-in-the-u.s/2013/crime-in-the-u.s.-2013/violent-crime/rape.

FBI. (2014g). *Robbery*. Retrieved from https://www.fbi.gov/about-us/cjis/ucr/crime-in-the-u.s/2013/crime-in-the-u.s.-2013/violent-crime/robbery-topic-page.

Glaun, D. (2015). *2015 Springfield homicides: List of murders in Massachusetts' 3rd-largest city*. Retrieved from http://www.masslive.com/news/index.ssf/2015/07/2015_springfield_homicides.html.

Lynch, J., & Addington, L. (2007). Introduction to the Uniform Crime Reporting Program. In *Understanding crime statistics: Revisiting the divergence of the NCVS and UCR*. New York, NY: Cambridge University Press.

Massachusetts Department of Elementary and Secondary Education. (2016). *School and district profiles*. Retrieved from http://profiles.doe.mass.edu/Default.aspx.

Massachusetts Family Institute. (2014). *Fatherless in Massachusetts: The economic and social costs to our commonwealth*. Retrieved from http://www.mafamily.org/wp-content/uploads/2014/10/fatherlessness-report_FINAL.pdf.

McCarthy, J. (2014, November 21). Most Americans still see crime up over last year. Retrieved from http://www.gallup.com/poll/179546/americans-crime-last-year.aspx.

MGL c.265 § 23

Puzzanchera, C., Chamberlin, G., & Kang, W. (2015). *Easy access to the FBI's Supplementary Homicide Reports: 1980–2015*. Retrieved from http://www.ojjdp.gov/ojstatbb/ezashr/.

Tcherni, M. (2011). Structural determinants of homicide: The big three. *Journal of Quantitative Criminology, 27*(4), 475–496.

U.S. Census Bureau. (2010). *2009–2013 American community survey 5-year estimates.* Retrieved from http://factfinder.census.gov/faces/tableservices/jsf/pages/productview.xhtml?src=CF.

U.S. Census Bureau. (2013). *2009–2013 American community survey 5-year estimates.* Retrieved from http://factfinder.census.gov/faces/tableservices/jsf/pages/productview.xhtml?pid=ACS_13_5YR_B01001&prodType=table.

U.S. Census Bureau. (2015). *Quick facts: Massachusetts.* Retrieved from http://quickfacts.census.gov/qfd/states/25000.html.

Chapter 3

Policing in Massachusetts

Learning Objectives

- Learn about different law enforcement agencies in Massachusetts at the local and state levels.
- Learn about the selection process to become a police officer in Massachusetts.
- Familiarize yourself with some of the issues that law enforcement is currently facing.
- Understand how technology aids law enforcement in investigations.

Introduction

The term *police* refers to an institution of state authority that represents the will of the government through the enforcement of criminal laws and the maintenance of civil order. In the narrowest sense, police departments are assigned the duty of maintaining law and order (fighting crime) in the jurisdiction that they are sworn to protect and serve. However, a police officer's crime-fighting efforts are only a small part of his or her overall activities. Police officers are responsible for protecting all members of the community—including the most vulnerable citizens. In fact, the phrase "serve and protect" is a common motto of many police agencies.

The term *law enforcement* may be limiting in the scope and magnitude of what police officers do on a daily basis. Police officers today than can be viewed as troubleshooters or problem solvers, who—while serving the public—are more concerned with addressing quality-of-life issues in a community than they are arresting felons. Policing deals with the day-to-day issues in a community and tries to address problems before they become crimes. While the duties of police officers across the country are vast and complex, officers are charged with protecting and serving the public while protecting the constitutional rights of all citizens.

The word *police* is actually taken from the Greek word *polis*, meaning "city," indicating that even in ancient times, citizens worked together to bring order to the community. But the primary origins for policing in Massachusetts and across the country gets its origins from Great Britain. In 1829, ***Sir Robert Peel*** introduced the ***Metropolitan Police Act***, establishing the first organized police force in London. Composed of more than 1,000 men, the London police force was structured along military lines and wore a distinctive uniform (Seigel & Worrall, 2018).

Although every officer conducted some level of investigations, the earliest record of the position of detective was in 1842, and there were only a few people assigned the task of full-time investigations. The modern, fully functioning Criminal Investigation Unit did not appear until 1877. Because of the overwhelming success of the London Metropolitan Police, Sir Robert Peel became known as the "father of modern policing." His mantra was that the police force should be "policing by consent" of the people. One of his more famous sayings was "The police are the people and the people are the police." Policing in Massachusetts still looks eerily like its predecessor in London.

Today, typically, the terms *policing* and *law enforcement* are used interchangeably, but there are discernable differences between the two. *Policing* is a much broader concept than law enforcement, and police agencies carry out many different tasks other than simply enforcing laws. Police officers carry out a wide range of service-related activities that do not involve enforcing criminal laws. Policing often involves officers trying to solve problems before they become crimes, and thus the service-provider side of policing must be maintained and prioritized.

In contrast, the term *law enforcement* is the action of enforcing laws and ordinances, investigating criminal activities, and arresting offenders. This is the classic role of the police and the role that most people think of when they envision what a police officer is supposed to do or what they think an officer actually does. Crime control is the occupational mandate of law enforcement agencies. We pay law enforcement officers to do what they can do to control crime.

Similar to law enforcement agencies and organizations throughout the United States, police in Massachusetts are responsible for protecting people, enforcing laws, preventing crime, and providing services to citizens. The police are the initiators of the criminal justice process. That is, they are the first ones to have contact with witnesses, victims, and individuals who break the law. The police then decide whether to make an arrest or not. In this chapter, you will learn about the various law enforcement agencies throughout Massachusetts, the selection process for these organizations, and some of the issues facing law enforcement today.

Massachusetts Law Enforcement, Police Agencies, and Organizations

There are many state, local, county, and municipal law enforcement agencies that work throughout Massachusetts. Individuals working in these organizations are responsible for enforcing laws, responding to calls, patrolling the community, conducting traffic stops, obtaining warrants, collecting evidence, writing reports, and testifying in court. Virtually all cities and towns in Massachusetts have their own police agency as well as county sheriff departments in all 14 counties. Massachusetts has approximately 323 law enforcement agencies employing over 20,000 ***sworn police officers*** (FBI, 2014b) or officers who have the power to arrest and carry a firearm. This figure averages out to approximately 300 sworn officers for every 100,000 residents. In the following sections, you will learn more about some of the law enforcement agencies operating throughout the Commonwealth of Massachusetts.

State Police

The Massachusetts State Police is an agency within the Commonwealth of Massachusetts's Executive Office of Public Safety and Security. The Massachusetts State Police is the oldest state police agency in the United States (Commonwealth of Massachusetts, n.d.b). The organization began as State Constables in 1865, and the modern version of the Massachusetts State Police began in 1921. On July 1, 1992, there was a merger of many of the state-controlled police agencies into one agency within the Executive Office of Public Safety, now known as the Department of Massachusetts State Police. The former agencies included Division of State Police, Massachusetts Registry of Motor Vehicles Police, Massachusetts Capitol Police, and Metropolitan District Commission (MDC) Police Departments. The distinctive uniform (French blue shirts and electric blue pants), badge, and seal of the former Division of State Police would be retained by the newly formed Department of State Police. The Massachusetts Environmental Police remained a separate entity under the Department of Fisheries, Wildlife, and Environmental Law Enforcement.

The Massachusetts State police are responsible for criminal law enforcement and traffic vehicle regulation across the state. The Massachusetts State Police have ***jurisdiction*** to enforce laws across the commonwealth. They also analyze evidence and provide investigative services to cities and towns throughout Massachusetts. There are approximately 2,300 employees in the state police—1,500 of them are uniformed troopers and 400 are civilian support staff—making it the largest law enforcement agency in New England (Reaves, 2011).

The Massachusetts State Police Department is divided into seven individual assignment areas, known as ***troops***, throughout the state. Troop A covers the northeast region of the state; Troop B covers the western region of the state; Troop C covers the central region of the state; Troop D covers the southeastern region of the state; Troop E covers the entirety of Interstate 90 (also known as the Massachusetts Turnpike, which runs east and west through the state from the New York state border to the Atlantic Ocean at Boston Harbor); Troop F covers Boston's Logan International Airport and the state shore line; and Troop H covers the metropolitan Boston area. Because the state police patrol areas are broken into troops, the state police officers are affectionately known as troopers. The Massachusetts State Police maintains an air wing with a fleet of five turbine helicopters and one fixed wing aircraft. The primary duty aircraft is the multipurpose helicopter (Commonwealth of Massachusetts, n.d.e).

In addition to policing the state's highways, the Massachusetts State Police provides protection services for the governor, lieutenant governor, some elected officials, and visiting dignitaries. The state police further provides primary policing and law enforcement services to the Department of Conservation and Recreation Beaches and Parks, Massachusetts Port Authority Airports and Properties, Massachusetts Department of Transportation, and Massachusetts Water Resources Authority Facilities. The state police also provides policing support and assistance to municipal police departments.

The Massachusetts state seal is centered on the state police emblem. The seal contains a blue shield adorned with the image of a member of the Native American tribe "Massachusett." He holds a bow in his right hand and an arrow in his left hand. The arrow is pointing downward, signifying peace. The white star above the bow represents Massachusetts as one of the original 13 states. Around the shield is a blue ribbon with the Latin motto *Ense petit placidam sub libertate quietem* (by the sword we seek peace, but peace only under liberty). Above the shield is an arm holding a sword, which represents the first part of the motto (U.S. District Court for the District of Puerto Rico, n.d.).

History of the Massachusetts State Police

In the 1800s, the common title for police officers was *constable.* The Massachusetts State Police (MSP) traces its origin directly through legislation to the Massachusetts State Constabulary, which was the first statewide police agency in the nation. The creation of the State Constabulary was signed into law on May 16, 1865, by Massachusetts Governor John A. Andrews. This legislative act to establish a State Police Force founded the first statewide enforcement agency in the nation. The establishment of the State Police Force in 1865 was unprecedented, but the actual Massachusetts legislation that created the statewide police force would eventually be adopted and duplicated in various states throughout the country.

The first commander of the newly formed statewide police force was General King. His title was probably earned during the American Civil War. The agency remained small and rather informal until 1921, when the MSP was enlarged to comprise 50 officers stationed in barracks across the state with the primary mission of providing law enforcement to rural areas underserved by existing local police agencies. This law enforcement mission was initially performed by the officers on horseback, but they moved to motor vehicles in areas with upgraded roads. The MSP enlarged its mission to handle primary vehicular regulation on the commonwealth's interstate and limited-access highways after their development mid-century; during this period, it also established a presence in protecting Boston's Logan International Airport.

For much of the 20th century, the MSP was organized along militaristic lines with a heavy emphasis on the role of the barracks as well as uniformity in appearance and internal culture. Until recently, the MSP maintained one of the strictest regimens for physical size requirements for applicants. Efforts are being made presently to render the department more racially diverse as well as more inclusive of women and LGBT officers.

The State Police Community Action Teams (CAT) are unique units. The purpose of the CAT teams is to augment the traditional troop barracks with extra patrols to be used for various duties. The CAT teams are a combination of an anti-crime unit and a motor vehicle enforcement unit, and they have a very large amount of freedom. The units are not part of any troop barracks but rather elite units out of the other barracks and headquarters. Duties include the patrol of high crime areas in inner cities and major highways, traffic enforcement, and foot, bicycle, or vehicle patrol. They are also involved in undercover missions with local police departments and major traffic accidents. Furthermore, CAT troopers are responsible for dignitary escorts, funeral prisoner escorts, and security at high-risk trials, as well as many other special missions (MSP Museum and Learning Center, n.d.).

Table 3.1 Number of Sworn Police Officers in Massachusetts's Largest Cities, 2014

Agency	Number of Full-Time Sworn Officers
Boston	2,151
Worcester	440
Springfield	435
Cambridge	281
Lowell	232

Source: "Massachusetts: Full-Time Law Enforcement Employees by City, 2014" by FBI, 2014a.

Local Police

Similar to the rest of the country, the majority of police officers in Massachusetts work at the ***municipal***, or local, level. In Massachusetts, there are 314 local agencies representing different cities and towns. Of the 20,000 sworn police officers in Massachusetts, approximately 13,700 (Reaves, 2011), or 68% of the officers, are employed at the local level. These officers have the jurisdiction to apprehend criminal suspects, maintain order, and provide services in the city or town in which they are employed.

Table 3.1 provides the number of sworn police officers in municipal police departments in Massachusetts with populations greater than 100,000 people. As you can see, with over 2,000 sworn officers, Boston has the largest local police department in Massachusetts. Please see the section below for more information on the history of the Boston Police Department.

Profile: Sergeant John Soules, Pittsfield Police Department

The best part of my job, as clichéd as it sounds, is the ability to have a positive impact on people in my community. This job is not strictly arresting criminals and investigating crimes. There is a great deal of problem-solving involved in policing, and there is tremendous satisfaction in being able to assist a citizen with a problem or dilemma that they may be facing. Additionally, I serve in the same area where I was born and raised; I personally know many of the people here, and they know me. I enjoy the face-to-face interactions that are so crucial to police work. I also like the fact that when it comes to police work, no two days are ever the same. There is excitement, unpredictability, and a certain amount of freedom as long as you are answering your calls, doing your job, and making a positive impact on those you serve.

Policing is not an easy career, and there are many difficult aspects to the profession. One of the hardest parts of police work is witnessing some of the horrible things that happen to other human beings. Many times we are called because someone, somewhere, is having the worst day of his or her life. We see sadness, horror, and despair far more often than most civilians. We see firsthand the effects of addiction, violence, and death. Officers need to possess certain traits and characteristics in order to handle these weighty issues, and they should have healthy outlets which they can use to decompress.

As far as a successful policy goes, our department (like many others) relies heavily on a community policing philosophy. We work with many other agencies, community groups, and local leaders, and because of that, we have a good working relationship with those we serve. We have officers that do a tremendous amount of community outreach: coaching youth sports, assisting at-risk youth, and helping with local charities. We also participate in events, such as crime watch meetings, "coffee with a cop," recruitment events, and other forums, where we can interact with community members. There is a certain degree of mutual respect between the police department and the community, and in today's day and age, this is the only way a police department can operate effectively and with legitimacy.

One of the challenges with policing today is finding qualified individuals, specifically young people, who are willing to work in law enforcement during a particularly challenging time in the profession's history. Whether accurate or not, some citizens currently have a negative perception of policing in America. It was already difficult to convince young people to join a career that is dangerous, stressful, and has less than ideal working hours. Now the same individuals we are trying to recruit are exposed to countless media reports, which highlight the strain between society and police in some areas of the country. The best way to change this dilemma is recruitment efforts where those in the field can educate and inform potential candidates who are considering law enforcement professions. There, we can tell them about the benefits of the profession while dispelling some of the myths that currently surround policing. Also, as stated above, a community policing philosophy bolsters mutual trust between society and officers. This relationship makes it easier to show young people that policing is a noble profession with tremendous opportunities to serve.

Boston Police Department

The history of American law enforcement began in Boston. In 1631, the citizens of the town of Boston established a watch. In 1636, these watchmen patrolled the streets of Boston at night to protect the public from criminals, wild animals, and fire. The duties of the Boston watchmen increased as the population increased, and the town became a city. In 1838, a bill passed in the Massachusetts General Court that allowed the City of Boston to name and appoint police officers. The City of Boston founded a police force of six men under the supervision of a city marshal. The Boston Watch of 120 men continued to operate separately. This action paved the way for the creation of a formal Boston Police Department (BPD News, n.d.).

In 1854, the city replaced the Watch organizations with the Boston Police Department, which consisted of 250 officers. Each officer received payment of $2 per shift, walked his own beat, and was forbidden to hold outside employment. Rather than use the billhook of the old Watch, officers began to carry a 14-inch club. In the previous years, the city had annexed several neighboring towns and expanded police services to those areas (BPD News, n.d.).

At the beginning of the 20th century, the Boston Police Department grew to 1,000 patrolmen, and keeping the peace resulted in approximately 30,000 arrests annually. The role of the police also expanded, and with the introduction of the automobile came new procedures. Police duties now included regulating motor vehicle traffic and removing unruly passengers from streetcars. The Boston Police Department purchased its first patrol car in 1903 and its first patrol wagon in 1912. In later years, police would use motorcycles to deal with ever-increasing problem known as Boston traffic (BPD News, n.d.).

Today's Boston Police Department, with over 2,000 sworn officers, is the twentieth largest police agency in the country and the second largest in New England, behind the MSP. Officers in Boston serve a population of nearly 670,000 residents and an estimated additional 350,000 commuters daily. The Boston Police Department is divided into three zones and 11 neighborhood districts spread across the city, with each zone supervised by a deputy superintendent and every district headed by a captain. But BPD also occupies a very important part in American history (BPD News, n.d.).

Boston Police Strike of 1919

As American society changed during the turn of the 20th century, the police were expected to act more professionally. When police reform was the order of the day, civil disobedience within the BPD was at the forefront. When Boston police officers went on strike in 1919 and refused to protect and serve the city residents, there was heightened interest in police reform. Though often regarded as a pretty obscure event in American history, the ***Boston Police Strike of 1919*** was one of the most significant events in the history of American policing. The strike became a realistic option because police officers in the city were disgruntled and discontent with their social and political status in society. At that time in early American history, other professions were unionizing and increasing their standards of living, but police salaries and quality of life lagged behind, and officers were becoming increasingly unhappy with their weakened status in society. In Boston, the police had seen their wages lag badly behind other municipal workers during World War I, and their respect from average citizens was declining as well.

There was consensus that the Boston police officers of 1919 had validity in their work-related complaints. Their grievances fell into three categories: lengths of working shifts, working conditions, and most importantly, inequity in their pay. Finally, the policemen objected to the conditions under which they were forced to work, particularly in the crowded decay and disrepair of the police station. They wanted to unionize in order to increase their working conditions and, frankly, their lot in life.

Boston Police Commissioner Edwin U. Curtis refused to allow the formation of a police union and suspended the organizers from their jobs as Boston police officers in August 1919. Commissioner Curtis believed that if allowed to unionize, the police department would take orders from the union, thereby hampering discipline and, ultimately, his authority to command the officers. The commissioner banned the officers from associating with any outside organization and refused to sanction a police union. The Boston police officers' fraternal organization, the Boston Social Club, endured a month-long labor dispute but finally voted to become a union affiliated with the American Federation of Labor. The commissioner then began the process of suspending 19 Boston police officers, including the president and other officers of the union, for violation of his orders not to unionize. That evening, the Policemen's Union voted to protest the suspensions by striking at evening roll call the next day.

At 5:45 p.m. on Tuesday, September 9, 1919, at the beginning of the evening shift, 1,117 BPD officers conducted a full-scale work stoppage. This action removed 70% of the police force from protecting the public, and it was the first strike by public safety workers in U.S. history. With the vast majority of the City of Boston virtually unprotected, criminals took the opportunity to increase their law violation. Petty crimes escalated into looting, and rioting took place all over the city. With the police on strike, there were reports that assaults, rapes, vandalism, and looting went unpunished as the city's officials struggled to get replacement police officers in place. Governor Calvin Coolidge then mobilized the state militia in order to regain control over the city, which was spiraling into chaos. Public support turned against the police, and the strike was broken. Eventually, all the striking officers were fired and replaced by new recruits. The Boston Police Strike ended police unionism for decades and solidified power in the hands of police and city administrators.

The striking policemen in Boston were not allowed to recover their jobs, which went overwhelmingly to servicemen returning from the war. Despite appeals from the American Federation of Labor wanting reinstatement of the striking officers, they were not allowed to return to work. However, new officers were granted higher pay and additional benefits. Ironically, the strike obtained its objectives but not for the striking police officers. While the Boston Police Strike proved disastrous for unions in the short term, police were eventually allowed to form unions. After the strike, various local, state, and federal crime commissions began investigating the extent of crime and the ability of the justice system to deal with it and made recommendations to improve police effectiveness. However, with the onset of the Great Depression, justice reform became a less important issue than economic revival, and for many years, little changed in the nature of policing (Herwick, 2016).

County Agencies

There are 14 counties in the Commonwealth of Massachusetts. Barnstable, Bristol, Dukes, Nantucket, and Plymouth counties are in the southeastern part of the state, including the general Cape Code area and the islands of Massachusetts. The greater Boston area holds Suffolk, Middlesex, Norfolk, and Essex counties. These counties have the bulk of the population in the state. The remaining five counties, Worcester, Franklin, Hampshire, Hampden, and Berkshire, are located in central and western Massachusetts.

In Massachusetts, counties sheriffs have the primary responsibility of running the jails and houses of corrections. They also conduct transportation of inmates in custody and serve ***civil process***, or the handling and serving of legal documents, including summons, subpoenas, or restraining orders. Furthermore, the sheriffs' departments also have sworn deputies who can enforce criminal laws within their county, and they often serve as backup to local law enforcement. There are approximately 1,500 sworn officers working in county agencies throughout Massachusetts (Reaves, 2011).

Transit Police

The Transit Police, formally known as the Massachusetts Bay Transit Authority (MBTA) Transit Police, is a civil service police department within the Commonwealth of Massachusetts. The MBTA is the oldest transit system in the country, dating back to 1894. The MBTA operates a transit system comprised of 4 subway lines, 13 commuter rail lines, 5 passenger ferry routes, and 162 bus routes, covering approximately 3,250 square miles and operating roughly 2,200 vehicles on a daily basis. This transportation network is responsible for approximately 1.3 million passenger trips per day (Massachusetts Bay Transportation Authority, n.d.).

The Transit Police have an authorized strength of 266 sworn officers and 10 civilian employees. The majority of the Transit Police Department's efforts are focused on patrol in Boston and surrounding communities. The Transit Police have special divisions found in many police agencies such as SWAT, K-9 units, crisis negotiators, bomb squads, a motorcycle unit, intelligence unit, and even a civil disturbance unit.

The Transit Police have police powers anywhere within the 175 cities and towns served by the MBTA. Transit Police have the authority to make arrests and enforce the law on and off MBTA property. These officers are responsible for preventing crime, arresting and detaining violators of the law, recovering stolen property, and preserving the peace (Massachusetts Bay Transportation

Authority, n.d.). Currently, there are over 250 sworn officers working for the MBTA Transit Police (Reaves, 2011).

Regional and Joint Police Forces

The Northeastern Massachusetts Law Enforcement Council (NEMLEC) is a group of police and sheriff's departments from Middlesex and Essex Counties who share resources, knowledge, and personnel for the benefit of public safety. NEMLEC helps its member agencies to provide supplemental services to approximately 1.7 million people in Middlesex and Essex Counties. Officers from member agencies help other communities during an emergency or event requiring police services that surpass the community's existing resources. (NEMLEC, n.d.).

With shrinking budgets and increased demands, agencies must effectively manage their resources to provide public safety services in their communities, including patrol, 911 response, and criminal investigations. By coordinating the sharing of police personnel, NEMLEC offers members access to additional resources for emergencies or large events (NEMLEC, n.d.).

Special Police Officers

A ***special police officer*** is a specially trained licensed security officer, hired by private companies or public agencies, who underwent special training under the supervision of the MSP or Boston Police Department. Special Police Officers are officers that work at nontraditional police or security agencies such as colleges, universities, or hospitals.

The special police designation is intended to give public and private security and reserve police officers a modicum of police powers, the power to detain or arrest, in order for the agency or officers to police and protect their respective campuses or properties. State Special Police Officers get their police powers from the colonel of the MSP. The State Special Police Academy is held at the state police facility in New Braintree, Massachusetts, and it is a 16-week optional live-in paramilitary academy.

Before 1992, the Commissioner of Public Safety gave special police officers their police powers. However, this changed amid the merger of the Metropolitan Police, Registry of Motor Vehicles Police, and Capital Police with the MSP. At that point, the colonel of the Massachusetts State Police became the appointing authority for State Special Police Officers (Commonwealth of Massachusetts, n.d.a).

Other municipalities may also commission special police officers. The BPD has a Special Police Program that is run out of the ***William Cloran Training***

Academy. Special officers in the City of Boston are issued a license and badge, but they are not employed by the city. Special officers have the power to arrest people and can be licensed to carry a firearm on duty.

The training for a special officer must pass a 100-hour course of instruction including a written test approved by the police commissioner. Special officers are trained at the department's firing range on the use of deadly force, which the law permits, but only to the degree required to overcome what the department considers unlawful resistance. This regulation applies whether the officers are using firearms or not. Being a State or Boston Special Police officer does not insure that you are issued a license to carry a firearm. That determination often comes from the agency that hires the officers (William Cloran Academy, 2014).

Private Investigators

Aside from the public law enforcement agencies previously mentioned, Massachusetts also has 1,600 people employed as ***private investigators*** (Bureau of Labor Statistics, 2018). Private investigators offer investigative and security-related services to individuals and corporations. Private investigators in Massachusetts must be licensed with the State Police, and they must have previous law enforcement experience.

Law Enforcement Training in Massachusetts

Integrity, honesty, helpfulness, and dependability are all words that should be associated with the ideal of policing. The objective of any police department in Massachusetts is to hire applicants with these personal traits or to instill these traits in all who complete the police training. Recruiting and selecting its potential officers is an extremely important task. Furthermore, going through the selection and hiring process to become a police officer today is very different from most other jobs for which you could apply. For the right person, becoming a police officer could be the perfect career option with good pay, attractive benefits, and the satisfaction of helping others.

However, the screening process is often quite extensive and rigorous. Police officers in Massachusetts today are often better trained, better educated, better compensated, and more representative of the entire community than almost any other time in history. But a career in policing is not for everyone. To ensure that the right person is selected, hired, and trained, applicants go

Table 3.2 Requirements to Become a State Police Officer in Massachusetts

- Between 21 and 35 years old
- Satisfy requirements for appointment to MSP Academy
- Nonsmoker
- Not convicted of a felony or sentenced to incarceration for misdemeanor conviction
- Good moral character
- Massachusetts firearms license
- High school diploma or GED certificate
- Satisfy department's physical fitness, medical, and psychological standards
- U.S. citizen
- Massachusetts driver's license
- Massachusetts resident at time of appointment
- No visible tattoos

Source: "Recruitment" by Commonwealth of Massachusetts, n.d.d.

through a strict set of selection criteria and a battery of tests before being sworn in as a police officer. Although many jurisdictions have similar types of selection standards, many departments have agency-specific goals, and some are stricter than others. In the following sections, you will learn about the selection process needed to work in law enforcement at the state and local levels in Massachusetts.

State Police Officer Training

It is the responsibility of the Division of Standards and Training (DST) to ensure the standards for the MSP and that recruits receive up-to-date training and education. The DST is organized into two sections: *Standards* and *Training*. Officers in the Standards section are responsible for investigating citizen complaints filed against MSP. In addition, officers in this section conduct background investigations on state employees, investigate allegations of discrimination and sexual harassment, and issue licenses to private investigators. Officers in the Training section provide basic training to recruits, as well as professional development training to existing officers (Commonwealth of Massachusetts, n.d.h).

To be considered for the MSP, candidates must meet the requirements listed in Table 3.2. Furthermore, recruits must complete the MSP Academy. Recruits attend this academy for 25 weeks. They are required to live at the academy from Monday morning until Friday afternoon every week but are allowed to go home on the weekends. Their day begins at 5:30 a.m. every morning with

Table 3.3 Requirements to Become a Municipal Police Officer in Boston

- Massachusetts Police Officer Civil Service Examination
- Residency in Boston one year before the exam
- U.S. citizen
- High school diploma or equivalency certificate
- Between 19 and 40 years old on the date of the exam
- Not convicted of felony
- Able to obtain firearms permit
- Pass physical ability test

Source: How to Become a Police Officer, 2018.

physical training. After that, they attend academic courses until 8:00 p.m., and then they have personal time or time to study until the lights go out at 9:30 p.m. (Commonwealth of Massachusetts, n.d.c).

The training to become a member of the MSP is challenging. Recruits receive classroom instruction and physical training in a strict, paramilitary environment. The curriculum includes criminal law, motor vehicle law, evidence identification, firearms training, public speaking, self-defense tactics, defensive driving, patrol procedures, military drills, court procedures, ethics, diversity awareness, and community policing.

Local Police Training

Local law enforcement agencies also have basic requirements for selecting candidates. Although each department has its own set of selection criteria, they usually have similar standards. See Table 3.3 for the basic requirements for consideration as a candidate for the Boston Police Department.

Aside from these basic requirements, police departments conduct extensive background checks and drug tests for each candidate. They review the candidate's education, military, credit, and driving records. In addition, they conduct in-depth interviews with the applicant's partners, acquaintances, and former employers. They also look at social media accounts, such as Facebook, Instagram, and Twitter, to determine if information posted to these sites pose any red flags for candidates (Gaines & Miller, 2016).

Recruits for the local police are also required to attend the intensive Recruit Officer Course, which is a 20-week basic training program for full-time entry-level municipal officers. The Recruit Officer Course provides recruits with classroom instruction, practical exercises, and scenarios that give them the knowledge and skills needed to be a successful police officer. The training focuses on integrity and professionalism as well as addressing emerging trends and issues in policing. This training is led by the Municipal Police Training Committee (MPTC), an agency within the Executive Office of Public Safety and Security. The MPTC establishes standards and provides training to police officers throughout the Commonwealth of Massachusetts (Commonwealth of Massachusetts, n.d.f).

Current Issues and Trends in Policing

While everything has its ups and downs, the field of policing has had a couple of especially challenging years. According to a Gallup poll, the public's confidence in the police is the lowest it has been in over 20 years (Jones, 2015), and unless something changes, these negative perceptions will continue. In the following sections, we will address some of the issues plaguing law enforcement today, including the use of force, civil unrest, and recommendations to improve the existing system. In addition, we will discuss some of the technology that police officers in Massachusetts are using to help solve crimes.

Use of Force

Police use of force is necessary and permitted under special circumstances, including self-defense or defense of citizens. While there is no universal definition of the use of force, the International Association of Chiefs of Police (2001) describes the ***use of force*** as the "amount of effort required by police to compel compliance by an unwilling subject."

In potentially threatening situations, officers must respond quickly and apply force, if necessary. Sworn police officers are trained to judge a crisis situation and use force to control the situation (National Institute of Justice, 2016). Police should only use the amount of force needed to regain control of a situation or to protect themselves and citizens from harm. However, the level of force will vary depending on the situation.

There are two types of force used by police officers—nondeadly (less than lethal) and deadly force. The majority of cases in which force is used is nondeadly and is usually referred to as ***reasonable force***. Reasonable force is the degree of force that a reasonable person would use if force were necessary to protect the officer or other citizens from harm. On the other hand, ***deadly force*** is force used by a police officer that is likely to cause death.

Hyland, Langton, and Davis (2015) reported that between 2002 and 2011, there had been an average of 44 million people per year who have had contact with the police. Of those people, 1.6% experienced the threat or use of nondeadly force by police. Three quarters, or 1.2% of those people, perceived the use of force to be excessive. While this may not seem like a large percentage, some groups experienced higher percentages of excessive force during contact with the police. Specifically, 2.8% of non-Hispanic Black people reported the use of excessive force in their encounters with the police.

Over recent years, we too often hear about stories of unarmed Black men who have been killed by police officers—primarily White officers. In the summer of 2014, Michael Brown was shot and killed in Ferguson, Missouri by a White officer, and Eric Garner died after being placed in a chokehold by New York City police officers. Shortly after, the grand juries failed to indict the officers in each of these cases. Following these cases, there have been countless other deaths, including the killings of Tamir Rice in Cleveland, Freddie Gray in Baltimore, Alton Sterling in Baton Rouge, and Philando Castile in St. Paul.

Civil Unrest

As a result of these killings, there has been a national uproar concerning the relationship between the police and the Black community, creating a state of civil unrest. Often as a reaction to a particular incident, citizens will engage in protests or demonstrations to express their frustrations toward the police. Unfortunately, these situations have the potential to become aggressive, and they can create an atmosphere for rioting and violence.

For example, in July of 2016, Micah Xavier Johnson reportedly shot at a group of police officers in Dallas, killing five of them and injuring nine other officers and two civilians. This shooting happened after a ***Black Lives Matter*** protest against the police killings of two African Americans: Alton Sterling in Louisiana and Philando Castile in Minnesota. During this same time period, hundreds of people in cities across the country were arrested for protesting the deaths of Sterling and Castile (Karimi, Shoichet, & Ellis, 2016).

The *Black Lives Matter* movement was created in 2012 after the murder of unarmed 17-year-old African American, Trayvon Martin, and the subsequent acquittal of George Zimmerman who was acting as a community watch member. The *Black Lives Matter* movement operates as a watchdog organization to shine a public light on issues they feel are unjust. The *Black Lives Matter* movement is a chapter-based, citizen-oriented, national organization working for the validity of Black lives. They are working to rebuild the Black liberation movement. Rooted in the experiences of Black people in the United States, this movement is a call to action and a response to the injustice that befalls underrepresented populations (Black Lives Matter, n.d.).

Feeling the pressure, police officers have tried to sue the *Black Lives Matter* movement, claiming the group's civil unrest gave way to actions that physically caused officers harm. In September, 2017, U.S. District Judge Brian Jackson ruled in Baton Rouge, Louisiana that Black Lives Matter is a social movement, like the Tea Party or the Civil Rights Movement, and therefore cannot be sued. The judge reiterated that Black Lives Matter is not an entity capable of being sued.

President's Task Force on 21st Century Policing

The President's Task Force on 21st Century Policing was created by an executive order signed by former President Barack Obama in December 2014. President Obama created this task force in response to the civil unrest in Ferguson, Missouri following the shooting of an unarmed African American, Michael Brown, by a White Ferguson police officer. The task force had 11 members that included academics, law enforcement officials, and civil rights activists (President's Task Force on 21st Century Policing, 2015).

The co-chairs of the task force were Philadelphia Police Commissioner Charles H. Ramsey and George Mason University Professor Laurie Robinson who taught the Criminology, Law, and Society program. Chief Ramsey is a 45-year police veteran and led the Washington DC Metropolitan Police for 19 years and the Philadelphia police for nearly 10 years. Professor Robinson twice served as the assistant attorney general for the U.S. Department of Justice Office of Justice Programs.

The task force created recommendations to help law enforcement and communities across the nation to build trust. The final report, which was released in 2015, called for additional data on police shootings, the public's attitudes toward police, and the removal of policies rewarding police for making more arrests. The task force released an update to the report, stating that nine states and cities across the country had adopted the task force's recommendations. However, with 18,000 police departments in the United States, many members of the task force expressed frustration with these numbers.

The task force was responsible for identifying best practices to promote effective crime reduction while building trust with the community. These recommendations were broken into six pillars (President's Task Force on 21st Century Policing, 2015):

1. *Building Trust and Legitimacy.* Promoting trust and ensuring legitimacy through transparency, accountability, and recognition of past and present obstacles.

2. *Policy and Oversight.* Developing policies on key topics while also implementing formal checks and balances as well as data collection and analysis.
3. *Technology and Social Media.* Balancing the embrace of technology and digital communications with local needs, privacy, and monitoring.
4. *Community Policing and Crime Reduction.* Encouraging the implementation of policies that support community-based partnerships to reduce crime.
5. *Training and Education.* Emphasizing the importance of effective training and education through partnerships with local and national training facilities.
6. *Officer Wellness and Safety.* Endorsing practices that support officer wellness and safety through the reevaluation of shift hours through data collection and analysis to help prevent officer injuries.

It is clear that unless something changes, perceptions of the police nationwide and the relationship between police and communities will only continue to get worse. Consequently, it is important for law enforcement agencies across the nation to implement the suggestions provided by the task force.

Technology and Forensic Science

Police are relying more on modern day technology to increase their effectiveness at solving crimes. The use of technology continues to be more prevalent in policing with the increased use of social media, cellphones, crime-mapping software, digitization, facial recognition software, and advances in forensic science. Over the past few decades, technology has transformed the way that police officers do their job and has proven to be helpful in solving crimes.

The MSP Crime Laboratory is the primary forensic science facility in Massachusetts providing services, including DNA analysis, fingerprint identification, and chemical analysis of evidence. This lab provides forensic services throughout the commonwealth, and there are various sections and units located throughout Massachusetts (Commonwealth of Massachusetts, n.d.g). Some of these units include the following:

- The *Arson and Explosives Unit* receives evidence from crime scenes involving suspicious fires and explosions. Using state-of-the-art equipment, this unit identifies ignitable liquid evidence or explosive residue to help police solve investigations.
- The *CODIS Unit*, or Combined DNA Index System, manages CODIS. Individuals convicted of felonies in Massachusetts are required to submit

a blood sample to the crime laboratory, and the profile of the offender is entered into the state and national CODIS databases. Crime scene DNA evidence can then be compared to other case samples and is useful in catching suspected criminals.

- The *Crime Scene Response Unit* is responsible for on-site technical assistance at crime scenes. Chemists from this unit collect, test, and analyze evidence to aid in the reconstruction of events.
- The *DNA Unit* analyzes forensic samples from crime scenes to include or exclude potential suspects in a particular crime.
- The *Drug Identification Unit* analyzes contraband seized by the MSP and examines the items for controlled substances such as marijuana, cocaine, or heroin.
- The *Identification Section* maintains fingerprint identification records. These records can help law enforcement agencies identify suspects by matching recovered prints to those of known criminals.

Finally, police in Boston began to use ***body cameras*** as part of a pilot program in 2016 (Enwemka, 2016). A body camera is a video recording system used by law enforcement to record their interactions with the public in hopes of increasing both officer and citizen accountability. The camera is intended to accurately capture the actions of police officers and citizens, aiding police reports in complex situations. Although this technology is new, the idea is that it will strengthen relationships between the police and the community.

Conclusion

After reading this chapter, you should be more familiar with the different levels of law enforcement within the Commonwealth of Massachusetts. You should also be familiar with the requirements to become a police officer in Massachusetts. Finally, you should be aware of some of the challenges and issues facing law enforcement today. It is more important than ever for police officers to uphold their oath of office and to protect and serve their communities with honesty and integrity.

Key Terms

Black Lives Matter: Chapter-based, citizen-initiated national movement working for the validity of Black lives in America and acts as a watchdog group against police brutality.

Body Camera: Video recording system used by law enforcement to record their interactions with the public.

Boston Police Strike: A work stoppage conducted by the police in an attempt to improve wages and working conditions for patrolmen and recognition for its trade union.

Civil Process: The handling and serving of legal and court documents, including summons, subpoenas, and restraining orders.

Deadly Force: Force applied by a police officer that is likely to cause death.

Jurisdiction: Legal authority for police to enforce laws within a specific geographic area.

Metropolitan Police Act: An 1829 law that stablishing the first organized police force in London.

Municipal: Relating to a city, town, or its governing body.

Private Investigator: Person hired by individuals or corporations to undertake investigatory law services.

Reasonable Force: Degree of force appropriate to protect a police officer or other citizens.

Sir Robert Peel: Known as the father of modern policing, introduced the Metropolitan Police Act in 1829, establishing a modern police force in London.

Special Police Officer: A specially trained licensed security officer, hired by private companies or public agencies, who underwent special training under the supervision of the Massachusetts State Police or Boston Police Department.

Sworn Police Officer: Police officer who has been sworn in under oath and has the authority to arrest citizens and carry a firearm.

Troop: Assignment areas for police in the Massachusetts State Police.

Use of Force: Amount of effort required by police to compel compliance by an unwilling subject.

William Cloran Training Academy: A training academy for special police officers in Boston.

Related Websites

Boston Police Department
 http://bpdnews.com/
Commission on Accreditation for Law Enforcement Agencies
 http://www.calea.org/
Massachusetts Chiefs of Police Association
 http://www.masschiefs.org/
Massachusetts Municipal Association
 https://www.mma.org/
Massachusetts State Police
 https://www.mass.gov/orgs/massachusetts-state-police

Review Questions

1. Explain the term "sworn officer."
2. Why is jurisdiction an important concept?
3. How do county sheriff's departments differ from municipal police departments?
4. What is a private investigator?
5. Why is it important to have an extensive selection process for potential police officers?
6. What are the requirements to work as a State Police Officer in Massachusetts?
7. What are the requirements to work in a municipal agency in MA, such as the BPD?
8. What is the difference between *reasonable* force and *deadly* force?
9. What is the significance of the President's Task Force on 21st Century Policing?
10. What is the significance of the Massachusetts State Police Crime Laboratory?

References

Black Lives Matter. (n.d.). *Homepage.* Retrieved from https://blacklivesmatter.com/.

BPD News. (n.d.). *History.* Retrieved from http://bpdnews.com/history/.

Bureau of Labor Statistics. (2018). *Occupational employment and wages, May 2017.* Retrieved from http://www.bls.gov/oes/current/oes339021.htm#st.

Commonwealth of Massachusetts. (n.d.a). *History of the SSPO Program.* Retrieved from http://www.mass.gov/eopss/funding-and-training/law-enforce/msp-acad/sspo/history.html.

Commonwealth of Massachusetts. (n.d.b). *Massachusetts State Police.* Retrieved from http://www.mass.gov/eopss/agencies/msp/#.V5Ygd_krLIU.

Commonwealth of Massachusetts. (n.d.c). *State Police Academy.* Retrieved from http://www.mass.gov/eopss/funding-and-training/law-enforce/msp-acad/academy-overview.html.

Commonwealth of Massachusetts. (n.d.d). *Recruitment.* Retrieved from http://www.mass.gov/eopss/agencies/msp/msp-recruit-prog/recruitment-information.html.

Commonwealth of Massachusetts. (n.d.e). *Massachusetts State Police Troop boundaries.* Retrieved from http://www.mass.gov/eopss/law-enforce-and-cj/law-enforce/msp-troops/troop-boundaries.html.

Commonwealth of Massachusetts. (n.d.f). *Guide: Requirements of all student officers.* Retrieved from https://www.mass.gov/guides/requirements-of-all-student-officers.

Commonwealth of Massachusetts. (n.d.g). *Forensic testing sections.* Retrieved from http://www.mass.gov/eopss/law-enforce-and-cj/criminal-investig/crime-lab/sections-and-units/.

Commonwealth of Massachusetts. (n.d.h). *Massachusetts State Police.* Retrieved from https://www.mass.gov/orgs/massachusetts-state-police.

Enwemka, Z. (2016, April 29). *Boston Police will roll out body camera pilot program, but policy questions remain.* Retrieved from http://www.wbur.org/news/2016/04/29/boston-police-body-cameras-pilot.

FBI. (2014a). *Massachusetts: Full-time law enforcement employees by city, 2014.* Retrieved from https://ucr.fbi.gov/crime-in-the-u.s/2014/crime-in-the-u.s.-2014/tables/table-78/table-78-bystate/Table_78_Full_time_Law_Enforcement_Employees_Massachesetts_by_Cities_2014.xls.

FBI. (2014b). *Full-time law enforcement employees by state, 2014.* Retrieved from https://ucr.fbi.gov/crime-in-the-u.s/2014/crime-in-the-u.s.-2014/tables/table-77.

Gaines, L., & Miller, R. (2016). *Criminal justice in action: The core.* (8th ed.). Boston, MA: Cengage Learning.

Herwick, E. B. (2016). *The Boston police strike that impacted labor for generations.* Retrieved from https://www.wgbh.org/news/post/boston-police-strike-impacted-labor-generations.

How to become a police officer. (2018). Retrieved from https://www.boston.gov/departments/police/how-become-police-officer.

Hyland, S., Langton, L., & Davis, E. (2015). *Police use of nonfatal force, 2002–11.* Retrieved from http://www.bjs.gov/content/pub/pdf/punf0211.pdf.

International Association of Chiefs of Police. (2001). *Police use of force in America, 2001.* Alexandria, VA: Author.

Jones, J. M. (2015, June 19). *In U.S., confidence in police lowest in 22 years.* Retrieved from http://www.gallup.com/poll/183704/confidence-police-lowest--years.aspx.

Karimi, F., Shoichet, C. E., & Ellis, R. (2016, July 9). *Dallas shooting: 5 officers die, suspect identified.* Retrieved from https://www.cnn.com/2016/07/08/us/philando-castile-alton-sterling-protests/index.html.

Massachusetts Bay Transportation Authority. (n.d.). *MBTA Transit Police.* Retrieved from http://www.mbta.com/transitpolice/the_department/default.asp?id=18850.

MSP Museum and Learning Center. (n.d.). *MSP history.* Retrieved from https://www.mspmlc.org/history.

National Institute of Justice. (2016). *Police use of force.* Retrieved from http://www.nij.gov/topics/law-enforcement/officer-safety/use-of-force/pages/welcome.aspx.

NEMLEC. (n.d.). *Who we are.* Retrieved from http://www.nemlec.com/.

President's Task Force on 21st Century Policing. (2015). *Final report of the President's Task Force on 21st Century Policing.* Washington, DC: Office of Community Oriented Policing Services.

Reaves, B. A. (2011). *Census of state and local law enforcement agencies, 2008.* Retrieved from http://www.bjs.gov/content/pub/pdf/csllea08.pdf.

Seigel, L., & Worrall, J. (2018). *Essentials of criminal justice.* (10th ed.). Boston, MA: Cengage.

U.S. District Court for the District of Puerto Rico. (n.d.). *The Massachusetts state flag.* Retrieved from https://www.prd.uscourts.gov/massachusetts-state-flag.

William Cloran Academy. (2014). *Homepage.* Retrieved from http://bostonspo.com/.

Chapter 4

Massachusetts Criminal Law

Learning Objectives

- Familiarize yourself with federal, state, and local laws.
- Learn how laws are created in Massachusetts.
- Understand the difference between criminal law and civil law.
- Explain the difference between procedural law and substantive law.
- Examine criminal laws in Massachusetts.

Introduction

In this chapter, we will discuss some of the criminal laws in Massachusetts. First, we will examine different types of laws: federal, state, and local. Second, we will discuss how laws are created in the commonwealth. Third, we will address the differences between criminal and civil laws. Finally, we will examine some Massachusetts criminal laws to see how certain offenses are defined in the state. We will be examining the same crime categories that we covered in Chapter 2: homicide, forcible rape, robbery, aggravated assault, burglary, motor vehicle theft, larceny-theft, and arson.

Types of Laws: Federal, State, and Local

This section briefly discusses how criminal laws can be enacted at any level of government. According to the U.S. Constitution, the U.S. Congress and Senate have the power to pass federal laws (U.S. Const. art. I, §8). These laws deal with interstate commerce, regulation of certain firearms, drug-related offenses, and money laundering, among other criminal actions.

Additionally, states have the power to ***enact*** laws. The Tenth Amendment of the U.S. Constitution states that all powers not delegated to the federal government are reserved to the states (U.S. Const. amend. X). Therefore, state legislatures enact laws on behalf of the states, many of which deal with criminal violations. The process of passing laws in Massachusetts is discussed in the following section.

Finally, laws can also be enacted at the local level. For example, cities can enact laws by the vote of the city council. Laws at the local level often relate to the health and welfare of residents, and they are only valid in the city in which they were enacted. For example, the Town of Middleborough banned the use of silly string in 2001, stating that its use negatively impacted the safety and welfare of town residents. Violators of this local bylaw face up to $300 in fines (Town Clerk's Office, 2011). However, this law is only valid in Middleborough and would not have to be adhered to in any other city or town in Massachusetts or the United States.

How Laws Are Created in Massachusetts

Laws in Massachusetts are enacted primarily through the state legislature, which is divided into two branches. The 160 members of the House of Representatives and the 40 members of the Senate work together to create laws for the commonwealth. Lawmaking officially begins when bills are filed in the House or Senate clerk's office. The bills are then assigned to one of 21 committees, each of which is responsible for a particular area of interest (e.g., education, healthcare, taxation) (Galvin, 2012).

Next, the respective committee schedules a public hearing for the bill, allowing citizens and legislators to express their opinions on the bill. After the public hearing, members of the committee meet to examine the public testimony and discuss whether or not they think the bill should pass. The committee then makes recommendations in a report that is submitted to the clerk for a first reading. Both favorable and adverse reports are referred to the Committee on Steering and Policy in the Senate or placed in the Orders of the Day for the next session in the House.

Once a favorable bill is reexamined in a second reading, a vote is taken by all of the members of the House or Senate. If the bill receives another favorable vote, it is referred to the Committee on Bills. This committee examines the bill to ensure its constitutionality before returning it for a third reading to the respective House or Senate, which then votes to pass the bill to be engrossed.

Once a bill is engrossed in one legislative branch, it must go through three readings and engrossment in the other branch. Finally, both the House and the Senate vote to enact the bill. After the bill is enacted, it goes to the governor, who can sign it into law, veto it, or return it to the legislature with suggested changes. Once the governor signs a bill, or two thirds of both legislative branches override the governor's veto, the bill becomes law, and it usually goes into effect within 90 days (Galvin, 2012).

Criminal Law vs. Civil Law

Both ***criminal laws*** and ***civil laws*** regulate the conduct of citizens. Civil laws focus on private wrongs of which the state has little interest. In civil suits, one party brings an action against another party in a court of law, and a judge or jury resolves the dispute between parties. Civil suits primarily deal with ***breaches of contract*** or ***torts***. Breaches of contract occur when one of the parties to a contract violates the terms of that contract. Torts do not involve a violation of the terms of a contract, but they do involve a violation of the rights of an injured party. Examples of torts include wrongful death suits, negligent infliction of personal injury, and trespassing. In civil cases, the damages sought by the injured party are usually monetary (Scheb & Scheb, 1999).

Unlike civil law, the state has a significant interest in criminal law. Criminal laws are enforced by the government, prosecuted by the government, and punished by the government. Moreover, criminal law includes the statutes that define conduct prohibited by the government because said conduct threatens or harms the public safety and welfare of citizens. In addition, the state also establishes punishment for the commission of criminal acts (Gardner & Mallicoat, 2012). Depending on the crime and the circumstances surrounding the crime, punishment ranges from monetary fines to capital punishment. However, because Massachusetts does not recognize capital punishment, life in prison would be the most severe punishment that could be imposed in the commonwealth for violation of state law.

Criminal law differentiates between serious crimes and less serious offenses. For more serious crimes, known as ***felonies***, offenders can receive a sentence of one year or more in state prison. Examples of felonies include homicide, forcible rape, arson, aggravated assault, and robbery. On the other hand, ***misdemeanors*** are less serious crimes, which are punishable by fines or less than 1-year imprisonment in a house of correction. Examples of misdemeanors include petty theft, public drunkenness, disorderly conduct, and gambling (Gardner & Mallicoat, 2012).

Boston's Fugitive Slave Case of Anthony Burns

While slavery was clearly thriving in the American South, activists in Massachusetts and a trial in Boston were prominent in the push toward abolition. The case of an escaped slave from Virginia who was found and arrested in Boston and ordered to be returned to slavery in Virginia put Boston in the national and moral spotlight. This case attracted national attention, had far reaching implications, and would dramatically alter the relationship between North and South forever. The 1854 Boston trial sent 50,000 people into the streets in protest and invigorated the abolition movement in the United States, resulting in the removal of a Boston Judge and an attack on U.S. Marshals at the federal courthouse in Suffolk County.

In 1853, 19-year-old ***Anthony Burns*** escaped slavery in Virginia and fled north as a stowaway aboard a ship sailing from Richmond to Massachusetts. After landing in Boston, he found a job as a store clerk at a clothing shop on Brattle Street and joined the nearby Twelfth Baptist Church, which was located on Phillips Street on Beacon Hill at the time. Burns hoped to put the painful memories of slavery behind him and build a new life of freedom, hard work, and worship. When his location was discovered, his former slave owner traveled to Boston and sought to reclaim him under the ***Fugitive Slave Act of 1850.***

On May 24, 1854, Anthony Burns was found and arrested as he quietly walked down Court Street in Boston on his way home from work. He was arrested not far from the federal court house that would later seal his fate. Fugitive slaves had long caused conflict between the antebellum South and North. In fact, the framers of the U.S. Constitution, after heated debates, compelled Northern citizens to cooperate with Southern masters in reclaiming their runaway slaves with the Fugitive Slave Clause in Article 4 of the Constitution.

But many abolitionists in the North, especially in places like Boston, had worked tirelessly to undermine the fugitive slave clause by helping transport escaped slaves to Canada or the free Black communities of the North. One such underground group was the Boston Vigilance Committee. Boston in 1854 was not just the abolitionist capital of America but also the North's intellectual center. Some of the most important writers, thinkers, and intellects in the country lived in or around Boston. Many of these progressive thinkers shared abolitionist sentiments, including William Lloyd Garrison, Ralph Waldo Emerson, Henry David Thoreau, and poet John Greenleaf Whittier. The week of Burns's arrest coincided with a large Boston convention being held by abolitionists and women's rights groups. Famed author Harriet Beecher Stowe happened to be in town along with hundreds of abolitionists from across the North. Beecher Stow's 1852 novel *Uncle Tom's Cabin* helped to radicalize White middle-class and upper-class Northerners against slavery.

Burns was placed in a jail cell on the third floor of Boston's federal courthouse on Court Street in downtown Boston until he stood before Judge Edward Loring. The Boston Vigilance Committee organized a huge meeting at Boston's historic Faneuil Hall. Some 5,000 irate antislavery protesters attended. While the White abolitionists were meeting in Faneuil Hall, members of Boston's African American community were meeting at the same time at the nearby Tremont Temple. After the meeting, the Black community rushed to the courthouse in an attempt to rescue Burns. Hundreds of people ran from the Faneuil Hall meeting to help the Tremont Temple protesters. An estimated 2,000 antislavery protesters mobbed Court Square unsuccessfully attempting to free Burns.

On June 2, 1854, as Judge Loring was prepared to hand down his decision, the City of Boston was placed under martial law. Because of the large size of the crowds and violent protests by abolitionists and citizens of Boston, federal troops were called in to help during and after the trial. Judge Loring decided to abide by the Fugitive Slave Act of 1850 and ordered that Anthony Burns return to Virginia, placing him back into slavery. At 2:00 p.m., Burns was escorted out of the courthouse (the building that is now known as the location of the Boston School committee), surrounded by a large contingent of Marines. Some 50,000 Bostonians lined streets in protest. Burns was marched down to Boston's Long Wharf to begin his long voyage back to Virginia and slavery.

Boston would never be the same again. At a huge July 4th outdoor meeting held in nearby Framingham a month after the Burns decision, Massachusetts journalist and abolitionist, William Lloyd Garrison made his point with fire. He stood before the crowd and burned a copy of the Fugitive Slave Act of 1850, a copy of Judge Loring's written decision in the Burns case, and a copy of the U.S. Constitution, condemning it as "a covenant with death and an agreement with hell."

Philosopher and abolitionist Henry David Thoreau believed that Northern silence in the face of the injustice against Burns and his three million fellow slaves could no longer continue. He favored civil disobedience to improve the government. Thoreau planted the seeds of civil war when he stated that they needed recognize a higher law than the Constitution or the decision of the majority. He further asserted that Northern states like Massachusetts should dissolve its union with the slaveholding states.

Eventually Reverend Leonard A. Grimes of the Twelfth Baptist Church would succeed in buying Burns's freedom for $1,300. Anthony Burns returned to Boston as a free man. He later studied at Ohio's Oberlin College and then became a Baptist minister. On July 27, 1862, just seven weeks before Lincoln would issue his Emancipation Proclamation, 28-year-old Burns died in Canada from tuberculosis. He was the last escaped slave in the United States to be returned to the South under the Fugitive Slave Act (MassMoments, n.d.).

Procedural Law vs. Substantive Law

Furthermore, criminal law can also be divided into ***procedural*** and ***substantive law***. Procedural law dictates the formal steps that the criminal justice system needs to take to ensure individual rights. These laws determine procedures such as filing a criminal charge after an arrest, trial proceedings, and matters regarding sentencing. On the other hand, substantive laws define crimes such as homicide, forcible rape, and arson, as well as the punishment associated with the particular crime (Gardner & Mallicoat, 2012).

Substantive laws require proof of two elements for an act to be considered criminal: (1) a wrongful act (***actus reus***) and (2) criminal intent (***mens rea***). Therefore, an act must not only be prohibited by law, but the offender must also intentionally engage in the act. For example, in the crime of arson, the *actus reus* would be the act of burning another person's property, and the *mens rea* would be the deliberate intent to set the fire. It is not necessary to show why a person committed a crime, only that the person intentionally committed an act prohibited by law (Scheb & Scheb, 1999).

Criminal Laws in Massachusetts

In this chapter, we will discuss some of the substantive laws in Massachusetts. These laws are laid out in Part IV, Title I of the Massachusetts General Laws, which are laws codified according to the subject matter. The General Laws dictate crimes and their associated punishments for a variety of crimes, including crimes against people, crimes against property, forgery, and money laundering. We will cover four specific crimes against people (homicide, forcible rape, robbery, and aggravated assault) and four crimes against property (burglary, motor vehicle theft, larceny-theft, and arson). These crimes were chosen because they comprise the eight Part I index crimes, reported to the Uniform Crime Reporting (UCR) Program, as discussed in Chapter 2 (The 190th General Court of the Commonwealth of Massachusetts, 2018).

Homicide

Homicide is defined as the killing of a human being by another human being. Because homicide is the most severe crime someone could commit, the laws regarding this crime are very complex. In fact, without a law degree, it is difficult to understand all of the intricacies surrounding homicide laws. In Massachusetts, criminal homicide can fall under one of two categories—murder or manslaughter. We will be examining the basics of criminal homicide, including first- and second-degree murder as well as voluntary, involuntary, and vehicular manslaughter.

Murder

As stated in Massachusetts law, first-degree murder is defined as "murder committed with deliberately premeditated malice aforethought, or with extreme atrocity or cruelty, or in the commission or attempted commission of a crime punishable with death or imprisonment for life" (MGL c.265 §1).

The term deliberate ***premeditation*** refers to the thinking process that the defendant used when killing the victim. In the case of deliberately premeditated murder, the actions were planned, and the defendant had time to think about the consequences of his actions before committing the killing. In addition, ***malice aforethought*** must be proved to make out a case of first-degree murder. This means that the defendant intended to kill the victim or intended to cause the victim severe bodily harm without a legal justification for the killing (e.g. self-defense) (Scheb & Scheb, 1999).

Alternatively, killings that lack premeditation, but are especially atrocious or cruel, can be classified as first-degree murder. During a trial, a jury determines if there is sufficient evidence for the killing to possess extreme atrocity or cruelty. Members of the jury consider factors, such as the amount of suffering the victim endured, the severity of injuries, and the type of weapon used during the murder, to determine if the crime falls within this category (Kickham, n.d.a).

A homicide can also be classified as first-degree murder if it occurs during the commission of a felony punishable by life in prison. The underlying felony must be inherently dangerous, such as armed robbery. For example, in the event of a bank robbery, someone may be killed. Even though there was no intent for someone to get killed, there was intent to commit another felony punishable by life in prison. Therefore, the intent would be carried over from the original felony, and the defendant could be found guilty of first-degree murder.

A first-degree murder conviction in Massachusetts has an automatic sentence of life in prison without the possibility of parole (MGL c.265 §2).

Relatedly, a "murder which does not appear to be in the first degree is murder in the second degree" (MGL c.265 §1). We will discuss two types of murder that are often classified as second-degree murder. First, an unlawful killing committed with malice aforethought, but without deliberate premeditation, is usually considered second-degree murder. In this case, the offender had intent to cause serious bodily injury with no legal justification, but he had not thought about the commission of the crime beforehand. Secondly, second-degree murder can also include a murder committed during the commission of a felony not punishable by life imprisonment (Kickham, n.d.b). The original felony is typically a property crime, such as burglary or motor vehicle theft, rather than a crime against a person.

In Massachusetts, second-degree murder has an automatic sentence of life in prison with the possibility of parole after 15 years (MGL c.265 §2).

Manslaughter

Other than first-degree and second-degree murder, a person can also be charged with ***manslaughter*** in Massachusetts. Manslaughter is the unlawful killing of a human being by another human being in the absence of malice. In this chapter, we will discuss three categories of manslaughter—voluntary, involuntary, and vehicular manslaughter.

Even though they are governed by the same statute, Massachusetts statutory law does not differentiate between voluntary and involuntary manslaughter. Instead, Massachusetts common law, or law derived from the courts, defines these categories of manslaughter. ***Voluntary manslaughter*** is the killing of another human being in the heat of passion upon reasonable provocation or sudden combat or from the excessive use of force in self-defense (Massachusetts Murder Defense, n.d.b).

Instances where the death of the victim occurs in the heat of passion or during a fight constitute voluntary manslaughter. In this type of manslaughter, the defendant is provoked by a situation that causes him to lose control of his emotions. The law would consider a homicide voluntary manslaughter if the killing happened as a result of circumstances that would cause a reasonable person to become so angry that he would be unable to restrain himself in a similar situation. Furthermore, the law requires that the time between the provocation and the killing be brief and that a reasonable person would not have had time to "cool off" and reflect upon the situation. One example that could reduce murder charges to voluntary manslaughter is a spouse finding his partner in bed with another person. In those circumstances, the defendant becomes angry on account of the situation, loses control, and kills one of the other parties. The loss of control removes the element of malice that is necessary for a murder conviction.

Voluntary manslaughter can also occur in instances of self-defense. Although someone can use force to defend himself from imminent harm, excessive force resulting in the death of his attacker could result in a conviction of voluntary manslaughter in Massachusetts.

As with voluntary manslaughter, involuntary manslaughter is defined by common law, rather than statutory law, in Massachusetts. ***Involuntary manslaughter*** may be committed in one of two ways: (1) an unintentional killing caused by wanton or reckless conduct or (2) an unintentional killing resulting from battery (Massachusetts Murder Defense, n.d.a). Under the first condition, a person can be convicted of involuntary manslaughter if he unintentionally kills someone due to wanton or reckless conduct. In this case, there must also be a high likelihood that the reckless conduct had the potential to harm someone and that the defendant was aware of the potential harm when he committed the act. For example, operating a vehicle in a reckless manner, such as playing "chicken," could constitute involuntary manslaughter if one of the parties is killed. A reasonable person is aware that playing this type of game has the potential to inflict serious bodily harm or death on another person.

The second way a defendant could be convicted of involuntary manslaughter is if he committed a battery that resulted in the unintended death of another human being. Even though the defendant may not have intended to kill the victim, he knew that the original act, such as striking someone over the head with a bottle, could cause bodily harm, though not likely death or serious bodily injury. In this case, the prosecution must show that the defendant should have known that his conduct was likely to result in harm to another person.

The maximum sentence for both voluntary and involuntary manslaughter in Massachusetts is 20 years in state prison (MGL c.265 § 13).

In addition to voluntary and involuntary manslaughter, someone can be convicted of ***motor vehicle homicide*** in Massachusetts. Someone who kills another human being while operating a motor vehicle on a public way in a reckless or negligent manner and is under the influence of alcohol or another intoxicating substance can be convicted of felony motor vehicle homicide. The maximum sentence for felony motor vehicle homicide is 15 years in state prison. In addition, someone can be convicted of misdemeanor motor vehicle homicide if he kills someone while operating a motor vehicle on a public way either (1) in a reckless or negligent manner or (2) is under the influence of alcohol or another intoxicating substance. The maximum penalty for misdemeanor motor vehicle homicide is two-and-a-half years in a county jail or house of correction. Furthermore, the first time someone is convicted of either felony or misdemeanor motor vehicle homicide, his or her driver's license is revoked for 15 years. Subsequent convictions of this crime result in a lifetime revocation of one's driver's license (MGL 90 § 24G).

Forcible Rape

There are two primary categories of sex offenses governed by Massachusetts law—nonforcible sex offenses and forcible sex offenses. Nonforcible sex offenses include sexual acts between an offender and a victim who is not able to give consent. The most notable nonforcible sex offense is statutory rape, where one of the parties is underage and consequently is unable to give consent. We will cover forcible sex offenses in this section, specifically forcible rape.

In Massachusetts, anyone who has sexual intercourse or unnatural sexual intercourse with another person, compelling that person to submit by force and against his or her will, can be convicted of ***forcible rape*** (MGL c.265 §22). Sexual intercourse or unnatural sexual intercourse requires penetration of the vagina, anus, or mouth. In addition, a male sex organ, fingers, or a foreign object can be used to penetrate any of the aforementioned orifices. Furthermore, force can include the threat of bodily injury as well as actual physical force.

Finally, anyone can be an offender or a victim of forcible rape in Massachusetts, regardless of gender. It does not matter if the defendant and alleged victim were married or dating at the time of the rape. As long as the prosecution can determine that the defendant penetrated the victim forcibly and against his or her will, the defendant can be convicted of forcible rape.

In Massachusetts, a first-time conviction of forcible rape has a maximum sentence of 20 years in state prison, and a subsequent conviction can result in life imprisonment. Moreover, a conviction of forcible rape involving the use of a firearm mandates a minimum sentence of 10 years in state prison (MGL c.265 §22).

Robbery

Robbery is a serious violent offense that usually involves an assault or battery. Note that robbery is different than the various categories of property theft, which will be discussed shortly, because robbery entails stealing from someone using force or the threat of force. In this section, we will discuss both armed and unarmed robbery and their respective penalties in Massachusetts.

A person who is "armed with a dangerous weapon, assaults another and robs, steals or takes from his person money or other property which may be the subject of larceny" (MGL c. 265 §17) can be convicted of ***armed robbery***. Simply put, armed robbery involves stealing something from someone by use of force and a dangerous weapon, such as a firearm or a knife.

The maximum sentence for armed robbery is life imprisonment in state prison. Furthermore, if the offender disguised his face (with a mask, for example) during the robbery, the first armed robbery conviction results in a mandatory minimum sentence of 5 years in state prison; subsequent armed robbery convictions while disguised result in a minimum of 15 years in state prison.

Unarmed robbery is similar to armed robbery except that it does not involve the use of a deadly weapon (MGL c.265 §19). This crime still involves the unlawful taking of another person's property by force, but the offender does not use a weapon. The maximum sentence for unarmed robbery in Massachusetts is life imprisonment. Similar to armed robbery, unarmed robbery also mandates minimum sentences for an offender wearing a disguise. For the first conviction while disguised, the minimum sentence is 5 years in state prison, and for subsequent convictions, the minimum is 10 years in state prison.

Aggravated Assault

You will recall from Chapter 2 that the UCR defines aggravated assault as "an unlawful attack by one person upon another for the purpose of inflicting severe or aggravated bodily injury" (Federal Bureau of Investigation, 2014), and this type of assault is usually accompanied by the use of a weapon.

In Massachusetts, aggravated assault is often classified as ***aggravated assault and battery*** but does not require the use of a deadly weapon. You have probably heard the term *assault and battery* before because the crimes of assault (threat of violence) and battery (actual violence) almost always accompany each other. That is, the threat of violence usually precedes the act of violence itself. In Massachusetts, an assault and battery charge can be elevated to an aggravated assault and battery if the victim sustains a serious bodily injury during the incident. Serious bodily injury can refer to an injury resulting in permanent disfigurement, impairment of a bodily function, or the risk of death. In addition, the charges could also be increased to aggravated assault and battery if the victim was pregnant at the time of the incident or if the victim had a restraining order against the offender.

In Massachusetts, the maximum sentence for an aggravated assault and battery conviction is five years in state prison. (MGL c.265 § 13A).

Burglary

Burglary is the breaking and entering of a house at night with the intent of committing another felony, such as larceny (MGL c.266 § 14). According to Massachusetts General Law, there are several elements necessary for a crime to be considered burglary. First, burglary is specific to a house or a dwelling where one sleeps, such as an apartment, hotel, or even a hospital. In addition, the offender must physically break into and enter the dwelling. This can include breaking through a window or knocking down a door, but it can also include something as simple as opening and walking through an unlocked door or opening a window and climbing through. Furthermore, the crime of burglary only happens at nighttime, which is legally considered between one hour after sunset and one hour before sunrise. Finally, the offender does not have to successfully commit another felony to be charged with burglary as long as he has the intention of committing one.

All of these elements must be present for the offender to be convicted of burglary in Massachusetts. The prosecutor must prove that the defendant unlawfully entered the dwelling at night with the intent to commit a felony. If any of these elements is missing, the offender would likely be charged with another crime, such as trespassing or breaking and entering, rather than burglary.

The maximum penalty for burglary in Massachusetts is 20 years in state prison (MGL c. 266 § 15). However, a burglary charge can also be increased to armed burglary if the defendant was armed with a dangerous weapon or to aggravated burglary if the offender injured someone in the dwelling at the time of the offense. If convicted of aggravated or armed burglary, a defendant could face life imprisonment in state prison (MGL c.266 § 14).

Motor Vehicle Theft

Anyone who steals a motor vehicle or receives, possesses, or conceals a motor vehicle that he knew or had reason to know was stolen can be convicted of ***motor vehicle theft*** in Massachusetts (MGL c. 266 § 28). Also, stealing any parts of a vehicle or intentionally damaging a motor vehicle can constitute motor vehicle theft.

Prosecutors can prove that a defendant knew a motor vehicle was stolen by showing that a vehicle's vehicle identification number (VIN) was intentionally removed, destroyed, or altered. Similarly, if a defendant is in possession of a motor vehicle with an altered VIN, it is sufficient evidence that he knew the motor vehicle was stolen.

The maximum sentence for motor vehicle theft in Massachusetts is 15 years in state prison, 2.5 years in a county jail or house of correction, a fine up to $15,000, or both imprisonment and a fine.

Larceny-Theft

Larceny-theft is the taking of someone else's property without his or her consent with the intent to permanently deprive the owner of its use and enjoyment. Property can include a number of possessions, including money, securities, deeds to property, animals, and electronic data. The monetary value of the property stolen typically determines whether the offender is convicted of ***petty larceny*** or ***grand larceny***. If the value of the property is less than $250, the act is usually classified as petty larceny; however, if the value of the property exceeds $250, it is classified as grand larceny (MGL c.266 § 30).

Grand larceny is a felony in Massachusetts, and it is punishable by up to five years in state prison, two years in a county jail, or a $25,000 fine. On the other hand, petty larceny is classified as a misdemeanor in Massachusetts and is punishable by imprisonment in a county jail for up to one year or a fine up to $300.

It is important to note that robbery and larceny are not the same crime. Robbery involves unlawfully taking someone else's property from their person or their immediate control with the use of force or the threat of force. Larceny does not involve the use of force, only the unlawful theft of someone's property. Let's consider an example. In the first scenario, an offender threatens to harm a victim at the train station if the victim does not give the offender his money and his smartphone. Frightened for his life, the victim gives the offender the money is his wallet ($100) and his smartphone. In the second scenario, an offender sees a person at the train station who is not watching her bag. The offender reaches into the bag and steals $100 and a smartphone. Even though the value of the stolen property is the same in both scenarios ($100 and a smartphone), the first scenario included the element of force, which would qualify it as robbery, as opposed to larceny.

Arson

Anyone who wilfully and maliciously sets fire to or burns a dwelling can be convicted of ***arson*** in Massachusetts (MGL c.266 §1). Note that the entire building does not have to be destroyed by the fire for the act to be classified as arson. A prosecutor only has to prove that part of the building was burned on account of a fire purposely set by the defendant. According to Massachusetts General Law, the building must be an actual dwelling, attached to a dwelling, or burned as a result of the dwelling being set on fire. If a person is convicted of burning a dwelling in Massachusetts, he or she could face up to 20 years in state prison.

If someone is convicted of maliciously burning a building other than a dwelling, he can be sentenced up to 10 years in state prison. This can include the burning of a church, court house, college, bank, warehouse, office building, store, or any other building not considered a dwelling (MGL c.266 §2).

Conclusion

The goal of criminal law is to regulate conduct to ensure the safety and welfare of citizens at the federal, state, and local levels. This chapter has discussed different types of laws and how they are made and has also examined eight crime categories and how they are defined and punished in Massachusetts.

After reading this chapter, readers should be familiar with some of the provisions in Massachusetts criminal laws.

Key Terms

Actus Reus: "Wrongful act."

Aggravated Assault and Battery: Assault and battery in which the victim sustains a serious bodily injury.

Anthony Burns: A fugitive slave from Virginia whose Boston trial attracted national attention and ignited riots and protests in Boston. Burns was the last escaped slave in the United States to be returned to the South under the Fugitive Slave Act.

Armed Robbery: The crime of taking money or property from a person by means of force and the use of a deadly weapon.

Arson: The criminal act of deliberately setting fire to a building or property.

Assault and Battery: Combination of assault (threat of violence) and battery (physical violence).

Breach of Contract: Violation of a provision in a legally enforceable contract, allowing the injured party the right to remedy the matter in a court of law.

Burglary: Breaking and entering of a home at night with the intent of committing another felony.

Civil Law: Branch of law pertaining to suits outside of criminal practice; pertains to rights or people in contract, tort, or real estate law.

Criminal Law: Statutes that define conduct prohibited by the government because the conduct threatens or harms public safety and welfare; also establishes punishment to be imposed for commission of such acts.

Enact: To establish by law.

Felony: Serious crime for which a person may be imprisoned for over one year.

Forcible Rape: Natural or unnatural sexual intercourse by force and against the will of the victim.

Fugitive Slave Act of 1850: A law that compelled Northern citizens to cooperate with Southern masters in reclaiming their runaway slaves.

Grand Larceny: Theft of property with a value exceeding $250.

Homicide: Killing of a human being.

Involuntary Manslaughter: Unintentional killing of another person as the result of wanton or reckless conduct.

Larceny-theft: Taking of someone else's property without his or her consent.

Malice Aforethought: Intention of killing or harming another human being.

Manslaughter: Unlawful killing of another person without malice.

Massachusetts General Laws: Statutes of the Commonwealth of Massachusetts that have been codified.

Mens Rea: "Guilty mind" or criminal intent.

Misdemeanor: Less serious offense, punishable by a fine or imprisonment up to one year.

Motor Vehicle Homicide: Homicide resulting from the negligent operation of a motor vehicle.

Motor Vehicle Theft: Criminal act of stealing a motor vehicle.

Petty Larceny: Theft of property valued at less than $250.

Premeditation: Deliberate plan to commit a crime.

Procedural Law: Law regulating governmental procedure.

Substantive Law: Law that defines criminal offenses and specifies punishments.

Tort: A wrong other than a breach of contract, whereby the remedy is a civil suit for damages.

Unarmed Robbery: The crime of taking money or property from a person by means of force but without the use of a deadly weapon.

Voluntary Manslaughter: Intentional killing of a human being without malice and usually happening during the heat of passion.

Related Websites

Boston College Law Review
http://bclawreview.org/

Boston University Law Review
http://www.bu.edu/bulawreview/

General Laws of Massachusetts
https://malegislature.gov/Laws/GeneralLaws

Harvard Law Review
http://harvardlawreview.org/

Massachusetts Law Review
http://www.massbar.org/publications/massachusetts-law-review

Massachusetts Legislature
https://malegislature.gov/

Review Questions

1. What are the differences between federal, state, and local laws?
2. How are most laws created in Massachusetts?

3. What are the differences between criminal and civil law?
4. Discuss the differences between a misdemeanor and a felony.
5. What is the difference between procedural and substantive law?
6. What would classify a homicide as first-degree murder?
7. Discuss the differences between voluntary and involuntary manslaughter.
8. What is forcible rape?
9. What is the difference between an armed robbery and an unarmed robbery?
10. Distinguish an assault from a battery.
11. Differentiate between an assault and battery and an aggravated assault and battery.
12. What elements are necessary for someone to be convicted of burglary in Massachusetts?
13. How can a prosecutor prove that a defendant knew a motor vehicle was stolen?
14. What are the penalties for arson in Massachusetts?
15. What is the difference between petty larceny and grand larceny?

References

Federal Bureau of Investigation. (2014). *Crime in the United States 2014*. Retrieved from https://ucr.fbi.gov/crime-in-the-u.s/2014/crime-in-the-u.s.-2014/offenses-known-to-law-enforcement/aggravated-assault.

Galvin, W. F. (2012). *Lawmaking in Massachusetts*. Secretary of the Commonwealth of Massachusetts. Retrieved from http://www.sec.state.ma.us/trs/trslaw/lawidx.htm.

Gardiner, C., & Mallicoat, S. L. (2012). *California's criminal justice system*. Durham, NC: Carolina Academic Press.

General Laws. (2018a). *CHAPTER 90 (Section 24G)*. Retrieved from https://malegislature.gov/Laws/GeneralLaws/PartI/TitleXIV/Chapter90/Section24G.

General Laws. (2018b). *CHAPTER 265 (Sections 1, 2, 13, 13A, 17, 19, 22)*. Retrieved from https://malegislature.gov/Laws/GeneralLaws/PartIV/TitleI/Chapter265.

General Laws. (2018c). *CHAPTER 266 (Sections 1, 2, 14, 15, 28, 30)*. Retrieved from https://malegislature.gov/Laws/GeneralLaws/PartIV/TitleI/Chapter266.

Kickham, W. (n.d.a). *First degree murder*. Law Offices of William D. Kickham, Esq. and Associates. Retrieved from http://criminal.attorneywdkickham.com/lawyer-attorney-1946532.html.

Kickham, W. (n.d.b). *Second degree murder*. Law Offices of William D. Kickham, Esq. and Associates. Retrieved from http://criminal.attorneywdkickham.com/lawyer-attorney-1947086.html.

Massachusetts Murder Defense. (n.d.a). *Involuntary manslaughter*. Retrieved from http://www.massmurderdefense.com/pages/manslaughter-in.html.

Massachusetts Murder Defense. (n.d.b). *Voluntary manslaughter*. Retrieved from http://www.massmurderdefense.com/pages/manslaughter-v.html.

MassMoments. *Fugitive slave Anthony Burns arrested*. (n.d.). Retrieved from https://www.massmoments.org/moment-details/fugitive-slave-anthony-burns-arrested.html.

Scheb, J. M., & Scheb, J. M. (1999). *Criminal law and procedure* (3rd ed.). Belmont, CA: Wadsworth.

The 190th General Court of the Commonwealth of Massachusetts. (2018). *General Laws: Part IV*. Retrieved from https://malegislature.gov/Laws/GeneralLaws/PartIV.

Town Clerk's Office. (2011). *Town of Middleborough by-laws 1927*. Middleborough, MA: Author.

U.S. Const. amend. X

U.S. Const. art. I, §8

Chapter 5

Courts in Massachusetts

Learning Objectives

- Learn about the structure of the court system in Massachusetts.
- Familiarize yourself with the appellate process.
- Recognize the importance of the Massachusetts Board of Bar Examiners.
- Familiarize yourself with the actors in the courtroom.
- Understand what happens before, during, and after a trial.
- Distinguish between the different types of evidence.
- Learn about the significance of specialty courts.

Introduction

Each of the 50 states in the United States has its own court system with a unique set of rules governing the court system's establishment and practices. While there are many similarities among the 50 court systems, there are also some differences. Nevertheless, the primary function of the courts is to settle disputes between parties. You will recall from the previous chapter that civil law usually involves disputes between two private parties. In civil cases, it is the court's primary role to settle disputes between private parties. On the other hand, criminal law includes statutes that define conduct prohibited by the state. In criminal cases, the courts determine whether or not a person is guilty of a crime. That is, the courts settle disputes between the state and individuals who violate the state's legal codes.

In this chapter, we will examine the court system that is unique to Massachusetts. By the end of the chapter, you will be familiar with the structure of the courts, the actors in the courts, and the events that occur before, during, and after a trial in Massachusetts. In addition, you will also learn about the role of specialty courts in Massachusetts.

Figure 5.1 Diagram of the Massachusetts Court System

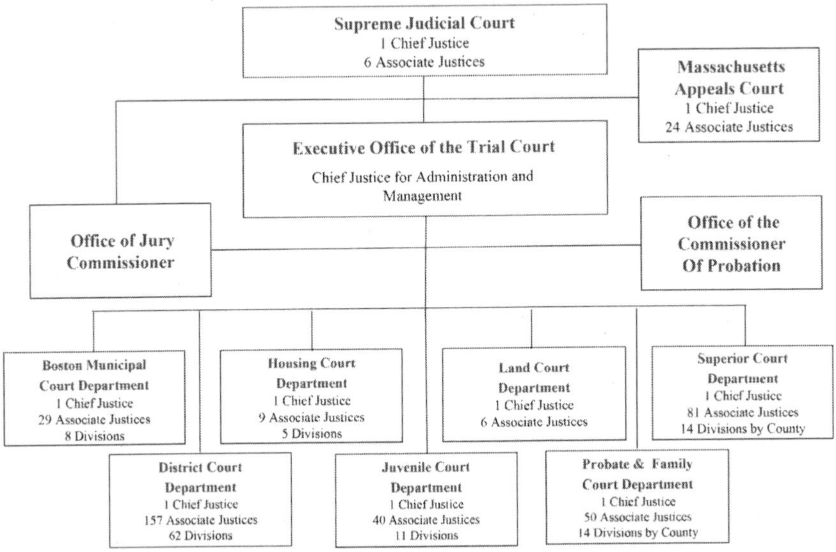

Source: Massachusetts Court System, 2012. Retrieved from http://www.mass.gov/courts/docs/sjc/docs/court-sys-chart-2012.pdf.

Structure of the Courts

The Massachusetts court system is comprised of the *Executive Office of the Trial Court*, seven *trial court* departments, the *Appeals Court*, the *Supreme Judicial Court*, the *Office of Jury Commissioner*, and the *Office of the Commissioner of Probation* (Commonwealth of Massachusetts, n.d.k). All of these components will be discussed in detail throughout this section. Refer to Figure 5.1 for a diagram of the Massachusetts court system.

The Executive Office of the Trial Court

The Executive Office of the Trial Court enables joint leadership of the Trial Court by the chief justice of the Trial Court and the court administrator. This office has many functions, including supporting research and planning, specialty court administration, judicial education, grants management, and general administration and communication (Commonwealth of Massachusetts, n.d.f).

Cases in Massachusetts are first tried in one of the seven trial court departments (i.e., *Superior, District, Boston Municipal, Housing, Juvenile, Land*, and

Probate and Family). Each case begins in the trial court that has ***jurisdiction***, or the authority to make legal decisions, over the issue at hand. Regardless of the department, trial courts are the first court to hear a case, so they have what is known as ***original jurisdiction***, or the authority to hear a case for the first time.

Even though the trial court departments differ in their ***subject matter jurisdiction***, or the authority of a court over the nature of a case, they all share the same function—to determine the facts of a case. The seven trial court departments seen throughout the Commonwealth of Massachusetts are discussed below.

Superior Court

The Superior Court in Massachusetts is a court of ***general jurisdiction***, meaning that it has the authority to hear any case that arises within its geographical area. Usually, the Superior Court hears felonies and civil cases seeking remedies over $25,000. Eighty-two Superior Court justices sit in 20 superior courthouses across the Commonwealth of Massachusetts (Commonwealth of Massachusetts, n.d.p).

District Court

The District Court Department has 159 judges who sit in 62 courts across Massachusetts. This court department hears a variety of cases, including criminal, civil, juvenile, mental health, and housing matters. The criminal jurisdiction of the District Court Department includes felonies punishable by up to five years in state prison, misdemeanors, and violations of city or town ordinances. For civil cases, district court judges hear matters with a monetary remedy not exceeding $25,000; small claims up to $7,000; restraining orders; and civil motor vehicle infractions (Commonwealth of Massachusetts, n.d.e).

Boston Municipal Court

The Boston Municipal Court Department has 30 judges who sit in eight court divisions within the City of Boston, including Brighton, Central Division (downtown), Charlestown, Dorchester, East Boston, Roxbury, South Boston, and West Roxbury. Judges in this court hear both criminal and civil matters. Criminal cases heard in this court include misdemeanors and felonies punishable by up to five years in state prison. In addition, the types of civil cases include civil actions not exceeding $25,000; small claims not exceeding $7,000; mental health matters; restraining orders; and violations of city ordinances (Commonwealth of Massachusetts, n.d.d).

Housing Court

There are 10 judges who serve in five divisions of the Housing Court Department—Central, Eastern, Northeast, Southeast, and Western. This court has jurisdiction over matters regarding residential housing, including zoning, general nuisance issues, and landlord-tenant matters (Housing Court Department, 2018).

Juvenile Court

The Juvenile Court Department has general jurisdiction over cases involving delinquency, youthful offender cases, care and protection of children needing assistance, and adoption. The mission of this court is to protect children from abuse and neglect, rehabilitate juveniles, and protect the public from delinquency. There are 41 judges in 11 divisions of the juvenile court across the state (Commonwealth of Massachusetts, n.d.i).

Land Court

The Land Court Department has jurisdiction over the registration of property titles, foreclosure and redemption of real estate tax liens, and most other property matters. There are seven judges on the land court, which is located in Boston (Commonwealth of Massachusetts, n.d.j).

Probate and Family Court

The Probate and Family Court Department has subject matter jurisdiction over family and probate matters including divorce, child support, custody, adoption, wills, and trusts. There are 14 divisions of probate and family court throughout Massachusetts (Commonwealth of Massachusetts, n.d.m).

Overview of the Appellate Process

As mentioned earlier, cases are initiated in the trial courts. However, if a party is not satisfied with the outcome from one of the trial courts, that party can make an appeal. The Massachusetts court system provides the accused with the right to have his or her trial court proceeding reviewed in an appellate court. The appellate courts, which include the Appeals Court and the Supreme Judicial Court (SJC), do not retry cases. Rather, they review proceedings from the trial courts to ensure the proceedings were fair (Commonwealth of Massachusetts, 2018c). Appellate courts have what is known as ***appellate jurisdiction***, or the authority to review decisions and to change outcomes that were decided in a lower court.

The appellate process starts with the prosecution and defense presenting ***briefs***, or written arguments, to the appellate court. Grounds for an appeal include claims that the trial judge did not apply the law correctly, the trial was conducted unfairly, or that the law applied violated the U.S. Constitution or the Massachusetts State Constitution.

Once the briefs are received by the appellate court, a case is scheduled for an oral argument, whereby each attorney presents the arguments to the justices who decide the case. With the exception of first-degree murder convictions and certain limited matters, most appeals begin in the Appeals Court. If the party is still not satisfied with the decision of the Appeals Court, that party can apply for further appellate review by the SJC.

Massachusetts Appeals Court

Established in 1972, the Appeals Court is the court in which most appeals from the trial courts begin. In addition to cases from the trial courts, the Appeals Court also receives cases from the Appellate Tax Board, Department of Industrial Accidents, and Commonwealth Employment Relations Board. The Appeals Court considers appeals regarding both civil and criminal cases, which the exception of first-degree murder, which go directly to the SJC (Commonwealth of Massachusetts, n.d.a).

The Massachusetts Appeals Court is composed of a chief justice and 24 associate justices, and it typically sits in panels of three justices. The panels regularly alternate so that each justice can sit with all of the other justices. After hearing an oral argument, as discussed earlier, the panel will write an ***opinion***, or decision, regarding the case. The Appeals Court in Massachusetts considers nearly 1,500 cases annually (Commonwealth of Massachusetts, n.d.a).

Massachusetts Supreme Judicial Court

The Massachusetts SJC traces its history back to the high court of the British Province of Massachusetts Bay, which was chartered in 1692, and it is the oldest functioning appellate court in the United States. It is the highest court in Massachusetts, and originally, the SJC sat one chief justice and four associate justices. Today the court consists of a chief justice and six associate justices who hear appeals on a wide range of criminal and civil cases. Once they have heard an oral argument, the SJC issues a written opinion of the majority of the justices regarding the case (Commonwealth of Massachusetts, n.d.q).

Furthermore, the SJC also holds single justice sessions for a variety of reasons, including bar discipline proceedings, petitions for admission to the bar, or motions about cases on trial or appeal. The SJC decides approximately 200 cases every year, while the single justices decide an additional 600 cases. Aside from its appellate functions, the SJC also makes rules for the operation of the lower courts in Massachusetts and is responsible for the supervision of the judiciary and the bar (Commonwealth of Massachusetts, n.d.q). The SJC sits at the John Adams Courthouse at One Pemberton Square in the Government Center section of downtown Boston.

Massachusetts High Court Says Black Men May Have Legitimate Reason to Flee Police

Black men who try to avoid an encounter with Boston police by fleeing may have a legitimate reason to do so and should not be deemed suspicious according to a ruling by the Massachusetts Supreme Judicial Court. The high court cited data collected from Boston police department from 2007–2010, as well as a 2014 report by the American Civil Liberties Union (ACLU) of Massachusetts, that found African Americans were disproportionately stopped and searched by Boston police.

A seminal case in the ruling was the December 18, 2011, arrest of Boston resident Jimmy Warren during the investigation of a burglary. Officers were given a description of the suspects as three Black men: one wearing a black hooded sweatshirt, one wearing a red hooded sweatshirt, and the other wearing dark clothing. A Boston police officer later saw Warren and another man (both wearing dark clothing) walking near a park. When the officer approached the men, they both ran. Warren was later arrested and searched. No contraband was found on him, but police recovered an unlicensed .22 caliber handgun in a nearby yard. Warren was charged with unlawful possession of a firearm and later convicted.

In its ruling, the Massachusetts SJC made two major findings: the justices said that the police did not have the right to stop Warren in the first place, and the fact that Warren ran away should not be used against him. On the first point, the court said the description of the break-in suspects' clothing was vague, making it impossible for police to reasonably and rationally target Warren or any other Black man wearing dark clothing as a suspect. The court said the ubiquitous clothing description and the officer's hunch was not enough to justify the stop.

The court ruling stated, "lacking any information about facial features, hairstyles, skin tone, height, weight, or other physical characteristics, the victim's description contributed nothing to the officers' ability to distinguish the defendant from any other Black male wearing dark clothes and a hooded sweatshirt in Roxbury."

On the second point, the court noted that state law gives individuals the right to not speak to police and even walk away if they are not charged with anything. The court said when an individual does run away, the action does not necessarily mean the person is guilty. BPD and ACLU reports that document racial profiling must be taken into consideration with cases involving black men.

The court ruling stated "we do not eliminate flight as a factor in the reasonable suspicion analysis whenever a Black male is the subject of an investigatory stop. However, in such circumstances, flight is not necessarily probative of a suspect's state of mind or consciousness of guilt. Rather, the finding that Black males in Boston are disproportionately and repeatedly targeted for FIO [Field Interrogation and Observation] encounters suggests a reason for flight totally unrelated to consciousness of guilt. Such an individual, when approached by the police, might just as easily be motivated by the desire to avoid the recurring indignity of being racially profiled as by the desire to hide criminal activity. Given this reality for Black males in the City of Boston, a judge should, in appropriate cases, consider the report's findings in weighing flight as a factor in the reasonable suspicion calculus."

The SJC concluded that police lacked reasonable suspicion for an investigatory stop in this case. This opinion looks at police encounters through the eyes of a Black man who might justifiably be concerned that he will be the victim of racial profiling.

The ACLU's report found that between 2007 and 2010, 63% of Boston police encounters were with African American citizens, though at that time the city's African American population was just 24%. The report said that taking into account high-crime neighborhoods did not explain the inequality.

The court ruling also cited the Boston Police Department analysis, which showed that African Americans were 8% more likely to be stopped repeatedly and 12% more likely to be searched and frisked, even when controlling for factors like criminal history, gang affiliation, and violent crime areas (Enwemeka, 2016).

Office of Jury Commissioner

The Office of Jury Commissioner (OJC) is in charge of the management and selection of jurors in Massachusetts. The OJC is a department within the judicial branch and is under the supervision of the Supreme Judicial Court. Correspondingly, the jury commissioner is appointed by the SJC to be the head of the OJC.

It is the responsibility of the OJC to provide the trial courts and grand jury with an adequate number of random and representative jurors from a pool of eligible jurors. Thus, the Office of Jury Commissioner creates a master juror list for each district, issues summonses for potential jurors to report for jury duty, and engages in disciplinary actions against people who do not comply with their jury service.

Office of the Commissioner of Probation

The Office of the Commissioner of Probation supervises probation services throughout the Commonwealth of Massachusetts. Probation is a court-ordered sentence, whereby an offender remains in the community under the supervision of a probation officer. Because the sentence of probation is a form of community-based corrections, it will be discussed in further detail in Chapter 6 (Corrections).

The ***Massachusetts Trial Court Probation Service***, more commonly referred to as the ***Massachusetts Probation Service*** (MPS), is the commonwealth's primary supervisory law enforcement agency. It was created in 1878 and is the first probation agency established in the United States. The probation department was created based on the work of ***John Augustus***, the Boston area bootmaker who is credited as being the "Father of Probation" in the United States because of his pioneering crusade for more lenient sentences for convicted criminals based on their individual backgrounds.

John Augustus: Boston Bootmaker and Father of Probation

John Augustus, who was born in Woburn, Massachusetts in 1785, later moved to Boston and became a successful bootmaker. Augustus did not drink alcohol and believed that abusers of alcohol could be reformed by being shown kindness, understanding, and continuous moral persuasion rather than through criminal conviction, incarceration, or harsh punishment. He became interested in the legal process and often visited the criminal courts in Boston.

This new calling as a volunteer probation officer started in 1841 when John Augustus attended police court. He was especially touched by the plight of a person convicted of public intoxication who begged the court not to incarcerate him and promised to give up alcohol in return for his freedom. Augustus, sensing hope for the man's rehabilitation, asked to supervise the offender in an attempt to show the man the evils of his drinking ways and an attempt to clean him up and make him a productive citizen. The judge allowed it, and Augustus paid the man's bail. The offender was ordered to appear in court three weeks later for sentencing. The man returned to court completely sober and clean, accompanied by Augustus. To the astonishment of all in attendance, his appearance and demeanor had dramatically changed. The judge was favorably moved, and the man was allowed to go free. This man became the first probationer in American history.

Augustus thus began an 18-year career in probation. Not every offender helped by Augustus was an alcohol abuser, nor did he take on the cause of all prospective probationers. He paid close attention to evaluating whether or not a candidate would likely prove to be a successful subject for probation. Augustus studied extra-legal factors such as the offender's character and age as well as the people, places, and things apt to influence the person. He used his own money for bail or received financial aid from other residents of Boston who believed in his cause; several of these followers continued the program after his death.

Augustus was subsequently credited with founding the investigations process, one of three main concepts of modern probation, the other two being intake and supervision. Augustus, who kept detailed notes on his activities, was also the first to apply the term "probation" to his method of treating offenders. By 1858, it is reported that John Augustus posted bail for nearly 2,000 people, and reports state that only 10 of these people forfeited their bond. The first probation statute, enacted in Massachusetts shortly after this death in 1859, was widely attributed to his efforts. There is a plaque memorializing John Augustus posted on the old Boston School Committee headquarters building at 26 Court Street in downtown Boston (Law Library—American Law and Legal Information, n.d.).

Massachusetts Board of Bar Examiners

The Massachusetts Board of Bar Examiners (BBE) evaluates the qualifications of individuals pursuing admission to the Massachusetts Bar. The BBE aims to ensure that all lawyers meet minimum standards before they can practice law within the Commonwealth of Massachusetts. The BBE meets this responsibility by administering a semi-annual Massachusetts Bar Examination to evaluate candidates on their character and fitness, legal knowledge, and educational background (Commonwealth of Massachusetts, n.d.c).

The BBE considers good character "to embody that degree of honesty, integrity, and discretion that the public and members of the bench and the bar have the right to demand of a lawyer" (Commonwealth of Massachusetts, 2017b). When evaluating character and fitness, the BBE considers past conduct of the candidate regarding honesty, trustworthiness, diligence, and reliability. Subsequently, the BBE ensures that candidates have not engaged in unlawful conduct, academic misconduct, neglect of financial responsibilities, evidence of drug or alcohol dependency, or disciplinary action by a professional disciplinary agency. Additionally, candidates seeking admission to the bar in Massachusetts must also meet academic standards and have completed an academic program in a law school approved by the American Bar Association (Commonwealth of Massachusetts, 2017b).

Once an individual seeking admission to the bar has satisfied the necessary conditions required by the Massachusetts BBE, he or she is eligible to take the Massachusetts Attorney's Oath, which states the following:

> I (repeat the name) solemnly swear that I will do no falsehood, nor consent to the doing of any in court; I will not wittingly or willingly promote or sue any false, groundless or unlawful suit, nor give aid or consent to the same; I will delay no man for lucre or malice; but I will conduct myself in the office of an attorney within the courts according to the best of my knowledge and discretion, and with all good fidelity as well to the courts as my clients. So help me God (MGL c.221 §38).

After the individual has taken this oath, he or she becomes a member of the Massachusetts Bar. All members of the Massachusetts Bar are expected to adhere to the Massachusetts Attorney's Oath throughout their legal careers. If a lawyer strays from this oath as amplified by the Massachusetts Rules of Professional Conduct, the unethical conduct or behavior is examined by the Board of Bar Overseers and the SJC (Commonwealth of Massachusetts, n.d.b).

Actors in the Courts

Many different positions within the courts help court proceedings run efficiently. In this section, we will discuss the function of some of these positions, including judges, prosecutors, defense attorneys, and juries.

Judges

Judges serve a variety of functions in court proceedings. However, their primary function is to oversee the trial process. During a trial, judges monitor the conduct of the attorneys and witnesses and resolve questions about evidence and procedure (Siegel, 2011). Judges also listen to evidence presented in a case and make decisions based on how the facts apply to legal codes. In jury trials, judges also determine what evidence can be presented to a jury. In addition, if a defendant is found guilty, the judge determines the offender's sentence (Gardiner & Mallicoat, 2012).

Currently, there are 411 judicial positions in Massachusetts: 7 justices in the SJC, 25 in the Appeals Court, and 379 in the trial courts. Judges in Massachusetts serve "lifetime" appointments, but they are required to retire at age 70 (Healy, 2012).

In addition, Massachusetts has 85 clerk-magistrate positions that serve the District Court Department, Housing Court Department, Juvenile Court Department, and Boston Municipal Court. The clerk-magistrate positions are also lifetime appointments, but they have no mandatory retirement age. Clerk-magistrates are responsible for the administration and management of the court, and they serve as judicial hearing officers in small claims cases and procedural criminal matters (Healy, 2012).

According to the Massachusetts Constitution (Chapter 2, Section 1, Article 4), the governor has the authority to nominate and appoint all judicial officers, including clerk-magistrates, with the approval of the governor's council.

Profile: Laura Gentile, Clerk-Magistrate, Hampden County Superior Court

The best part of the job is being in the courtroom, especially for major cases, such as homicides. This type of work is very eye-opening because it provides insight on different lifestyles that the average middle-class person never experiences. Working in the courts allows you the opportunity to work with people from all walks of life, and you can project yourself into the lives of people who are less fortunate than yourself. For example, Laura recalled a former case when a defendant had hidden a firearm under the mattress of his child's crib. It was Christmastime, and she was buying toys for her child while someone was hiding weapons under the mattress of his child. What hits home the most in these cases for Laura is that many kids face hardships from the beginning. While they are no different, some children have guns hidden under their beds, while other children have toys under their beds.

The single-most rewarding part of her job was when Mark Schand, who had been wrongfully convicted of murder, was released in 2013. Schand served nearly 30 years in state prison for a murder he did not commit. With the help of the Innocence Project, new evidence was uncovered regarding the identification of the true killer. He was granted a new trial based on that evidence. His conviction was overturned, and the prosecution did not bring further charges. Schand was brought to court for that hearing, and he was released there from. In order for Mr. Schand to be released directly from court, the staff remained after working hours to tie up loose ends so he could be released from court rather than have to return to prison. Laura recounted how overwhelming, yet rewarding, that moment was—especially because Schand and his family were so thankful that the staff had stayed. She felt that the least she could do was stay an extra 30 minutes, as this man had spent nearly 30 years in prison for a crime he did not commit.

The hardest part of the job is the same thing she considers to be the best part of the job. That is, it is difficult seeing people, day in and day out, who struggle. This is particularly true when you have to watch young people go to jail. And it is especially heartbreaking in cases when you think the jury got the verdict wrong. While the jury usually gets it right, there have been a handful of times when Laura was confident they did not.

Regarding policies, one policy Laura disagrees with are mandatory minimum sentences. These policies give people a false sense of security and disproportionately target low-level drug offenders. She feels that it would be more appropriate to deal with offenders on a case-by-case basis. Judges and probation officers have a good understanding of each individual's background, and they can determine which offenders can be supervised within the community and which ones need to be incarcerated. In most cases, treatment is more beneficial than sending offenders to jail. Plus, it is more beneficial for taxpayers.

The biggest challenge the Hampden County Superior Court currently faces is resources. The building is outdated, and it is not conducive to the amount of cases they process, as her court is the busiest criminal court in the commonwealth. In addition, she noted that the security guards are great, but they do not have the resources they need, and she fears that something could go wrong. The equipment is also outdated. For example, they are finally starting to scan documents, and they are just getting video conferencing. Laura believes that video conferencing would provide many benefits, especially reduced travel costs and convenience for lawyers and other personnel who do not live or work in the Springfield area.

To remedy this problem, she mentioned that the courts need more resources. Historically, the trial courts are slow to change. Massachusetts courts are among the oldest in the country, and they tend to resist change. But it is clear that nothing will change until they have additional resources.

Overall, Laura loves her job and enjoys working for the courts. If she had to give advice to young people entering the profession, she mentioned that jobs within the court system are great jobs. The pay, benefits, and pensions are very good. The jobs are hard to get, but there are many opportunities within the courts and probation departments throughout the commonwealth.

District Attorneys (Prosecutors)

In criminal cases, ***district attorneys*** represent the government or the people in the Commonwealth of Massachusetts. It is their job to prosecute criminal cases. In Massachusetts, district attorneys are elected, and they serve a term of four years. There are 11 district attorneys throughout the commonwealth, and they typically represent a district at the county level. Furthermore, district attorneys must live in the district they represent and must also be a member of the Massachusetts Bar (MGL c.12 §12).

District attorneys hire assistant district attorneys who are responsible for the management of activities in the office as well as prosecutorial duties. These lawyers appear in the courts throughout Massachusetts, and they represent the interest of the commonwealth. Their caseloads include felonies, misdemeanors, and cases involving juvenile delinquency, among other matters.

Defense Attorneys

Defense attorneys represent the ***defendant***, or the person or entity accused of a crime in a criminal prosecution. There are two types of defense attorneys—private defense attorneys and public defenders. If a defendant can afford to do so, he hires a private defense attorney. If a defendant cannot afford a private attorney, he is assigned to a public defender.

It is the job of the Massachusetts Committee for Public Counsel Services to arrange for the legal representation of ***indigent defendants***, or individuals who cannot afford a private defense attorney. The majority of representation is provided for by nearly 3,000 private attorneys who accept appointments for indigent defendants (Committee for Public Counsel Services, n.d.).

Profile: Dunn & Phillips, P.C. (Neil Phillips, Attorney; Sergeant Reggie Miller, Springfield Police; Cherish Wright and Maame Dufie Kyei, Legal Assistants)

This profile was a collaborative effort from several members of the staff at the Dunn & Phillips, as well as Sergeant Miller, who leads the Springfield Police Department's Community Policing Unit. When asked about the best part of the job, they unanimously mentioned "helping people."

Furthermore, they agreed that the most rewarding part of the job was bonding with people in the community. Sergeant Miller stressed that they are making strides to get the City of Springfield back to what is was back in the day. Currently, the city is very impoverished, many residents are unemployed, and the drug problem has become increasingly worse. Neil mentioned that the most rewarding part of the job was forming bonds with clients. At Dunn & Phillips, they want their clients to know that they can reach out for help at any time.

Cherish mentioned that the hardest part of the job is giving bad news to clients. You build bonds with clients, and it is very difficult to give any bad news to them. Phillips mentioned that the most difficult part of the job is making sure the door stays open. There are so many practicing attorneys in the area, and the field of law is very competitive. To be competitive, they focus on giving their clients the best service possible, concentrating on the bonds they have with their clients. He added that it is important to reinvent yourself every day and to engage in constant networking with the community.

Sergeant Miller mentioned that the most challenging part of the job for him was seeing the system not work the way that it is intended to. Sometimes the system does not allow law enforcement to help people. The law is often slow to react to the needs of society. In many instances, the police want to help people, but there might not be a law against a particular behavior yet. For example, up until a couple of years ago, people could lawfully take pictures up other people's skirts (i.e., "upskirting"). Thankfully, however, this act is now illegal.

Sergeant Miller also mentioned that a challenging part of his job is media coverage of law enforcement. Good news does not sell the way that bad news does. The media will often turn up to broadcast events, making the police or the city look bad, but they rarely show up for the good events. They do not accurately depict all of the ways that police help people and positively engage with the community. Sergeant Miller stressed how we must change the image of the police, and having the media highlight positive things the police are doing is a great place to start.

In regards to a successful program or policy, Sergeant Miller mentioned that the Community Policing Unit, or the C3 unit, in Springfield has been working well. This unit works closely with Roca, an organization that helps young people to learn prosocial skills and disrupts the cycle of incarceration. They also work closely with the Center for Human Development, a social service organization in Western Massachusetts. The police in the area recognize that arresting everyone will not solve the city's problems. Instead, they must focus on helping people in the community and getting them the services they need, including services to help with addiction.

As far as giving advice to young people entering the profession, Phillips stressed the importance of listening rather than talking. The people in the community have a lot to say, but they are not always heard. Sergeant Miller corroborated this statement, adding "big ears, little mouth." In addition, he mentioned that it is important to treat the members of the community the way that you want to be treated, regardless of race, color, ethnicity, or other defining characteristics.

Juries

The right to a jury trial is protected by the U.S. Constitution in criminal trials by the Sixth Amendment and in civil trials by the Seventh Amendment. Furthermore, the right to a jury trial is also stated in the Constitution of the Commonwealth of Massachusetts (Part 1, Article 15). The role of the jury is to review facts and make decisions in court proceedings and to ensure a fair and impartial trial for the people in Massachusetts.

Massachusetts has a long history of implementing the jury system within the commonwealth and throughout the nation. The *trial by jury* was brought to the New World by the Pilgrims in 1620, who landed at what was formerly known as Plymouth Colony, located in Massachusetts. Moreover, in 1860, Massachusetts was the first state in the United States to grant the right and obligation of jury service to African Americans. Massachusetts was also the first state to adopt the one-day or one trial system in its jury courts, which is currently the standard used throughout the United States. In this system, qualified citizens that have been impaneled on a case have jury duty for either one day or the duration of one trial (Commonwealth of Massachusetts, n.d.l).

You will recall that the Office of Jury Commissioner randomly selects potential jurors from a master juror list. This list contains the names of residents in the

351 cities and towns across the Commonwealth of Massachusetts. Any U.S. citizen who is 18 years old and older, lives in Massachusetts for at least six months of the year, and can speak and understand English, is eligible for jury service every three years (Commonwealth of Massachusetts, n.d.n).

In Massachusetts, there are two types of juries—trial juries and grand juries. Trial jurors serve under the one-day or one trial system, as mentioned above. They hear and evaluate evidence for one criminal case and determine if there is reasonable doubt that a defendant committed the crime in question. Grand jurors, on the other hand, fulfill a longer jury service—typically three months. These jurors hear evidence from the district attorney's office to determine if there is enough ***probable cause***, or reasonable grounds, to criminally charge offenders by way of the indictment before they go to trial (Commonwealth of Massachusetts, 2018a).

Pretrial Activities

Court procedure can be very complicated, so this section will briefly introduce several of the most important activities that occur before a criminal trial begins. Although every case is different, most cases follow the same basic procedures before trial.

Booking

After a suspect has been arrested for suspicion of breaking the law, a police officer takes the suspect into custody to be booked at the police station. During ***booking***, the suspect is photographed, fingerprinted, and asked questions to ascertain his identity.

Shortly after the arrest, a judge, clerk-magistrate, or bail commissioner determines if the suspect will be released on bail, as well as the amount of bail (MGL. c.276 § 58). ***Bail*** (or bond) is the monetary amount determined for the conditional release of the suspect to ensure that he returns for subsequent court proceedings. The amount of bail is usually returned to the accused person, provided he appears at his next court appearance.

Arraignment

An ***arraignment*** is the first court appearance after the accused has been arrested. Recall that in Massachusetts a grand jury establishes if there is probable cause to criminally charge offenders by way of indictment, which is the process that begins a criminal case in Superior Court. In district and juvenile courts, a clerk-magistrate determines if there is probable cause to charge offenders by way of a complaint. During the arraignment, the accused is formally told which charges are being brought against him, as determined by the grand jury or the clerk-magistrate. At this time, the accused is also advised of his constitutional rights, and a court appointed attorney is appointed if the defendant cannot afford a private attorney.

During the arraignment, the defendant also enters a plea of *not guilty, guilty*, or *nolo contendere* (no contest). *Not guilty* means that the defendant denies the charges brought against him or he wants a trial. *Guilty* means the defendant admits to the charges, and a date is set for sentencing. Finally, *no contest* means the defendant is not pleading guilty but is willing to be sentenced as if he were found guilty (Commonwealth of Massachusetts, n.d.r).

Plea Bargaining

The defense attorney and the assistant district attorney prosecuting the case discuss plea options for the defendant instead of going to trial. A ***plea bargain*** is an agreement between the prosecution and the defense in which the accused agrees to plead guilty to a lesser charge. For example, under a plea bargain, a charge of possession of heroin with intent to distribute could be reduced to simple possession of heroin.

The practice of plea bargaining is advantageous for several reasons. Most importantly, plea bargaining saves the courts resources. Trials can drain the courts of resources because they can be very costly and time-consuming. Not only do they require the time of attorneys and judges, but they also rely on jurors, who often lose pay to fulfill their jury service. Furthermore, the prosecution favors a plea bargain because a guilty plea ensures them a "win" (i.e., a conviction), whereas a trial could result in a "loss" if the defendant is not found guilty. In addition, if the defendant is found guilty, it could be in his best interest to plead guilty to a lesser charge rather than risk going to trial and facing a harsher sentence.

However, note that there are also disadvantages to plea bargaining. First, it encourages defendants to waive their constitutional rights to a trial. In addition, plea bargains also may result in violent offenders receiving more lenient sentences than if they went to trial. Finally, plea bargaining can also result in an innocent person being convicted of a crime he did not commit. Defendants may be convinced that it is preferable to plead guilty and receive a lighter sentence rather than risk a more stringent sentence after trial (Siegel, 2011).

Pretrial Motions

Before the case goes to trial, the prosecutor and defense attorney appear before a judge to make pretrial motions. They discuss whether there are any technical grounds to dismiss the case, including unlawful searches and seizures, illegally obtained confessions, and other matters related to the defendant's mental competency (Doerner, 2012). In addition, the attorneys set boundaries for the trial at the pretrial motions. They discuss which evidence can go to trial, which witnesses can testify, and which evidence can go to trial.

During a Trial

The defendant's guilt or innocence is determined at a trial. In some cases, a jury decides if the defendant is guilty or not guilty at a ***jury trial***; in other cases, a judge makes a decision without a jury at a ***bench trial***. Defendants usually choose to have a jury trial because they want a jury of their peers determining their guilt or innocence. It is important to note that anyone who is accused of a crime is innocent until proven guilty. Therefore, it is the job of a prosecutor to convince the judge or jury beyond a reasonable doubt that the defendant is guilty (Commonwealth of Massachusetts, n.d.h)

We will next discuss some of the common events that occur in most trials. Specifically, we will discuss some of the trial proceedings, including opening arguments, the state's presentation of evidence, the defense's presentation, closing arguments, and jury deliberation.

Jury Selection

As noted earlier, the OJC has a master juror list from which they randomly select potential jurors. Once individuals have been summoned for jury duty, they arrive at the courthouse at their specified date and time. The pool of prospective jurors from which a jury is selected is called a ***venire***.

Once the venire has assembled, the process of ***voir dire*** (to speak the truth) begins. Voir dire is the process by which prospective jurors are questioned by the attorneys to determine if they are able to be fair and impartial members of the jury. If a potential juror indicates bias toward the defendant or the case (e.g., the juror knows the defendant, has a prejudice toward the defendant, or has already formed an opinion on the case), either of the attorneys can ask the judge to dismiss the potential juror. This request is known as a ***challenge for cause***, and there is no limit on the number of these objections (Siegel, 2011).

Another request to remove a potential juror is known as a ***peremptory challenge***, whereby the attorneys can excuse potential jurors without disclosing their reasoning. For example, a prosecutor might not want a nightclub owner as a juror in a drunk driving case, because based on the individual's occupation, he may be more sympathetic to the defendant. Each side has a limited number of peremptory challenges. In Massachusetts, for crimes punishable by life in prison, each side is entitled to 12 peremptory challenges. In other criminal cases decided by a 12-person jury, each side has up to four peremptory challenges, And in cases decided by a six-person jury, each side is entitled to two peremptory challenges (Commonwealth of Massachusetts, 1979a).

Once the jury has been selected, the jurors are sworn in. The following oath is administered to the jurors: "you shall well and truly try the issue between the commonwealth and the defendant, (or the defendants, as the case may be) according to your evidence; so help you God" (MGL c.234 § 29)."

Opening Statements

After the jury is seated and the criminal complaint is read to the jurors, the prosecutor and defense attorney make their opening statements. The prosecution's opening statement familiarizes the judge and jury with the criminal charges in the case, summarizes the facts it expects to prove, and discusses how the state will prove that the defendant is guilty beyond a reasonable doubt. That is, the state must convince the jury that there is no reasonable doubt the defendant committed the crime in question. Following the prosecutor, the defense attorney may give an opening statement in which he discusses why the defense believes that the defendant is not guilty of the charges.

The purpose of the opening statements is to give the jury a summary of the trial so that as the evidence unfolds, the jury will have an understanding as to how each piece of evidence relates to the whole case. Both attorneys discuss the evidence that will be presented at trial, including witnesses and physical evidence. Opening statements are important because they give both attorneys a chance to explain their view of the case to the jury before the trial begins.

State's Presentation

After the opening statements, the state begins its case by offering various types of evidence to the court. Types of evidence include testimonial evidence, real evidence, and circumstantial evidence (Siegel, 2011). ***Testimonial evidence*** is given to the courtroom by witnesses, sworn under oath, about what they saw or heard regarding the case. Witnesses may include police officers, citizens, or experts on a particular subject. ***Real evidence*** refers to evidence that is tangible and can be brought into the courtroom for the judge and jury to see. This can include a weapon, such as a knife or a firearm, allegedly used in the commission of the crime at hand. Real evidence could also include photographs or diagrams of the crime scene. Finally, ***circumstantial evidence*** is evidence indirectly used to prove a fact. For example, pretend one of the witnesses saw the defendant and the victim go into another room. The witnesses heard the defendant say he was going to shoot the victim, heard a shot, and saw the defendant leave the room with a gun. This is an example of circumstantial evidence. The jury can draw a reasonable conclusion based on inferences that the defendant shot the victim, even if the witness did not see the shooting.

Individuals called as witnesses by a lawyer give testimony through ***direct examination***. In direct examination by the prosecutor, the prosecutor questions a witness to present evidence related to the state's case. After the prosecutor has finished questioning the witness, the defense attorney conducts a ***cross-examination*** of the witness. During the cross-examination, the defense attorney can challenge parts of the witness's testimony, including the witness's accuracy of what he or she saw or heard. The intention is for the defense to undermine some of the facts of the prosecution's case. After the defense attorney has completed the cross-examination, the prosecutor may conduct a second direct examination, or redirect examination, to clarify any questions that may have come up during the cross-examination. Furthermore, the defense may also recross-examine the witness, if necessary. After all the prosecution's witnesses are questioned, the prosecution rests, and it is time for the defense to give its presentation if it chooses.

Defense's Presentation

After the prosecution rests, the defense attorney may enter a motion for a ***directed verdict*** in which he asks the judge to order the jury to return a verdict of not guilty (Commonwealth of Massachusetts, 1998). The defense attorney asks the judge to determine if the state has proved its case against the defendant or not. If the judge agrees that the state has failed to prove guilt beyond a reasonable doubt, the trial ends.

However, if the judge denies the motion for a directed verdict, the defense may call its witnesses to the stand for direct examination. During this part of the trial, the defense may introduce new evidence to raise doubts about the prosecution's case. After direct examination, the state can cross-examine the defense's witnesses. Once examination of the witnesses has concluded, the closing arguments begin.

Closing Arguments

Closing arguments are the last opportunity for the attorneys to address the jury. During these arguments, the two sides summarize the facts and evidence of the case to make their side look favorable to the jury. In Massachusetts, the defense speaks first during the closing argument, followed by the prosecution (Commonwealth of Massachusetts, 1979b). Once the closing arguments have concluded, the focus of the trial shifts to the jury.

Instructions to the Jury

Next, the judge instructs the jury on what issues they need to discuss to determine the defendant's guilt or innocence. Specifically, the judge discusses the information regarding the elements of the particular crime as well as the burden of proof necessary to obtain a guilty verdict. Once the judge has instructed the jury and provided them with a copy of the instructions, the jury leaves the courtroom to deliberate (Siegel, 2011).

Jury Deliberation and Verdict

Once the jurors have left the courtroom, they deliberate in private. During ***deliberation***, the jury discusses the facts and evidence of the case to determine a ***verdict***, or decision regarding the defendant's guilt or innocence. During the trial, jurors must avoid talking to anyone about the case. In addition, they must avoid newspapers, television, or Internet searches related to the case. This ensures that outside sources or the media do not influence their decisions.

If a jury cannot reach a unanimous verdict, the trial may result in a ***hung jury***. In this situation, the prosecutor may bring the defendant to trial again in hopes of obtaining a conviction.

However, juries are usually able to reach a verdict. Once they have reached their verdict, they reconvene in the courtroom to deliver it. If the jury finds the defendant not guilty, he is released from the criminal process. However, if he is found guilty, he enters the post-trial phase, as discussed below (Siegel, 2011).

Post-Trial Activities

If the defendant is found guilty, the next step is the sentencing phase. Before sentencing, the judge often orders a presentence investigation before imposing the actual sentence. Also, Massachusetts has structured sentencing guidelines that judges may consider when imposing a sentence. The use of a presentence investigation and sentencing guidelines will be discussed in this section as well as the sentencing hearing (Siegel, 2011).

Presentence Investigation

After an individual has been found guilty, the judge orders a presentence investigation by the probation department. For the presentence investigation, the probation officer looks into the nature of the criminal case and reports information to the court about the convicted individual's prior criminal record. The report contains prior criminal or juvenile prosecution records in which the defendant was convicted. The report also contains information about the history of the defendant, including education, marital status, and employment, which will be helpful in determining the individual's sentence (Commonwealth of Massachusetts, 2008).

Sentencing Guidelines

In 1994, the Massachusetts Sentencing Commission was created to promote truth in sentencing with the establishment of uniform sentencing guidelines. The sentencing commission is part of the judicial branch, made up of nine voting members appointed by the governor and six nonvoting members. The voting members are made up of judges, prosecutors, and defense attorneys. The nonvoting members include the commissioner of corrections, commissioner of probation, the secretary of public safety, the chairman of the Massachusetts Parole Board, the president of the Massachusetts Sheriff's Association, and a victim witness advocate (MGL c. 211E § 1).

The commission's sentencing guidelines were established to "promote fairness and reduce disparity while preserving that degree of judicial discretion necessary to fashion the sentence appropriate for the individual offender and the specific offense" (Commonwealth of Massachusetts, 2018b). Consequently, the sentencing commission recommends sentencing policies for the Commonwealth of Massachusetts that

- punish the offender
- promote public safety
- meet the purposes of sentencing, including the following:
  - reflecting the seriousness of the offense
  - providing just punishment for the offender
  - affording deterrence to criminal conduct

  - protecting the public from the defendant
  - providing the defendant with educational or vocational training
- provide fairness in sentencing to avoid sentencing disparities for defendants with similar criminal records who have been convicted of similar crimes, but allowing for judicial discretion and flexibility to allow for mitigating or aggravating circumstances on a case-by-case basis
- make rational decisions to balance criminal justice resources with protecting public safety
- offer a wide range of intermediate sanctions to accommodate different levels of offender behavior (MGL c.211E §2)

The sentencing commission is responsible for enacting the sentencing guidelines into law, and these guidelines are used in criminal cases throughout the commonwealth. The guidelines are based on the seriousness of the offense, the offender's prior history, the offender's amenability to rehabilitation, and the availability of criminal justice resources. Likewise, the guidelines determine which sentencing sanctions are appropriate for particular crimes. The list of sanctions includes standard probation, intensive supervision probation, community service, home confinement, day reporting centers, substance abuse treatment, fines, vocational training, counseling, and imprisonment, among other sanctions (MGL c.211E §3). Refer to Figure 5.2 to see an example of a sentencing guideline grid used in Massachusetts.

The sentencing guidelines provide judges with a range of sentencing options for a particular offense, unless he has a reason for departing from the said guidelines. The most common reason for a judge to depart from the guidelines would be the presence of an aggravating or mitigating circumstance. An ***aggravating circumstance*** is any circumstance that increases the seriousness of the crime, thus increasing the offender's punishment. For example, when considering the crime of robbery, this crime could be viewed as more severe if the offender caused serious bodily injury to the victim. Therefore, the degree of harm inflicted upon the victim would be considered an aggravating circumstance and may warrant a harsher sentence than that specified in the guidelines (Siegel, 2011).

On the other hand, a ***mitigating circumstance*** is a circumstance that does not justify a criminal act but may lessen the defendant's degree of culpability as well as his sentence. For example, imagine that four individuals are involved in robbing a bank—three males committed the actual robbery, and the girlfriend of one of the offenders drove the getaway car but did not play as significant a role in the robbery as the other offenders. Consequently, her minor role could be considered a mitigating circumstance, warranting a lesser sentence than that specified in the guidelines (Siegel, 2011).

Figure 5.2 Portion of Massachusetts Sentencing Guidelines

Level	Illustrative Offenses	Sentence Range				
6	Manslaughter (Involuntary) Armed Robbery (No gun) A&B DW (Significant Injury)	40–60 Mo.	45–67 Mo.	50–75 Mo.	60–90 Mo.	80–120 Mo.
5	Unarmed Robbery Stalking in Violation of Order Unarmed Burglary Larceny ($50,000 and over)	12–36 Mo. IS-IV IS-III IS-II	24–36 Mo. IS-IV IS-III IS-II	36–54 Mo.	48–72 Mo.	60–90 Mo.
	Criminal History Scale	A No/Minor Record	B Moderate Record	C Serious Record	D Violent or Repetitive	E Serious Violent

Sentencing Zones		Intermediate Sanctions Levels	
(dark shading)	Incarceration Zone	IS-IV	24-Hour Restriction
(light shading)	Discretionary Zone (Incarceration/Intermediate Sanction)	IS-III	Daily Accountability
		IS-II	Standard Supervision

Source: Commonwealth of Massachusetts, 2017a. Retrieved from http://www.mass.gov/courts/court-info/trial-court/sent-commission/ma-sentencing-grid-gen.html.

Sentencing Hearing

The judge is typically responsible for imposing the criminal sentence at the sentencing hearing. The sentence is based on the information reported in the presentence investigation and the recommendations of the sentencing guidelines. Depending on the seriousness of the offense and the offender's prior history, the offender can be sentenced to any number of sanctions, including fines, probation, substance abuse treatment, imprisonment, or any combination of these sanctions (Siegel, 2011).

Specialty Courts

In addition to the courts already covered in this chapter, the commonwealth also has specialty courts, or problem-solving courts, to address the unique needs of certain offenders. Specialty courts in Massachusetts include drug courts, mental health courts, veterans treatment courts, and homeless courts, which will be discussed in this section. These courts were established not only to address the needs of offenders but also to promote public safety and maximize the efficiency of limited criminal justice resources.

Drug Courts

Drug courts attempt to address drug or alcohol addiction, which are underlying issues correlated with criminal behavior. This type of court is overseen by a drug court judge, and these courts provide intensive probation, mandate treatment, require regular drug testing, and impose graduated sanctions for noncompliance. Furthermore, substance abuse treatment specialists and probation officers develop and monitor treatment protocols and manage the caseloads for the drug court participants.

Currently, Massachusetts has over 20 drug courts across the state. The adult drug courts operate in the following district court locations: Ayer, Barnstable, Brockton, Cambridge, Chelsea, Concord, Dudley, Fall River, Greenfield, Hingham, Lawrence, Lynn, Malden, New Bedford, Newton, Orange, Pittsfield, Plymouth, and Quincy, Springfield, Taunton, and Worcester. There are also drug court sessions in the Charlestown, Dorchester, East Boston, and South Boston divisions of the Boston Municipal Court. Furthermore, there is also a juvenile drug court that operates in New Bedford, Fall River, and Taunton (Commonwealth of Massachusetts, n.d.o).

Mental Health Courts

Mental health courts provide an alternative to incarceration for defendants who have mental illness or a co-occurring disorder (e.g., mental health issues and substance abuse issues). These courts allow mentally ill offenders to remain in the community on probation while receiving the community-based services they need. As part of this program, mental health court participants must participate in community-based treatment for at least three months and meet regularly with their specialty court team. Currently, there are three mental health courts within the Boston Municipal Court, and the Springfield District Court and Plymouth District Court also hold sessions for mentally ill offenders (Commonwealth of Massachusetts, n.d.o).

Veterans Treatment Courts

Veterans treatment courts handle cases that involve offenders with a history of military service. This type of specialty court coordinates with community providers and the veterans service delivery system to improve public safety and address the issues of veterans such as post-traumatic stress disorder (PTSD). Participants of veterans treatment court are required to abstain from drugs and alcohol, receive treatment, and have weekly contact with the court. There are several veterans treatment courts in Massachusetts—the Boston Veterans Treatment Court in the Boston Municipal Court, the Norfolk County Veterans Treatment Court in the Dedham District Court, the Middlesex County Veterans Treatment Court in the Lawrence District Court, the Middlesex County Veterans Treatment Court in the Framingham/Natick District Court, and the Western Massachusetts Veterans Treatment Court in the Holyoke District Court (Commonwealth of Massachusetts, n.d.o).

Homeless Courts

Homeless Courts are specialty courts that serve the Boston Municipal Court Department, as well as Cambridge District Court. This type of court helps homeless offenders find permanent housing, employment, and government benefits. Furthermore, upon completion of substance abuse treatment, job training, or mental health treatment, offenders may have their open or pending warrants removed. In addition, their cases are often dismissed if they work to address their behaviors and addictions that originally contributed to their criminality (Commonwealth of Massachusetts, n.d.o).

Conclusion

After finishing this chapter, readers should be familiar with the structure and role that the courts play in the criminal justice system in Massachusetts. The Massachusetts court system is very complex and is composed of many different actors. Even though each actor plays a different role, they all work together to achieve justice throughout the Commonwealth of Massachusetts.

Key Terms

Aggravating Circumstance: Circumstance that increases the seriousness of a given crime, increasing the offender's punishment.

Appellate Jurisdiction: Authority of a court to review decisions and change outcomes that were decided in a lower court.

Arraignment: Criminal proceeding in which a judge informs the defendant of the charges against him, and the defendant enters a plea of guilty, not guilty, or no contest.

Bail: Monetary amount set as a condition of pretrial release to ensure the return of the accused at subsequent proceedings.

Bench Trial: Trial in which a judge determines the guilt or innocence of a defendant without a jury.

Booking: Procedure by which law enforcement record details of an arrest and charges against a suspect, including the crime for which the arrest was made, information used to identify the suspect, and other pertinent facts related to the arrest.

Brief: Written legal argument, stating the legal reasons in support of a party's position or appeal based on statutes, case precedents, and reasoning applied to the facts in the particular situation.

Challenge for Cause: Request that a potential juror be dismissed because there is reason to believe he cannot serve as a fair and impartial juror.

Circumstantial Evidence: Evidence presented in a criminal trial that permits conclusions indirectly establishing the existence or nonexistence of a fact.

Cross-Examination: Process whereby an attorney interrogates witnesses of the opposing side during a criminal trial.

Defendant: Person or entity accused of a crime in a criminal prosecution.

Defense Attorney: Attorney who represents the defendant in a criminal trial.

Deliberation: Phase of a criminal trial at which the jury meets in private to discuss the evidence presented in court to decide whether a defendant is guilty or innocent.

Direct Examination: Questioning of one's own witness during a trial.

Directed Verdict: Right of a judge to direct a jury to acquit a defendant because the state did not prove the elements of the crime or has not established guilt according to law.

District Attorney: Attorney who represents the Commonwealth of Massachusetts in a criminal trial.

General Jurisdiction: Power of a court to hear any type of case that arises within its geographical area.

Hung Jury: Trial jury selected to make a decision in a criminal case regarding a defendant's guilt or innocence who cannot reach a verdict due to divisions in opinion.

Indigent Defendant: A defendant who cannot afford a private defense attorney.

John Augustus: A Boston area bootmaker who was the first person to supervise a probationer and is credited with being the "Father of Probation."

Jurisdiction: Authority of the courts to make legal decisions.

Jury Trial: Judicial proceeding to determine a defendant's guilt or innocence by a body of persons sworn to render a verdict based on law and evidence.

Massachusetts Trial Court Probation Service: More commonly referred to as the **Massachusetts Probation Service** is the commonwealth's primary supervisory law enforcement agency.

Mitigating Circumstance: Information about the defendant that does not justify or excuse a criminal act but which may lessen the defendant's degree of culpability.

Opinion: Legal document stating the reasons for a judicial decision.

Original Jurisdiction: Authority of a court to hear a case for the first time.

Peremptory Challenge: Dismissal of a potential juror by the prosecution or defense for unexplained reasons.

Plea Bargain: Agreement between the prosecution and defense in which the accused agrees to plead guilty to a lesser charge or to a particular sentencing recommendation.

Probable Cause: Evidence discovered through logical inquiry that would lead a reasonably prudent person to believe an accused person has committed a crime warranting prosecution.

Real Evidence: Evidence that is tangible and can physically be brought into the courtroom for the judge and jury to see.

Subject Matter Jurisdiction: Power of a court over the nature of a case and the type of remedy sought.

Testimonial Evidence: Evidence obtained from a witness who makes a sworn statement or declaration of fact about a criminal case.

Venire: The panel of prospective jurors from which a jury is selected.

Verdict: Formal decision made by a jury concerning the questions submitted to it during a trial.

Voir Dire: The process by which prospective jurors are questioned by counsel and the court before being selected to serve on a jury.

Related Websites

Committee for Public Counsel Services
http://www.publiccounsel.net/
Mass Legal Services
http://www.masslegalservices.org/
Massachusetts Bar Association
http://www.massbar.org/
Massachusetts Board of Bar Examiners
http://www.mass.gov/courts/court-info/sjc/attorneys-bar-applicants/bbe/
Massachusetts Court System
http://www.mass.gov/courts/
Massachusetts District Attorneys Association
http://www.mass.gov/mdaa/

Review Questions

1. List and describe the functions of the seven trial court departments in Massachusetts.
2. What is the difference between trial courts and appellate courts?
3. Describe the appeals process in Massachusetts.
4. What is the role of the Massachusetts Board of Bar Examiners?
5. How are judges selected in Massachusetts?
6. What is the difference between district attorneys and defense attorneys?
7. What is an indigent defendant?
8. Explain the difference between a trial jury and a grand jury.
9. What happens during booking?
10. What is the purpose of bail?
11. Explain what happens during an arraignment.

12. What is a plea bargain?
13. What are the advantages and disadvantages of engaging in plea bargaining?
14. Explain the purpose of pretrial motions.
15. Differentiate between a bench trial and a jury trial.
16. What is the difference between a challenge for cause and a peremptory challenge?
17. What is the purpose of an opening statement?
18. List and describe the different types of evidence that can be used during a trial.
19. Explain the difference between a direct examination and a cross-examination.
20. What is a directed verdict?
21. What happens during jury deliberation?
22. What is the purpose of a presentence investigation?
23. What is the significance of sentencing guidelines?
24. List and describe the different types of specialty courts in Massachusetts.

References

Committee for Public Counsel Services (n.d.). *Home.* Retrieved from http://www.publiccounsel.net/.

Commonwealth of Massachusetts. (n.d.a). *About the Appeals Court.* Retrieved from http://www.mass.gov/courts/court-info/about-mass-courts/appeals-hist-gen.html.

Commonwealth of Massachusetts. (n.d.b). *Massachusetts Board of Bar Overseers.* Retrieved from https://www.massbbo.org/.

Commonwealth of Massachusetts. (n.d.c). *Seeking admission to the bar in Massachusetts.* Retrieved from https://www.mass.gov/seeking-admission-to-the-bar-in-massachusetts.

Commonwealth of Massachusetts. (n.d.d). *Boston Municipal Court Department.* Retrieved from http://www.mass.gov/courts/court-info/trial-court/bmc/.

Commonwealth of Massachusetts. (n.d.e). *District Court Department.* Retrieved from http://www.mass.gov/courts/court-info/trial-court/dc/.

Commonwealth of Massachusetts. (n.d.f). *Executive Office of the Trial Court.* Retrieved from http://www.mass.gov/courts/court-info/trial-court/exec-office/.

Commonwealth of Massachusetts. (n.d.g). *Housing Court Department.* Retrieved from http://www.mass.gov/courts/court-info/trial-court/hc/.

Commonwealth of Massachusetts. (n.d.h). *The pre-trial, trial, and verdict process.* Retrieved from https://www.mass.gov/info-details/the-pre-trial-trial-and-verdict-process.

Commonwealth of Massachusetts. (n.d.i). *Juvenile Court.* Retrieved from https://www.mass.gov/orgs/juvenile-court.

Commonwealth of Massachusetts. (n.d.j). *Land Court.* Retrieved from https://www.mass.gov/orgs/land-court.

Commonwealth of Massachusetts. (n.d.k). *Massachusetts court system.* Retrieved from https://www.mass.gov/orgs/massachusetts-court-system.

Commonwealth of Massachusetts. (n.d.l). *Jury Duty.* Retrieved from https://www.mass.gov/jury-duty.

Commonwealth of Massachusetts. (n.d.m). *Probate and Family Court.* Retrieved from https://www.mass.gov/orgs/probate-and-family-court.

Commonwealth of Massachusetts. (n.d.n). *Master juror list information for city & town clerks.* Retrieved from https://www.mass.gov/master-juror-list-info-rmation-for-city-town-clerks.

Commonwealth of Massachusetts. (n.d.o). *Specialty courts.* Retrieved from http://www.mass.gov/courts/programs/specialty-courts/.

Commonwealth of Massachusetts. (n.d.p). *Superior Court.* Retrieved from https://www.mass.gov/orgs/superior-court.

Commonwealth of Massachusetts. (n.d.q). *About the Supreme Judicial Court.* Retrieved from http://www.mass.gov/courts/court-info/about-mass-courts/sjc-hist-gen.html.

Commonwealth of Massachusetts. (n.d.r). *Your arraignment or first appearance in court.* Retrieved from http://www.mass.gov/ourts/selfhelp/criminal-law/arraignment.html.

Commonwealth of Massachusetts. (1979a). *Criminal Procedure Rule 20: Trial jurors.* Retrieved from https://www.mass.gov/rules-of-criminal-procedure/criminal-procedure-rule-20-trial-jurors.

Commonwealth of Massachusetts. (1979b). *Criminal Procedure Rule 24: Opening statements; arguments; instructions to jury.* Retrieved from https://www.mass.gov/rules-of-criminal-procedure/criminal-procedure-rule-24-opening-statements-arguments-instructions-to.

Commonwealth of Massachusetts. (1998). *Civil Procedure Rule 50: Motion for a directed verdict and JNOV.* Retrieved from http://www.mass.gov/courts/case-legal-res/rules-of-court/civil-procedure/mrcp50.html.

Commonwealth of Massachusetts. (2008). *Criminal Procedure Rule 28: Judgment.* Retrieved from https://www.mass.gov/rules-of-criminal-procedure/criminal-procedure-rule-28-judgment.

Commonwealth of Massachusetts. (2017a). Locate the appropriate grid cell/sentencing grid. In *Advisory Sentencing Guidelines.* Retrieved from https://www.mass.gov/files/documents/2018/07/10/Final%20Advisory%20Sentencing%20Guidelines%2020180621.pdf.

Commonwealth of Massachusetts. (2017b). *Supreme Judicial Court Rule 3:01: Attorneys.* Retrieved from https://www.mass.gov/supreme-judicial-court-rules/supreme-judicial-court-rule-301-attorneys.

Commonwealth of Massachusetts. (2018a). *Learn about grand jury service.* Retrieved from http://www.mass.gov/courts/jury-info/trial-and-grand-jurors/gand-jurors/.

Commonwealth of Massachusetts. (2018b). *Advisory sentencing guidelines.* Retrieved from https://www.mass.gov/doc/advisory-sentencing-guidelin-es.

Commonwealth of Massachusetts. (2018c). *Learn about the court appellate process.* Retrieved from https://www.mass.gov/info-details/learn-about-the-court-appellate-process.

Doerner, W. (2012). Florida courts. In *Florida's criminal justice system.* Durham, NC: Carolina Academic Press.

Enwemeka, Z. (2016). *Mass. high court says Black men may have legitimate reason to flee police.* WBUR. Retrieved from http://www.wbur.org/news/2016/09/20/mass-high-court-black-men-may-have-legitimate-reason-to-flee-police.

Gardiner, C. L., & Mallicoat, S. L. (2012). *California's criminal justice system.* Durham, NC: Carolina Academic Press.

Healy, M. W. (2012). A guide to the Massachusetts judicial selection process: The making of a judge. (2nd ed.). Boston, MA: Massachusetts Bar Association.

Law Library—American Law and Legal Information. (n.d.). *John Augustus.* Retrieved from http://law.jrank.org/pages/4568/Augustus-John.html.

MGL c.12 §12

MGL c.211E §1

MGL c.211E §2

MGL c.211E §3

MGL c.221 §38

MGL c.234 §29

MGL c.276 §58

MGL c.278 §4

Siegel, L. J. (2011). *Essentials of criminal justice* (7th ed.). Boston, MA: Cengage Learning.

The 188th General Court of the Commonwealth of Massachusetts. (2018). *Constitution of the Commonwealth of Massachusetts (Chapter 2, Section 1)*. Retrieved from https://malegislature.gov/Laws/Constitution#chapterII SectionI.

U.S. Const. amend VI.

U.S. Const. amend VII.

Chapter 6

Corrections in Massachusetts

Learning Objectives

- Learn about the correctional system in Massachusetts.
- Understand the justifications for punishment.
- Familiarize yourself with the Massachusetts Department of Correction.
- Compare the different security levels within the Massachusetts Department of Correction.
- Recognize the difference between prisons and jails.
- Learn about the selection process to become a correctional officer in Massachusetts.
- Become familiar with community-based corrections within Massachusetts.

Introduction

As you are aware, there are three components to the criminal justice system—law enforcement, courts, and corrections. Remember that law enforcement is responsible for apprehending people who break the law. Also recall that the courts are responsible for determining an offender's guilt or innocence as well as sentencing an offender if he is found guilty. In this chapter, you will learn about the ***correctional system***. After someone has been convicted of a crime and sentenced to punishment, he or she becomes part of the correctional system. Essentially, this system includes all of the institutions and methods used to punish, control, and change the behavior of convicted offenders. Forms of punishment within this system include prisons, jails, probation, parole, and intermediate sanctions.

In this chapter, we will discuss the purposes of sentencing and why we punish offenders. We will then discuss the correctional system in Massachusetts, including the Department of Correction, houses of correction, becoming a corrections officer, probation, parole, and intermediate sanctions. As you read this chapter, keep in mind that there are approximately 90,000 people under correctional supervision in Massachusetts, accounting for 1.3% of all people under correctional supervision in the United States. Of those 90,000 people, approximately 70,000 are supervised in the community on probation or parole, and the other 20,000 are incarcerated in a prison or jail (Kaeble, Glaze, Tsoutis, & Minton, 2016).

Purposes of Sentencing

In Chapter 5, you learned that after a defendant is found guilty, he or she is sentenced to punishment. When considering different punishments, we want to be sure that these punishments are doing what they set out to do. Most importantly, are law enforcement keeping the public safe and ensuring that the offender will not commit another crime? In the following sections, we will discuss the four primary reasons for sentencing—retribution, deterrence, incapacitation, and rehabilitation (Gaines & Miller, 2016).

Retribution

Retribution is the oldest and the most common justification for sentencing. The concept of retribution is similar to how the Old Testament makes reference to "an eye for an eye." That is, if someone commits a crime, that person deserves to be punished. The principle of retribution is sometimes referred to using the Latin term ***lex talionis*** or the "law of talion." The English word talion (translated from Latin) means a retaliation authorized by law in which the punishment corresponds in kind and degree to the injury. The term *lex talionis* does not only refer to literal eye-for-an-eye codes of justice but rather applies to the broader concept and class of legal systems that specifies direct penalties for specific crimes, which are thought to be fitting in their severity: "let the punishment fit the crime." The concept of retribution also considers the principle of ***just deserts*** in that the severity of the punishment should be proportional to the severity of the crime. For example, someone who commits petty theft may be sentenced to pay a fine, while someone who commits first-degree murder may be sentenced to life without parole (Meyer, 2014).

Deterrence

The next justification for sentencing is ***deterrence***, and its goal is to prevent future crimes with the threat of punishment. The intention of deterrence is that society is sending a message to potential offenders that criminal acts will not be tolerated, and wrongdoers will be punished. There are two types of deterrence—***general deterrence*** and ***specific deterrence***. The idea behind general deterrence is that by punishing one individual, the general public will be discouraged from committing a similar act, given the possibility of punishment. For example, if someone is executed in the state of Texas, general deterrence would suggest that the general public would be discouraged from committing a crime that would warrant capital punishment. On the other hand, specific deterrence is targeting a specific individual who has already been punished for a particular crime. For instance, if Jane Doe has been convicted of a DUI and sentenced to jail before, specific deterrence would postulate that Jane Doe would (hopefully) not drink and drive again. The intention is that once that individual has already been punished for a particular act, she will be less apt to commit that act again, knowing that she has been punished for it in the past (Gaines & Miller, 2016).

Incapacitation

The next justification for punishment is ***incapacitation***, or the idea that incarcerating a criminal ensures that he is no longer a danger to society. According to this rationale, if a criminal is behind bars, he cannot harm anyone in the community for the duration of his prison term. This justification focuses on physically removing the offender from society to prevent future criminality. If he is behind bars, he cannot harm anyone in society (Gaines & Miller, 2016).

Rehabilitation

The final justification for punishment is ***rehabilitation***. The idea behind rehabilitation is that offenders do not commit crimes because they are evil, but rather they have behavioral patterns leading them to commit crime. For example, an offender could have a substance abuse problem or an issue with anger management. The criminal justice system recognizes that the root of the problem (i.e., addiction) is leading the individual to engage in criminal behavior, and unless that problem is addressed, the individual will continue to offend. Therefore, by intervening to change the offender's behavior patterns and attitudes, the hope is that the offender can be treated and will be less apt to engage in future criminality (Gaines & Miller, 2016).

Massachusetts Department of Correction

The Massachusetts Department of Correction's (DOC) vision is to promote positive change among inmates to minimize violence, victimization, and recidivism. Its mission is to "promote public safety by managing offenders while providing care and appropriate programming in preparation for successful reentry into the community" (Commonwealth of Massachusetts, n.d.e).

As mentioned earlier, there are approximately 20,000 people incarcerated in the Commonwealth of Massachusetts. Approximately 10,800 of those people are incarcerated in ***prisons*** operated by the DOC (Commonwealth of Massachusetts, n.d.d). Offenders housed in the MA DOC have been convicted primarily of ***felonies***, or serious crimes, such as violent crimes, property crimes, or drug offenses.

In terms of gender, approximately 95% of these inmates are male, while the other 5% are female. Regarding the racial and ethnic composition of the inmate population in the MA DOC, 43% identify as White, 28% as Black, 26% as Hispanic, 1% as Asian, 1% as American Indian, and 1% as "Other." Not including inmates with life sentences, the average time served in the MA DOC is 3.6 years for males and 2.8 years for females (Commonwealth of Massachusetts, n.d.d).

List of Facilities

The DOC has 17 institutions and four security levels—maximum, medium, minimum, and prerelease—to account for the different levels of security needed to supervise inmates. ***Maximum security*** refers to a custody level in which the design of the prison and the classification of the inmate require maximum supervision through heightened security inside and outside the prison. Inmates housed in maximum security prisons present an increased risk of escaping or hurting themselves, other inmates, or staff (Commonwealth of Massachusetts, n.d.c). Although inmates housed in ***medium security*** prisons are not as dangerous as those in maximum security facilities, they still pose some risk of escaping or hurting someone within the prison. Therefore, supervision is still constant. However, these inmates are more apt to follow the rules and regulations of the prison so that they have more job and program opportunities.

Inmates in ***minimum security*** and ***prerelease*** facilities have a greater amount of autonomy than those in maximum or medium security facilities. The goal of a minimum security facility is to give the inmate a greater sense of personal responsibility while still being supervised. Inmates in these facilities pose a low risk of escaping or of harming anyone. Furthermore, they have an increased level of programming and often have access to the community while being supervised. Finally, the goal of a prerelease facility is to reestablish inmate responsibility before their release. Prerelease inmates require minimal supervision, and they are often allowed to participate in work release or educational release in the community without being supervised (Commonwealth of Massachusetts, n.d.c).

The facilities operated within the MA DOC are listed below (Commonwealth of Massachusetts, n.d.f):

- *Boston Pre-Release Center* (BPRC) is a minimum security and prerelease facility housing male inmates. BPRC focuses on reintegration by increasing opportunities for employment and access to agencies and programs within the community.
- *Bridgewater State Hospital* is a medium security facility housing male inmates who are primarily ***civil commitments*** with or without criminal sentences. Many of these inmates pose a risk to public safety due to mental illness.
- *Lemuel Shattuck Hospital Correctional Unit* is a unit within the Lemuel Shattuck Hospital that provides secure medical care to both male and female inmates from state and county facilities in Massachusetts. Inmates are usually only housed at this facility while they need medical care, and they are not housed here long term.
- *Massachusetts Alcohol and Substance Abuse Center* is a minimum security facility that provides services to males civilly committed by the court for detoxification and substance abuse treatment for up to 90 days.
- *Massachusetts Treatment Center* is a medium security facility housing male sex offenders and sexually dangerous persons. It offers specialized treatment to reduce the risk of recidivism among sex offender populations.
- *MCI-Cedar Junction* is the DOC's reception and diagnostic center for male inmates to determine an inmate's classification and individualized program plan. Therefore, this is where all new male inmates within the MA DOC are initially placed. The Department Disciplinary Unit for serious discipline issues within the DOC is also located at this facility.
- *MCI-Concord* is a medium security facility for male inmates.
- *MCI-Framingham* is the MA DOC's primary facility for sentenced female offenders, and it is the oldest operating women's prison in the country.
- *MCI-Norfolk* is the largest medium security facility in Massachusetts. At this facility, the inmates live in dormitory-style units.
- *MCI-Plymouth* houses minimum and prerelease males, and its focus is on reintegration into the community.
- *MCI-Shirley* houses both medium and minimum security level inmates.

- *North Central Correctional Institution* houses medium and minimum security inmates.
- *Northeastern Correctional Center* houses minimum and prerelease criminally sentenced male inmates.
- *Old Colony Correctional Center* houses inmates in medium and minimum housing units. It is currently a mental health focused facility that provides mental health services and promotes rehabilitation and reentry.
- *Pondville Correctional Center* houses minimum and prerelease inmates.
- *South Middlesex Correctional Center* houses minimum and prerelease female inmates.
- *Souza Baranowski Correctional Center* is the only exclusively maximum security male facility in Massachusetts, and it is also the newest facility within the MA DOC. This is the facility that housed Aaron Hernandez, the now deceased former New England Patriots player sentenced to life without parole for a first-degree murder conviction.

Historical Prisons in Massachusetts

Charlestown State Prison was a correctional facility built in the Charlestown section of Boston in 1805. It sat at the intersection of Austin Street and New Rutherford Avenue on a 5-acre parcel of land. The original prison only had 90 cells. But early in its history, the state prison in Charlestown became notorious for its cruel and abusive conditions. The cells could barely hold a cot and did not have plumbing or windows. Inmates were given a bucket for waste, which they emptied once each day during their hour of free time (Charlestown Historical Society, n.d.).

The prison occupied the land that currently houses Bunker Hill Community College. The prison population quickly grew, and in 1828, 1,850 additional wings were built on the prison. In 1867, the Department Of Corrections converted a guardroom into additional prison cells. Due to overcrowding, in 1878 the state built a new prison, MCI-Concord, to replace the prison in Charlestown. Although prisoners were moved out of Charlestown, the prison in Concord quickly became over crowded so prisoners were moved back. A third wing was constructed in 1886 to help ease overcrowding (Charlestown Historical Society, n.d.).

In 1920, prisoners in the Charlestown State Prison were employed in a prison trade program and many learned how to manufacture automobile license plates. Keeping inmates occupied learning a trade or being educated was thought to placate inmates during the day and help make them less violent and cut down on prison unrest. Others were allowed to spend time in the prison library reading various books. Some notable prisoners in the Charlestown State Prison included ***Sacco and Vanzetti*** and ***Malcom X*** (O'Neil, 2012).

In a widely celebrated and controversial case, Italian-born Nicola Sacco and Bartolomeo Vanzetti were convicted of first-degree murder on July 14, 1921, and sentenced to death. As details of the trial and the men's suspected innocence became known, it is reported that protests on their behalf were held in several domestic and international cities. Prominent legal scholars, citizens, and academics pleaded for their pardon or for a new trial (Encyclopedia Britannica, 2018).

Responding to an influx of people calling for their pardon, Governor Alvan Fuller appointed a commission to investigate the case (Encyclopedia Britannica, 2018). After weeks of deliberation, the commission upheld the verdict, and they were executed in the electric chair at the Charlestown State Prison on August 23, 1927 (MassMoments, n.d.).

Investigations continued after their executions, as ballistics tests and incriminating statements by others known to the case intensified belief in their wrongful executions. On August 23, 1977, the 50th anniversary of the executions, Governor Michael Dukakis issued a proclamation that Sacco and Vanzetti had been unfairly tried and convicted and that "any stigma and disgrace should be forever removed from their names" (MassMoments, n.d.).

In 1946, 20-year-old Malcolm Little (Malcom X) was convicted of burglary and served seven years of a 10-year sentence in the Charlestown State Prison (O'Neil, 2012). While incarcerated, he joined the Black Muslims, a new branch of the Nation of Islam. Eager to learn to improve his life, he spent a lot of time in the prison library. He copied an entire dictionary page by page and read every book the prison library had in the areas of literature, history, philosophy, and science. When he was paroled in 1952, Malcolm X became a spokesman for the Nation of Islam and later became one of the country's most compelling and influential Black leaders.

Rioting, murder, assaults, and death had become routine occurrences in the Charlestown State Prison, which did not officially close until 1955. The last executions in Massachusetts were at Charlestown State Prison when ***Philip Bellino*** and ***Edward Gertson*** were electrocuted on May 9, 1947, for murder (- O'Neil, 2012).

Charles Street Jail, also known as the *Suffolk County Jail*, was located at 215 Charles Street in the old West End of Boston. The jail was first proposed by newly elected mayor, Martin Brimmer, in his 1843 inaugural address as a replacement for the old Leverett Street Jail that had been built in 1822. Construction on the jail began in 1848 and was completed in 1851. It was designed with input from prison reformer, Rev. Louis Dwight, a pioneer in American prisons. The project was based on the Auburn Plan, which was intended to keep inmates separated and unable to communicate with each other.

The guiding principles of the Auburn Plan were industrial work, obedience, and silence. The Auburn plan resulted in the construction of tiny individual cells and workshops and a rigid system of imposed silence and harsh punishments. Every inmate was assigned a number when they entered the jail, which served as his or her identity. Movement within the jail was performed in a regimented manner, known as the *lockstep*, which called for prisoners to march in an almost military-style human chain (Law Library—American Law and Legal Information, n.d.).

The original jail was built in the form of a cross with four wings made of the granite from the nearby Quincy Quarries. These four wings each extended from a central, octagon-shaped rotunda affectionately known as the guard room floor. This area had a 90-foot tall atrium with 30 arched windows, each 33 feet high, which provided ventilation and natural light. The winged corridors allowed segregation of prisoners by sex and type of offense. The original jail contained 220 granite 8-by-10 foot cells on four tiers (or levels). The Charles Street Jail was run by the Suffolk County Sheriff Department, and sheriff deputies handled the care, custody, control, and transport of all inmates assigned to the jail (Turkel, 2014). In 1973, the U.S. District Court ruled because of overcrowding, the jail violated the constitutional rights of the prisoners housed there. In 1990, the prison was ordered to close because the building was condemned because of inhumane living conditions. In May 1990, the inmates were moved into the new Nashua Street Jail one mile away, across from the Boston Garden, now known as TD Garden.

The building is now owned by the Massachusetts General Hospital. It has since been redesigned and reopened in the summer of 2007 as a 300-room luxury Liberty Hotel with a number of high end bars and restaurants. The old Charles Street Jail building is listed in the state and national Registers of Historic Places. The Liberty Hotel has retained much of the historic structure, including the famed rotunda (Turkel, 2014).

Recidivism Rates

A study examining ***recidivism*** rates of inmates released from the MA DOC in 2010 found that 21% of the inmates recidivated within one year of release, 11% with two years, and 7% within three years. Thus, the overall 3-year recidivism rate for this group of inmates was 39%. The MA DOC considers a recidivist to be an inmate released to the street from the MA DOC who is re-incarcerated in either a Massachusetts state or county facility or to a federal facility within three years of their release (Commonwealth of Massachusetts, n.d.d).

Massachusetts Jails and Houses of Correction

You have learned that people convicted of felonies are often sentenced to prison time in the MA DOC. However, people awaiting trial or those convicted of ***misdemeanors***, or less serious felonies, are often housed in a county ***house of correction***. In Massachusetts, county ***jails*** are typically for people accused of crimes who are awaiting trial and have not yet been convicted. On rare occasions, convicted felons may spend some time in a county jail. County houses of correction, on the other hand, are where people are housed if they are convicted in a district court of a felony and are sentenced for a period of incarceration not to exceed two-and-one-half years (Suffolk County Sheriff's Department, 2017).

Similar to other states, jails in Massachusetts are operated at the county level by an elected sheriff. Consequently, there are jails and houses of correction in each of the 14 counties in Massachusetts: Barnstable, Berkshire, Bristol, Dukes, Essex, Franklin, Hampden, Hampshire, Middlesex, Nantucket, Norfolk, Plymouth, Suffolk, and Worcester. Each county has at least one facility, and some of the larger counties have more than one facility, often to accommodate female inmates or to provide services to inmates after incarceration.

Profile: Jack Quinn, Superintendent, Berkshire County Jail and House of Correction

The best part of my job is the people I work with. These are the dedicated unsung and unseen heroes of law enforcement. They do an outstanding job 24 hours a day, seven days a week, and 365 days a year. This goes for the correctional officers, senior management, support staff, case managers, mental health professionals, education and substance abuse professionals, and medical personnel. All the way down to maintenance. When you can take a group of dedicated individuals and turn a jail and house of correction, which traditionally is a place of despair, into a place of hope that is when you know you have something special. Yes, we wear uniforms and have badges, and we are charged with care and custody, but we also incorporate a social work aspect to this field.

When you combine all of the above, and you see individuals released who have become productive members of society, you know you have obtained your goal. It is very rewarding to know you and your team were able to help these individuals succeed with their goals.

Our goal is making correctional facilities humane. Our profession is one of the oldest professions in the world. The word *correction* comes from correcting the behavior of the people who are sent to a correctional facility. The policy that works the best is "offering inmates as many programs as you can for them to succeed." With every individual that comes to us, we have to evaluate his or her risk and need. Once we figure out their risk need base, with their help and buy-in, you plug in the programs and set the road map where all parties will see success. This is not easy because you have to look at their criminogenic behavior, educational level, housing situation, employment, substance abuse, mental health, and any medical needs they may have. Our policy is an individualized approach including all of these different disciplines.

An ongoing problem we face is literacy. We are mandated to give two tests when inmates arrive—a TB test and a literacy test. If an inmate comes to jail and cannot read, what will happen if he leaves and still cannot read? He will not be able to get a job and succeed, and he will end up right back in jail. Nationally, if we had better programs to teach literacy, we would see more of the inmates make it on the outside. Consequently, our best program is what we call Big Head Books. This is a literacy program where the final product is filming the inmate and sending the DVD home so these individuals can read bedtime stories to their children. Of the 60 programs we run, I personally feel this is the best because it is connecting the inmates behind the wall to their families out in society. The hardest part of my job, without a doubt, is seeing the children of the individuals that are sent to us.

While the number one problem facing the agency is always funding, another large problem is how to address the opioid problem in the commonwealth. Here in New England, we have one of the largest opiate abuse problems nationwide. It affects every economic and social class. People have to remember we are the last stop for individuals who continue to struggle with this addiction. Unfortunately, everything else has failed prior to them coming to jail. The opiate addiction problem is one of the fastest growing issues I have seen in my 31 years in law enforcement. The consequences are devastating because of the amount of heroin deaths there has been both in Massachusetts and in Berkshire County.

Although there is not one solution to the opioid crisis, in my opinion, we should start by taking the individual out of the dysfunctional environment that they are living in day to day. The individual needs to be in a controlled environment, such as a correctional facility, so that we can address the opiate addiction that has led to their criminal behavior. I am talking about good evidence-based programming that is going to have a lifelong effect on their addiction issue, as well as their criminal behavior.

In Massachusetts, we are going down the path of demonizing correctional facilities as a whole. The correctional facilities that have the evidence-based programming that are dealing with the opioid crisis are being thrown in with the facilities that do not have these programs. Without incarceration, I also see the victimization of family members and loved ones repeatedly.

As far as the funding goes, we should start with the lawmakers in Massachusetts. They have set up recipes for failure by taxing the poor who are involved in the system. An example of that would be probation fees that most criminals cannot pay. They are sending them to jail because they cannot pay. Another example would be diversionary programs for substance abuse. Nobody comes to jail on his or her first probation violation. It is usually their sixth or seventh violation. That does not work. You need to fund correctional facilities. Of all the institutions that are involved in supervision of justice-involved people, we need to be able to implement programs better than anyone both inside the walls and outside when an inmate is released.

> Working at the jail and house of correction is the greatest starting point for young individuals starting out in law enforcement. A correctional officer needs to have excellent verbal skills and must be fair but firm and empathetic. This job helps them use those skills in the jail by providing care and custody to the inmates. They use the same tactics and have to learn to face situations similar to those in other aspects of law enforcement.

Becoming a Correctional Officer or Sheriff's Deputy in Massachusetts

Correctional officers and deputy sheriffs maintain the safety and security of inmates and staff within prisons and jails. Without correctional officers, correctional facilities would be in a state of chaos. Correctional officers observe the conduct and behavior of inmates, investigate suspicious inmate activity, and perform other duties related to the job. In Massachusetts, correctional officers are required to take a civil service examination and undergo 400 hours of training at the Basic Correction Officer Academy before becoming an officer.

At this academy, recruits become familiar with the MA Department of Correction's policies and procedures as well as working on physical conditioning. In the classroom, recruits learn about critical incidents and emergencies, stress management, ethics and professionalism, security procedures, communicable diseases, first aid, staff and inmate relations, inmate rights, and defensive tactics, among other topics. They are also required to meet physical fitness standards related to strength, flexibility, and aerobic capacity (Plymouth County Sheriff's Department, 2014). Applicants wishing to become a correctional officer in Massachusetts must also meet the following requirements:

- Be at least 21 years old at the time of appointment
- Have a high school diploma or GED equivalent
- Be a U.S. citizen
- Pass psychological, medical, and physical abilities examinations
- Complete a training program for corrections officers
- Cease smoking tobacco products
- Not have a felony conviction
- Be able to obtain a permit to carry firearms

Correctional officers perform a variety of duties within prisons and jails. Some officers supervise cell blocks and are responsible for the well-being of inmates within their cells. Others supervise work detail, and they are responsible for overseeing inmates who work in the cafeteria, laundry, or other areas of the facility. Some officers supervise inmates in shop or school, and they ensure that inmates do not cause problems during these sessions. Furthermore, some officers work in the prison yard to ensure that prisoners are not causing disruptions during outside recreation. Finally, some correctional officers are responsible for overseeing security at the prison gates or during visitations.

There are other corrections personnel, called correctional program officers, who are involved with the counseling and rehabilitation of inmates. These officers are responsible for performing classification duties, interviewing inmates, analyzing assessment information, and counseling inmates on programming. The minimum entrance requirements for this position in Massachusetts are at least two years of full-time professional experience in counseling, rehabilitation, or a related field. However, education can be substituted for experience. Furthermore, individuals seeking this position are also required to obtain a permit to carry firearms, have a valid driver's license, and complete the Basic Correction Officer Academy (Commonwealth of Massachusetts, n.d.b).

Aside from correctional officers, there are many other positions within correctional facilities, including accountants, administrative assistants, engineers, doctors, chaplains, librarians, recreation officers, among many other positions. Because prisons and jails operate 365 days a year, 24 hours a day, many support staff are needed to help with the everyday operations of the facility and with the care and supervision of the inmates.

Community Corrections in Massachusetts

Recall that there are approximately 90,000 people under correctional supervision in Massachusetts, and 70,000, or 78% of these people, are supervised within the community. ***Community corrections***, such as probation or parole, are important because they help with successful reintegration back into the community, and they provide a low-cost alternative to incarceration (Gaines & Miller, 2016).

The premise behind ***reintegration*** is to focus on preparing offenders for a successful return to the community so that they do not reoffend. Consequently, it is important for them to build ties to the community, such as obtaining employment or education and restoring family ties, so that they can become productive members of society. In addition, it is much more cost-effective to supervise offenders in the community, provided these offenders do not pose a high threat to public safety. For example, it costs the MA DOC an average of $53,000 per year to house an inmate (Commonwealth of Massachusetts, n.d.d) but less than $3,000 per year to supervise an offender in the community (Pew Charitable Trusts, 2009).

Probation

Probation is the most common form of punishment in the United States. While it is administered differently in different states, probation is essentially a sentence for convicted offenders in which the individual is allowed to remain in the community under the supervision of a probation officer. Probation has strong roots in the commonwealth, as Massachusetts was the first state in the nation to establish a probation agency in 1878. In addition, John Augustus, who we discussed earlier in a Chapter 5 text box, was known as the "father of probation." Augustus was one of the first to recognize the connection between substance abuse and crime, and he thought that people could be rehabilitated through treatment as opposed to incarceration (Commonwealth of Massachusetts, 2018b). To this day, probation in Massachusetts is still inspired by the vision of Augustus.

The mission of the Massachusetts Probation Service is to "increase community safety, support victims and survivors, and assist individuals and families in achieving long term positive change." Currently, the Massachusetts Probation Service is comprised of 105 probation departments and 18 community corrections centers throughout the commonwealth. It is managed by the Office of the Commissioner of Probation, a department of the Massachusetts Trial Court. At present, there are over 80,000 people under probation supervision in Massachusetts. Eighty percent of these people are males, and the other 20% are females (Commonwealth of Massachusetts, n.d.h).

Probation Officers

Probation officers are the individuals responsible for monitoring and enforcing the orders of the court for people on probation, and they work closely with these ***probationers*** to promote positive behavioral changes. They help refer probationers to various programs and services, including substance abuse counseling and job and educational training. Probation officers ensure offenders are using pro-social behaviors, making better decisions, and building healthy relationships. All of these positive changes in behavior lead to safer communities and fewer victimizations.

Probation officers often visit probationers at home and at work to make sure they are complying with the conditions of their probation ordered by the court. These conditions can include reporting to the probation officer on a regular basis, attending services and programs, paying fines, or going to treatment or counseling, among other things. In addition, probationers are required not to commit another offense while they are on probation. If a probationer does not comply with these conditions, the probation officer is responsible for bringing the offender before the court. The probation officer can then recommend additional conditions to improve the probationer's behavior, including jail time (Commonwealth of Massachusetts, n.d.k).

In Massachusetts, probation officers work in various courts throughout the commonwealth. For example, some probation officers work in the adult criminal courts, including the Boston Municipal Court, Superior Court, or District Court Department. Other probation officers work in the Juvenile Court Department, supervising children and young adults. Finally, other officers work within the Probate and Family Court Probation Departments, and they are responsible for investigating custody issues, resolving visitation disputes, and enforcing court orders regarding child support (Commonwealth of Massachusetts, n.d.a).

Intermediate Sanctions

Aside from imprisonment and probation, there are also what is known as ***intermediate sanctions*** to accommodate a more diverse range of criminals and the crimes they commit. Intermediate sanctions provide additional sentencing options that are more restrictive than traditional probation but not as restrictive as incarceration. These sanctions match a punishment and treatment for an individual offender with a program reflecting the individual's situation (Gaines & Miller, 2016).

Profile: Alfred E. "Alf" Barbalunga, Chief Probation Officer, MA Probation Services

The best part of the job is the opportunity to provide excellent customer service to members of the public, defendants, and probationers. I always say, "A small spark of employee kindness can put a colossal burst of sunshine into someone's day." Furthermore, being part of a probationer's journey to reach sobriety is particularly rewarding. When that probationer finally reaches the "promised land," rewards abound for both individuals.

One of the most successful programs in the agency has been the Electronic Monitoring (ELMO) Program, a nationwide leader monitoring offenders since April 2001. Currently, this 24/7 supervision tactic has approximately 3,000 participants utilizing the innovative technology. I believe execution and buy-in by the Massachusetts Probation Service leadership team, in tandem with the robust cost savings to the Commonwealth of Massachusetts taxpayers, has vaulted ELMO as the "go-to" supervision enhancement option.

The greatest problem facing probation is a lack of specialty courts, including, but not limited to, drug courts, homeless courts, veteran courts, and mental health courts. In order to change this, we would need legislative approval of additional funding.

The hardest part of the job is understanding that no matter how much time, energy, blood, sweat, and tears you invest in certain probationers, there will sometimes be negative outcomes.

Perseverance is needed for young people entering this profession today. The supply of MA Probation Service employment opportunities is drastically lower than the demand of interested applicants. I am a firm believer in arranging for an internship with our agency to find out if it is a good fit for that prospective applicant and conversely to broadcast some of the individual's excellent employment characteristics to the possible future employer.

There are many types of intermediate sanctions, and some of the more widely used ones are fines, community corrections centers, community service, and house arrest. All of these options allow the offender to be supervised within the community, and they provide a more cost-effective alternative than incarceration.

The intermediate sanction department of the Massachusetts Probation Service is known as the Office of Community Corrections (OCC). The OCC is responsible for establishing intermediate sanctions that offer a continuum of sanctions and services for people on probation, parole, and sometimes the MA DOC. There are two primary initiatives of the OCC—the Trial Court Community Service Program (CSP) and the statewide network of Community Corrections Centers (CCC). The CSP is responsible for developing community service projects and monitoring participants of these projects, and the CCC facilitates supervision by probation and parole agencies through integrated services (Commonwealth of Massachusetts, n.d.i).

Electronic Monitoring Program

The Massachusetts Probation Service's ELMO began in 2001 as an alternative to incarceration, providing greater accountability for probationers sentenced to ***house arrest***. Currently, there are nearly 3,000 offenders statewide being tracked by ELMO, and the idea is that the technology enhances the level of supervision for probationers who need additional surveillance.

There are two types of electronic monitoring devices used by ELMO—the radio frequency bracelet and the GPS bracelet. Offenders wearing the radio frequency bracelet can only leave their homes at specific times authorized by a judge. If the offender leaves at an unauthorized time, an alert notifies the ELMO command center that the individual is out of range so that a probation officer can quickly respond to the alert. For the GPS bracelet, the device tracks where the offender is 24 hours a day, seven days a week. If an offender enters an area he is not supposed to enter, the command center is notified so a probation officer can quickly get in touch with the offender. Furthermore, if a probationer tampers with either type of device, the command center is alerted, and an arrest warrant is issued for the offender (Commonwealth of Massachusetts, 2018a).

Parole

The Massachusetts Parole Board is an agency under the Executive Office of Public Safety. This agency is responsible for granting ***parole*** and supervising parolees. Every year, the parole board conducts at least 10,000 release hearings, supervises more than 8,000 parolees, and provides reentry services to approximately 700 offenders leaving prisons in Massachusetts without postrelease supervision (Commonwealth of Massachusetts, n.d.g).

In Massachusetts, the parole board is comprised of seven members who are appointed by the governor to serve 5-year terms. Each board member must have at least five years of experience in one of the following fields: parole, probation, law enforcement, law, psychology, sociology, or social work (Commonwealth of Massachusetts, n.d.j).

The parole board uses their discretion to release an offender from confinement after he or she has served part of his sentence in prison. ***Parolees***, or individuals who are granted parole, remain under supervision and must adhere to the conditions of their parole as determined by the parole board. The agency also helps parolees find housing, employment, and other services so they can successfully transition back into the community from prison.

Conclusion

After reading this chapter, you should be familiar with the correctional system in Massachusetts. The majority of offenders are supervised in the community, but others are supervised in prisons or jails. The overarching goal of this system is to punish and treat offenders so they do not reoffend.

Key Terms

Bellino and Gertson: Philip Bellino and Edward Gertson were the last people to be executed in Massachusetts. They were executed in the electric chair at the Charlestown State Prison on May 9, 1947.

Charles Street Jail: also known as the *Suffolk County Jail*, located at 215 Charles Street in the old West End of Boston and was operated from 1851–1990.

Charlestown State Prison: A state-run correctional facility in the Charlestown section of Boston from 1805 to 1955 and was the location of the last execution in the state.

Civil Commitment: Legal process through which an individual is deemed to have symptoms of psychiatric disease and is court ordered into treatment in a mental institution, correctional facility, or the community.

Community Corrections: Correctional supervision of offenders within the community as an alternative to incarceration.

Correctional Officer: Individual responsible for overseeing people who have been sentenced to serve time in jail or prison.

Correctional System: Institutions and methods used to punish, control, and change the behavior of convicted offenders.

Deterrence: Use of punishment as a threat to deter people from offending.

Felony: Serious crime for which a person may be imprisoned for over one year.

General Deterrence: Theory of punishment in which the law seeks to deter the public from engaging in criminal acts.

House Arrest: State of being confined to one's home as a sentence as an alternative to incarceration.

House of Correction: A facility operated by county sheriff which houses felons convicted in a district court and are sentenced for a period of incarceration not to exceed two-and-one-half years.

Incapacitation: Philosophy that crime can be prevented by detaining criminals in prison to physically separate them from the community, reducing criminal opportunities.

Intermediate Sanctions: Sanctions that are more restrictive than probation and less restrictive than imprisonment.

Jail: A facility operated by county government (sheriff) that holds people awaiting felony trials or those convicted of misdemeanors.

Just Deserts: Punishment that is deserved.

Lex Talionis (the law of talion): A retaliation authorized by law in which the punishment corresponds in kind and degree to the injury.

Malcom X (Malcolm Little): an outspoken leader of the Nation of Islam and an influential Black leader who served a 7-year sentence in the Charlestown State Prison for burglary.

Maximum Security Prison: A correctional facility designed to control dangerous felons and prevent escapes.

Medium Security Prison: A correctional facility that houses less dangerous inmates and uses less restrictive measures to prevent violence and escapes.

Minimum Security Prison: A correctional facility designed to allow inmates who pose a low security threat to have contact with the outside world.

Misdemeanor: Less serious offense, punishable by a fine or imprisonment up to one year.

Parole: Conditional release of an inmate before his sentence has expired.

Parolee: An individual released on parole.

Prerelease Facility: A type of correctional facility that provides a gradual transition from prison life to the community by means of reintegration through releases to work or educational programs.

Prison: A place of confinement for persons convicted of serious crimes.

Probation: Criminal sanction in which a convicted offender is allowed to remain in the community as an alternative to incarceration.

Probation Officer: An individual who supervises offenders who are on probation.

Probationer: A convicted offender on probation.

Recidivism: Refers to a person's relapse into criminal behavior after receiving a sanction or undergoing an intervention for a previous crime.

Rehabilitation: The process of improving a criminal's character so he will become a productive member of society.

Reintegration: Goal of corrections that focuses on preparing the offender for a successful return to the community without reoffending.

Retribution: Punishment inflicted on someone as vengeance for a criminal act.

Sacco and Vanzetti: In a widely celebrated and controversial case, Nicola Sacco and Bartolomeo Vanzetti were convicted of murder in 1921, sentenced to death, and executed in a case in which many believe they were wrongly convicted.

Sanction: Penalty for disobeying a law or rule.

Specific Deterrence: Method of punishment intended to discourage criminal behavior in a specific individual charged with a crime.

Related Websites

American Correctional Association
http://www.aca.org/aca_prod_imis/aca_member
American Jail Association
http://www.americanjail.org/
American Probation and Parole Association
https://www.appa-net.org/eweb/
Federal Bureau of Prisons
https://www.bop.gov/
Massachusetts Department of Correction
https://www.mass.gov/orgs/massachusetts-department-of-correction
Massachusetts Parole Board
https://www.mass.gov/orgs/massachusetts-parole-board
National Institute of Corrections
http://nicic.gov/
Office of the Commissioner of Probation
http://www.mass.gov/courts/court-info/probation/
The Sentencing Project
http://www.sentencingproject.org/

Review Questions

1. List and explain the four purposes of sentencing.
2. What types of inmates are housed in Massachusetts prisons?
3. Why is it important to have different levels of security among the various prisons?
4. What types of inmates are housed in Massachusetts jails?
5. What are the requirements to become a correctional officer in Massachusetts?
6. What are some of the duties and responsibilities that correctional officers perform?
7. Why is it important to have community-based corrections?

8. What is the role of a probation officer?
9. What is the significance of intermediate sanctions?
10. What are the differences between probation and parole?

References

Charlestown Historical Society. (n.d.). *Massachusetts State Prison, Charlestown.* Retrieved from https://charlestownhistoricalsociety.org/chs_events/massachusetts-state-prison-charlestown/.

Commonwealth of Massachusetts. (n.d.a). *Learn about the Office of the Commissioner of Probation.* Retrieved from http://www.mass.gov/courts/court-info/probation/office-of-the-commissioner-of-probation-gen.html.

Commonwealth of Massachusetts. (n.d.b). *Correctional Program Officer position summary.* Retrieved from http://www.mass.gov/eopss/law-enforce-and-cj/prisons/recruitment/correctional-program-officer-position-summary.html.

Commonwealth of Massachusetts. (n.d.c). *Prison security levels.* Retrieved from http://www.mass.gov/eopss/law-enforce-and-cj/prisons/doc-facilities/security-levels.html.

Commonwealth of Massachusetts. (n.d.d). *Frequently asked questions about the DOC.* Retrieved from http://www.mass.gov/eopss/agencies/doc/faqs-about-the-doc.html.

Commonwealth of Massachusetts. (n.d.e). *Massachusetts Department of Correction.* Retrieved from http://www.mass.gov/eopss/agencies/doc/.

Commonwealth of Massachusetts. (n.d.f). *Prison.* Retrieved from https://www.mass.gov/prison.

Commonwealth of Massachusetts. (n.d.g). *Massachusetts Parole Board.* Retrieved from http://www.mass.gov/eopss/agencies/parole-board/.

Commonwealth of Massachusetts. (n.d.h). *Massachusetts Probation Service.* Retrieved from http://www.mass.gov/courts/court-info/probation/.

Commonwealth of Massachusetts. (n.d.i). *Office of Community Corrections.* Retrieved from https://www.mass.gov/orgs/office-of-community-corrections.

Commonwealth of Massachusetts. (n.d.j). *Massachusetts Parole Board.* Retrieved from https://www.mass.gov/orgs/massachusetts-parole-board.

Commonwealth of Massachusetts. (n.d.k). *Find out what probation officers do.* Retrieved from https://www.mass.gov/service-details/find-out-what-probation-officers-do.

Commonwealth of Massachusetts. (2018a). *Learn about the Electronic Monitoring Program*. Retrieved from http://www.mass.gov/courts/court-info/probation/electronic-monitoring-program.html.

Commonwealth of Massachusetts. (2018b). *Learn about the Massachusetts Probation Service's famous firsts*. Retrieved from http://www.mass.gov/courts/court-info/probation/probation-firsts-gen.html.

Encyclopedia Britannica. (2018). *Sacco-Vanzetti case*. Retrieved from https://www.britannica.com/event/Sacco-Vanzetti-Case.

Gaines, L., & Miller, R. (2016). *Criminal justice in action: The core*. (8th ed.). Boston, MA: Cengage Learning.

Kaeble, D., Glaze, L., Tsoutis, A., & Minton, T. (2016). *Correctional populations in the United States, 2014*. Retrieved from https://www.bjs.gov/content/pub/pdf/cpus14.pdf.

Law Library—American Law and Legal Information. (n.d.). *Prisons: History—The Auburn plan*. Retrieved from http://law.jrank.org/pages/1776/Prisons-History-Auburn-plan.html#ixzz4uE42B4DL.

MassMoments. (n.d.). *Massachusetts executes Sacco and Vanzetti*. Retrieved from https://www.massmoments.org/moment-details/massachusetts-executes-sacco-and-vanzetti.html.

Meyer, J. F. (2014). *Retributive justice*. Retrieved from https://www.britannica.com/topic/retributive-justice.

O'Neil, H. (2012, February 27). *Where Sacco, Vanzetti and Malcolm X stayed in Charlestown*. Retrieved from https://patch.com/massachusetts/charlestown/sacco-vanzetti-malcolm-x-charlestown-prison.

Pew Charitable Trusts. (2009, March 9). *One in 31 U.S. adults are behind bars, on parole or probation* [Press release]. Retrieved from http://www.pewtrusts.org/en/about/news-room/press-releases/0001/01/01/one-in-31-us-adults-are-behind-bars-on-parole-or-probation.

Plymouth County Sheriff's Department. (2014). *Home*. Retrieved from http://www.pcsdma.org/co.html.

Suffolk County Sheriff's Department (2017). *FAQs*. Retrieved from http://www.scsdma.org/faqs/.

Turkel, S. (2014, December 10). *Former prison now luxury hotel: Liberty Hotel in Boston*. Retrieved from http://www.correctionsforum.net/article/former-prison-now-luxury-hotel-41629.

Chapter 7

The Juvenile Justice System in Massachusetts

Learning Objectives

- Learn about the evolution of the juvenile justice system.
- Understand the differences between the adult and juvenile justice systems.
- Become familiar with juvenile crime rates in Massachusetts.
- Familiarize yourself with the structure of the juvenile justice system in Massachusetts.
- Understand the juvenile justice process.
- Recognize when a juvenile would be transferred to adult court.
- Learn about different correctional treatment plans for juveniles.

Introduction

In this chapter, we will discuss how the juvenile justice system differs from the adult criminal justice system. Specifically, we will cover the evolution of the juvenile justice system, delinquency, juvenile crime rates, juvenile court processing, and juvenile corrections throughout the Commonwealth of Massachusetts.

Evolution of the Juvenile Justice System

Before the early 1800s, juvenile offenders were treated no differently than adult offenders. They were tried in the same courts and were sentenced to the same sanctions. However, this began to change as reformers recognized the correlation between deviant behavior and poverty, especially among children of immigrants. Thus, the child-saving movement was initiated, and reformers took steps to "save" children from social and familial circumstances that could be contributing to their delinquency (Gaines & Miller, 2014).

The Child-Saving Movement

Advocates of the child-saving movement supported the philosophy of ***parens patriae***. According to this philosophy, the state has a legal duty to care for children who are delinquent, neglected, or abused. The child-savers believed that rehabilitation and treatment, rather than punishment, should be the focus for juvenile offenders. Additionally, they thought that children should not be sentenced to the same prisons and punitive conditions as adult offenders.

The child-savers created some of the first programs for poverty-stricken youth, including the New York House of Refuge, which opened in 1825 (Gaines & Miller, 2014; Siegel, 2011). This house of refuge took at-risk youth off the street, removing them from the negative influences of their family and friends, and it reformed them through discipline and labor. In addition to completing school work, males often worked in shops or farms, while females carried out domestic work.

The Illinois Juvenile Court

As the nation's population was increasing due to industrialization, the number of juvenile offenders was also increasing. Because it was not possible for private organizations to adequately care for the growing population of at-risk youth, the child savers petitioned for government-run ***juvenile courts***. In 1899, the Illinois Juvenile Court Act was passed, and the Illinois legislature created the first juvenile court. This court handled violations of criminal law committed by people under 16 years of age, in addition to caring for neglected youth. Furthermore, this act also created a probation department to monitor youth within the community (Siegel, 2011). By the mid-1900s, every state in the nation had established a juvenile court modeled after Illinois's system (Gaines & Miller, 2014).

While the juvenile court movement rapidly spread throughout the nation, it did not initially adhere to constitutional rights or due process of the law for juveniles. For example, attorneys were not required for court proceedings, and juveniles were often urged to admit their guilt in court (violations of the Sixth and Fifth Amendments, respectively). However, this changed when, starting in the 1960s, the Supreme Court made several decisions that extended due process rights to juveniles.

For example, the Supreme Court limited judicial discretion when transferring juveniles to adult courts in *Kent v. United States* (1966). The Court held that basic due process rights must be extended to juvenile offenders if they were being transferred to adult court. The following year, in *In re Gault* (1967), the Court decided that juveniles have basic due process rights in all criminal proceedings, including the right to counsel, the right to confront and cross-examine witnesses, and the privilege against self-incrimination.

Furthermore, Congress enacted the Juvenile Justice and Delinquency Prevention (JJDP) Act in 1974, which established the Office of Juvenile Justice and Delinquency Prevention (OJJDP). The initial purposes of the JJDP Act were to fund programs in the juvenile justice system, deinstitutionalize status offenders so they were not detained in juvenile detention facilities or adult jails, and separate juveniles sentenced in adult facilities from the adult population (Office of Juvenile Justice and Delinquency Prevention, n.d.b).

History of Juvenile Justice in Massachusetts

The juvenile code and juvenile court system were established in Massachusetts in 1906. Although the goal of rehabilitation was recognized in the early system, juvenile offenders were regularly institutionalized and committed to adult correctional facilities. In addition, if a juvenile was charged with a crime punishable by life imprisonment, that offender was tried and sentenced in an adult court (Lindsay et al., 1994).

This rule continued until 1948, when Massachusetts amended the juvenile code so that juvenile delinquents were handed over to the custody of the Youth Service Board, which would then transfer the child to an appropriate facility. However, in the mid-1960s, the Youth Service Board was investigated by the U.S. Department of Health, Education, and Welfare (HEW) on reports of brutality. As a result of this investigation, HEW discovered many deficiencies throughout the existing system. Consequently, a reform bill restructured the juvenile corrections system into the current Department of Youth Services (DYS) in 1969 (Lindsay et al., 1994).

More recently, Massachusetts has moved away from the philosophy of *parens patriae* after the Juvenile Justice Reform Act was enacted in 1996. With escalating levels of juvenile violence across the nation, this act moved to criminalize serious cases of juvenile delinquency. Rather than focus solely on treatment for juvenile offenders, it combined elements of punishment with that of treatment. Furthermore, the "Youthful Offender" statute was also enacted in Massachusetts in 1996. This statute requires that all juveniles 14 years and older who are charged with murder are automatically treated as adults (Commonwealth of Massachusetts, n.d.d). This topic will be discussed in more detail later in the chapter when we discuss transferring juveniles to the adult system.

How the Juvenile Justice System Differs from the Adult System

As you are aware by now, there are two separate justice systems in Massachusetts—the adult criminal justice system and the juvenile justice system. While there are many similarities between the two systems, there are also many differences. Aside from the fact that the juvenile justice system has jurisdiction over people who were under 18 years old at the time they committed their crime, we will focus on some of the other differences, including juvenile delinquents and status offenders, neglected and abused juveniles, and differences in terminology.

Child Requiring Assistance vs. Juvenile Delinquent

One of the major differences between the two systems is that the state has the responsibility to care for minors whose behavior indicates their parents cannot control them. This minor is recognized as a "child requiring assistance (CRA)," formerly known as a ***status offender***. A status offender is a juvenile who has engaged in behavior that is deemed to be unacceptable for someone under a certain age. However, if the same act were committed by an adult, it would not warrant the attention of law enforcement. Status offenses in Massachusetts include disobeying lawful commands of parents or guardians, engaging in habitual truancy, failing to obey school regulations, and running away from home (MGL c.119 §21; Office of Juvenile Justice and Delinquency Prevention, 2014).

Juvenile delinquency, on the other hand, refers to any behavior that would also be criminal if an adult committed the same act. These acts include violent crimes such as homicide, forcible rape, robbery, and aggravated assault. They also include property crimes such as burglary, larceny-theft, motor vehicle theft, and arson. In Massachusetts, a juvenile delinquent is someone who committed a criminal act before reaching his or her 18th birthday.

Neglected and Abused Juveniles

In addition to juvenile delinquents and status offenders, the juvenile justice system also deals with cases of ***child abuse*** and ***neglect***. Child abuse refers to physical or emotional mistreatment of a child, whereas child neglect is a type of abuse when parents or guardians deny their children basic necessities such as food, shelter, or adequate care (Gaines & Miller, 2014).

Cases of child abuse and neglect in Massachusetts are handled by the Department of Children and Families (DCF). When a report has been filed indicating abuse or neglect, DCF investigates the suspected behavior and completes a written evaluation to determine if the behavior can be substantiated. The investigation includes a home visit to determine causes of the injuries, the identity of the person responsible, the name, age and condition of other children in the household, and an evaluation of the parents (MGL c.119 §51B).

If DCF determines there is reasonable cause that a child's health or safety is at risk, they are authorized to take the child into temporary custody to protect that child from further abuse or neglect. DCF aims to find all abused and neglected children safe, permanent homes with extended family, foster homes, or other residential placement. In addition, the department reports serious cases of child abuse and neglect to the district attorney and local law enforcement.

Terminology

Finally, the juvenile justice system uses different terminology than the adult system. For instance, a juvenile being "taken into custody" would equate to an adult being "arrested." Because the systems are distinct, it is important to have different terminology when referring to juvenile offenders (refer to Table 7.1).

Juvenile Crime in Massachusetts

Recall that we looked at crime trends in Massachusetts in Chapter 2. Remember that statistics from the ***Uniform Crime Reporting (UCR) Program*** provide us with official data on crime throughout the United States. The Federal Bureau of Investigation (FBI) publishes this report annually with data on a variety of crimes, including the eight index crimes—homicide, forcible rape, robbery, aggravated assault, burglary, motor vehicle theft, larceny-theft, and arson. In the following sections, we will be focusing on juvenile arrest rates for the index crimes.

In 2014, 9,186 people under the age of 18 were taken into custody in the Commonwealth of Massachusetts (Puzzanchera & Kang, 2017). What does this tell us? Do we have a problem with juvenile crime in Massachusetts, or do we need additional information to give us the whole picture?

If you think that we need more information, you are correct. These figures are counts of the number of juveniles who were taken into custody in Massa-

Table 7.1 Juvenile Court Terminology vs. Adult Court Terminology

Juvenile Court	Adult Court
Adjudicatory Hearing	Trial
Aftercare	Parole
Agree to a Finding	Plead Guilty
Delinquent	Criminal
Deny Petition	Plead not Guilty
Detention Hearing	Bail Hearing
Disposition	Sentence
Initial Appearance	Arraignment or Preliminary Hearing
Petition	File Charges or Indictment
Preventative Detention	Awaiting Trial in Jail
Take Into Custody	Arrest
Youth Correctional Facility	Prison

Source: "Criminal Justice in Action: The Core" by L. K. Gaines and R. L. Miller, 2014.

chusetts in 2014. Unfortunately, raw counts do not provide us with an accurate picture of crime. Instead, we want to look at ***crime rates***. Crime rates divide the number of offenses in an area by the number of people in that area for a given time period and multiply that number by a constant (often 1,000 or 100,000). By doing this, we can determine how many crimes occurred in a particular location for a consistent population.

By examining crime rates rather than counts, we can make different analyses, including state-by-state, city-by-city, and year-to-year comparisons. For example, let's consider the crime of aggravated assault among juveniles. Once we have consistent rates, we can see if juvenile aggravated assault is a problem in Massachusetts versus a neighboring state such as New Hampshire or Connecticut. Or we can determine if cities within Massachusetts, such as Boston, Worcester, or Springfield, have similar rates of aggravated assault. Furthermore, crime rates allow us to compare crime from one year to the next. So we could see if the rate of juvenile aggravated assaults in Massachusetts increased or decreased from one year to the next. All of this is important so that the criminal justice system can determine where it can most effectively allocate resources.

Juvenile Violent Arrest Rates in Massachusetts

In this section, we will be discussing juvenile arrest rates for the violent index crimes—homicide, forcible rape, robbery, and aggravated assault. The first thing we will do is compare juvenile violent arrest rates in Massachusetts with juvenile violent arrest rates nationwide. Figure 7.1 indicates that juvenile violent arrest rates have been declining from 2008 to 2014. Furthermore, Massachusetts has lower juvenile arrest rates than the national average for homicide, forcible rape, and robbery. However, for rates of aggravated assault, Massachusetts surpasses the national average. Nevertheless, it appears as though these rates have been decreasing over time and are converging with the national average. The juvenile justice system in the commonwealth has likely recognized this discrepancy and considered measures to reduce juvenile rates of aggravated assaults. Initiatives, such as Roca (which we will discuss later in this chapter), have contributed to fewer violent crimes.

Figure 7.2 provides a comparison of juvenile and adult violent arrest rates within Massachusetts from 2008 to 2014. For the most part, violent arrest rates have been decreasing for both juveniles and adults. When we look at the specific crime categories, rates of homicide and forcible rape are higher for adults than for juveniles. On the other hand, rates of robbery are higher for juveniles than adults, but they have been converging in recent years. Finally, rates of aggravated assault were higher for juveniles until 2010, when adult rates surpassed those of juveniles. Overall, official statistics indicate that robbery is currently the only violent index crime in Massachusetts where juvenile rates surpass that of their adult counterparts.

Juvenile Property Arrest Rates in Massachusetts

Now we will examine the juvenile arrest rates for the property index crimes—burglary, motor vehicle theft, larceny-theft, and arson. Figure 7.3 indicates that juvenile property crimes have been decreasing from 2008 to 2014. Furthermore, the graphs show that juvenile arrest rates are consistently lower in Massachusetts than they are across the United States.

Figure 7.4 indicates that juveniles in Massachusetts have consistently higher property arrest rates than their adult counterparts during the period, with the exception of adult rates being higher for larceny-theft from 2011 to 2014. These trends are different than what we observed in the comparison between juvenile and adult violent arrest rates. It was expected that juvenile property crime rates would be higher than that of their adult counterparts because many people experiment with crime as youth, but they stop once they are adults.

Figure 7.1 Juvenile Violent Arrest Rates, 2008–2014 (per 100,000 persons, 10–17 years old)

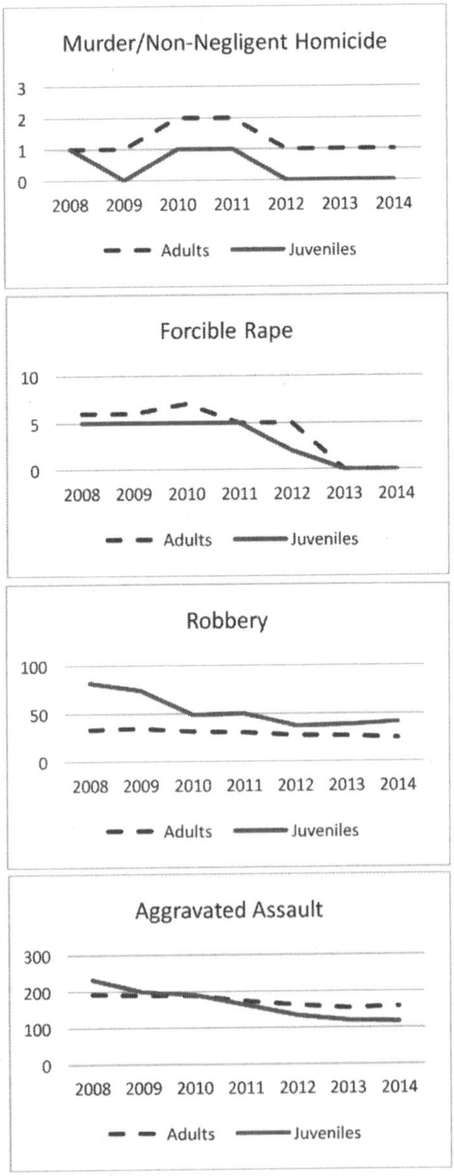

Source: "Easy Access to FBI Arrest Statistics 1994–2014" by C. Puzzanchera and W. Kang, 2017. Retrieved from http://www.ojjdp.gov/ojstatbb/ezaucr/ (compiled by authors).

Figure 7.2 Violent Arrest Rates for Juveniles and Adults in MA, 2008–2014 (per 100,000)

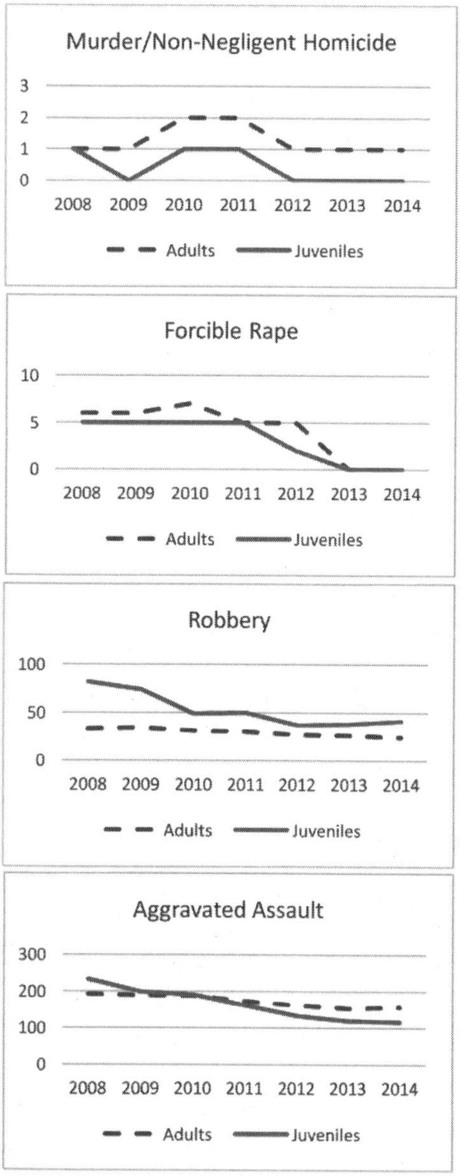

Source: "Easy Access to FBI Arrest Statistics 1994–2014" by C. Puzzanchera and W. Kang. Retrieved from http://www.ojjdp.gov/ojstatbb/ezaucr/ (compiled by authors).

Figure 7.3 Juvenile Property Arrest Rates, 2008–2014 (per 100,000 persons 10–17 years old)

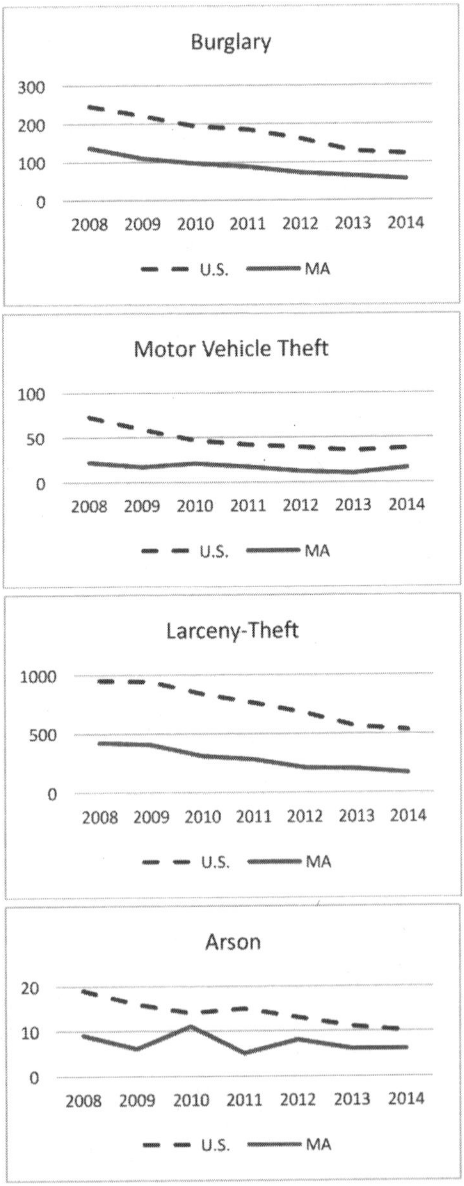

Source: "Easy Access to FBI Arrest Statistics 1994–2014" by C. Puzzanchera and W. Kang. Retrieved from http://www.ojjdp.gov/ojstatbb/ezaucr/ (compiled by authors).

Figure 7.4 Property Arrest Rates for Juveniles and Adults in MA, 2008–2014 (per 100,000)

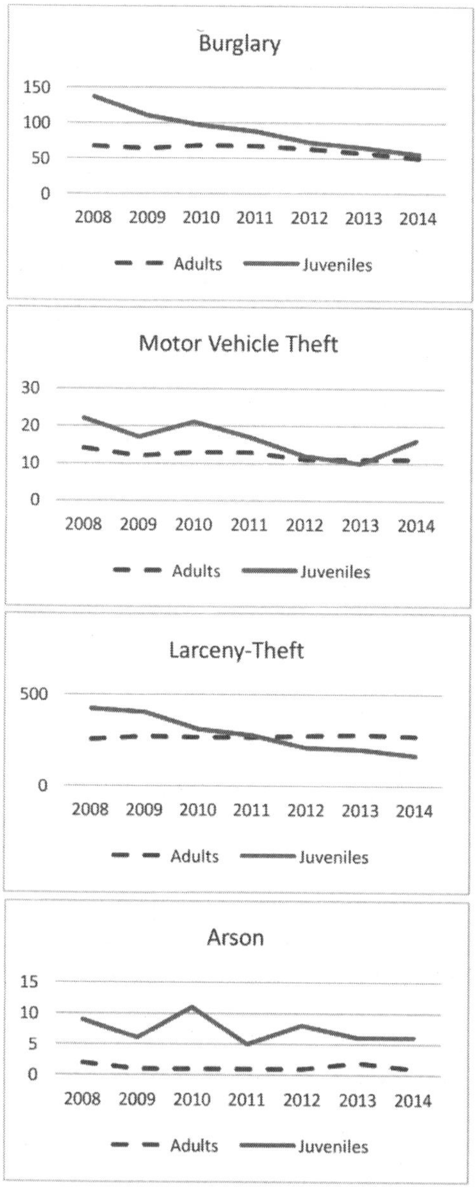

Source: "Easy Access to FBI Arrest Statistics 1994–2014" by C. Puzzanchera and W. Kang. Available at http://www.ojjdp.gov/ojstatbb/ezaucr/ (compiled by authors).

Structure of the Juvenile Justice System in Massachusetts

Now that you are familiar with the nature and extent of juvenile crime in Massachusetts, we are going to discuss how the juvenile justice system deals with minors who have broken the law. Similar to the adult system, the juvenile justice system has three components—law enforcement, courts, and corrections. Although there are separate court and correctional systems for juveniles and adults, there is only one law enforcement system. Throughout the following sections, we will be discussing the juvenile court, juvenile court procedure, and types of juvenile corrections used throughout the Commonwealth of Massachusetts.

Juvenile Court Department in Massachusetts

As mentioned earlier, the juvenile justice system is not limited to cases in which a minor has been taken into custody, but rather it deals with a variety of issues related to minors. The mission of the Juvenile Court Department in Massachusetts is to

> protect children from abuse and neglect, to promote opportunities for children to reside in a safe, stable, permanent family environment, to strengthen families, to rehabilitate juveniles, to protect the public from delinquent and criminal behavior and to decide all cases fairly and impartially with dedication, integrity and professionalism (Commonwealth of Massachusetts, n.d.b).

There are over 40 locations of the Juvenile Court Department across Massachusetts, and this court has jurisdiction over civil and criminal matters dealing with juveniles (Commonwealth of Massachusetts, n.d.b). Specifically, it deals with cases involving delinquencies, youthful offenders, care and protection petitions, children requiring assistance, adults contributing to the delinquency of a minor, adoption, guardianship, and termination of parental rights proceedings. Refer to Table 7.2 for the number and type of cases that were filed in the Juvenile Court Department in the fiscal year 2017.

In the following sections, we will be primarily discussing juvenile delinquency and youthful offender cases. Historically, status offenses were dealt with in the same manner as juvenile delinquency cases, but modern practices have moved

Table 7.2 Summary of Case Filings—Juvenile Court Department, FY 2017

Type of Case	#
Adoption	664
Adult Criminal	6
Application for Complaint	13,175
Care and Protection	3,462
Child Requiring Assistance	5,388
Contempt—Civil	13
Contributing to Delinquency	19
Delinquency	8,648
Equity	42
Failure to Cause	400
Guardianship	1,014
Harassment	462
Interstate Compact	13
Mentally Ill Person	23
Name Change	19
Paternity/Support	381
Substance Abuse	137
Support	2
Temporary Support	1
Young Adult Permanency Hearings	463
Youthful Offender	151
Total	34,483

Source: "State of the Massachusetts Trial Court, Fiscal Year 2017" by Executive Office of the Trial Court, 2018.

away from this treatment, and separate systems handle this distinct category. Most importantly, status offenders are often in need of human and social services rather than the administration of juvenile justice.

Initial Contact: Police Processing

The first contact between a minor and the criminal justice system usually happens when a police officer apprehends the juvenile in the commission of a crime or through a call for service (Gaines & Miller, 2014). Essentially, police officers exercise the same procedures that they would when dealing with adult arrests. However, additional protective procedures are extended to juveniles once they have been taken into custody in Massachusetts. First, the officer in charge of the police station or town lockup to which the minor has been taken must notify a juvenile probation officer and at least one of the child's parents or guardians. Furthermore, the child in custody must be placed in a separate and distinct place from their adult counterparts (MGL c.119 §67).

It is important to note that police often use a great deal of ***discretion*** when deciding to detain or release juveniles who have committed crimes or status offenses. While this decision is primarily based on the seriousness of the offense, the police officer also considers other factors. These include the ability of the parents to discipline the child, the child's previous contact with police and the justice system, and the level of cooperation on the part of the child (Siegel, 2011).

The Juvenile Court Process

Once the police have determined that a particular case requires attention, they notify the juvenile court system through a process known as ***referral.*** While most cases in juvenile court are referred by the police, anyone with a compelling reason can issue a complaint against a juvenile, referring that child to the system. Other individuals often concerned about the well-being of a juvenile include parents, relatives, school officials, or welfare agencies. Refer to Figure 7.5 for a flowchart illustrating the steps in the juvenile justice process.

Intake

Once a juvenile has been referred to the system, the next step is the ***intake*** process. During this process, court officials determine the appropriate path for the juvenile. The child is screened to determine whether he or she needs to be handled through formal or informal means. If the case is not dismissed at this stage, the juvenile will either proceed to juvenile court, be transferred

Figure 7.5 The Juvenile Justice Process

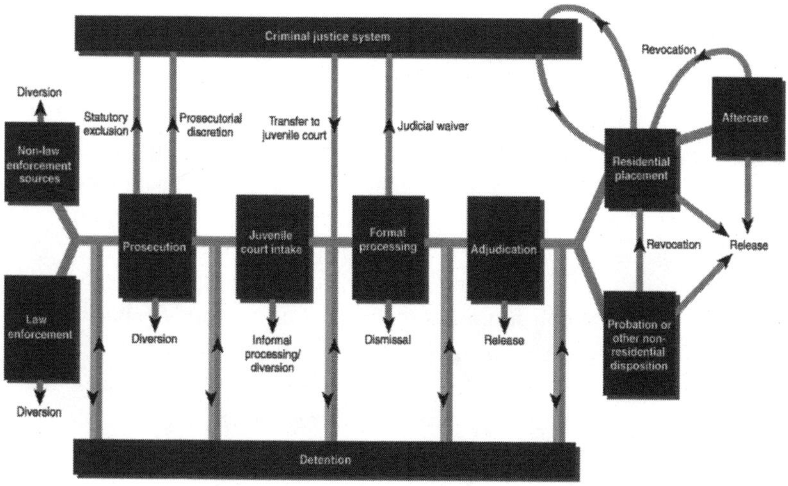

Source: Office of Juvenile Justice and Delinquency Prevention. Retrieved from https://www.ojjdp.gov/ojstatbb/structure_process/images/flowbluemedwebalt2.gif.

to adult court, or enter a diversion program. We will discuss all of these options in greater depth in the following sections.

Arraignment/Detention

If it has been determined a youth will proceed through juvenile court, an ***arraignment*** is the next step in the process. At the arraignment, the juvenile is formally charged with the crime he or she was accused of committing. During this time, the probation department also determines if the child qualifies for a court-appointed attorney, and it conducts a background investigation on the juvenile for information related to the proceeding. After the juvenile has been arraigned, the district attorney can request that the child be held on bail to ensure he or she will return for the next court appearance (O'Keefe, n.d.). Usually the juvenile is released into the custody of his or her parents, guardians, or DYS, provided the child will return for the next appearance in court (MGL c.119 §68).

However, the court may recommend that a juvenile is held in a secure detention facility if that child is a fugitive from another jurisdiction, has failed to appear for previous court proceedings, or presents a safety risk to individuals in the community. Under these circumstances, DYS provides special foster homes and detention homes for juveniles to be detained in temporary custody (MGL c.119 §68).

Trial

Juvenile trials are closed to the public except in cases when the juvenile is tried as a "youthful offender." A youthful offender is defined as the following:

> a person who is subject to an adult or juvenile sentence for having committed, while between the ages of fourteen and 18, an offense against a law of the commonwealth which, if he were an adult, would be punishable by imprisonment in the state prison, and (a) has previously been committed to the department of youth services, or (b) has committed an offense which involves the infliction or threat of serious bodily harm in violation of law or violated certain firearm statutes (MGL c.119 §52).

A juvenile trial can be either a bench trial or a jury trial. In a bench trial, a judge listens to the evidence to determine if the prosecution has proven its case. In a jury trial, a panel of six jurors hears the evidence and must decide a unanimous verdict of "delinquent" or "not delinquent." For youthful offender cases, the commonwealth requires a panel of 12 jurors (O'Keefe, n.d.).

At the trial, an assistant district attorney represents the Commonwealth of Massachusetts, while a defense attorney represents the juvenile. During the trial, the court listens to witness testimony and examines evidence related to the case. Throughout this process, the commonwealth has the burden of proving its case beyond a reasonable doubt. If ***proof beyond a reasonable doubt*** can be established or if the child voluntarily admits that he or she committed the crime in question, the juvenile is found to be a delinquent child (MGL c.119 §58). On the other hand, if a judge or jury determines that there is not enough evidence against the juvenile, the child is found to be not delinquent.

Furthermore, the court may also continue the case without a finding. In this situation, the juvenile admits there was sufficient evidence to warrant a delinquent finding (O'Keefe, n.d.). However, instead of going to trial, the juvenile and at least one parent or guardian agrees that the child be put on probation for a specified period of time. After successful completion of the terms of probation, the case is dismissed. On the other hand, if the juvenile does not complete the terms of probation, he or she is adjudicated a delinquent and sentenced appropriately (MGL c.119 §58).

Sentencing

After the juvenile has been adjudicated delinquent, the judge determines which steps will be taken toward rehabilitation and punishment. Recall that the sentencing phase of an adult trial is concerned predominantly with keeping the community safe from individuals who have been convicted. On the contrary, at a sentencing hearing for juveniles, the judge determines a sentence that will fit the needs of the child. The prosecutor and defense attorney offer their recommendations for sentencing based on the seriousness of the delinquent act, the juvenile's past criminal history, the juvenile's family background, and interviews with teachers and social workers.

Furthermore, victims often have the opportunity to give a ***victim impact statement*** at this phase in the proceedings. A victim impact statement is a written or oral statement allowing crime victims to tell the courtroom how they were affected physically, mentally, emotionally, and financially as a result of the perpetrator's actions. The judge considers the victim impact statement, as well as the suggestions of the prosecutor and defense attorney, prior to sentencing the juvenile.

Typically, juvenile delinquents are sentenced to probation or DYS commitment, which we will discuss later in the chapter. However, in youthful offender cases, the judge has a wider range of sentencing options. In these cases, the juvenile can be sentenced to (a) DYS commitment until his or her 21st birthday, (b) any sentence permitted by law in adult court, or (c) a combination of DYS commitment and sentencing permitted by law in adult court (MGL c.119 §58).

Waivers and Transfers to Adult Court

As mentioned earlier, some juveniles are transferred directly to adult court, a process whereby the juvenile court waives jurisdiction over the child. During the "Tough on Crime" era of the 1980s and 1990s, there was concern over violent juvenile offenders and the threat they posed to the community. Consequently, state legislatures expanded transfer laws requiring the prosecution of juveniles in adult criminal courts. All 50 states across the nation allow for juveniles to be tried as adults under certain circumstances. Each state has at least one provision for trying youth as adults in court. Transfer laws vary by state, but they fall into three general categories (Office of Juvenile Justice and Delinquency Prevention, 2011):

1. ***Judicial waiver*** laws allow the juvenile judge to determine whether a juvenile's case will be transferred to adult court. The decision is made at the discretion of the judge, and it is based on the offender's age, the nature of the offense, and the juvenile's criminal history.
2. ***Prosecutorial waiver*** laws define cases that can be heard in either juvenile or adult court. As long as age and offense circumstances are met, the decision of jurisdiction is at the discretion of the prosecutor.
3. ***Statutory exclusion*** laws grant adult courts jurisdiction over certain cases involving juvenile offenders. Depending on the state, these cases are typically reserved for homicide and serious felonies. If a case falls with the state's statutory exclusion category, it is filed in an adult criminal court.

While some states allow for all three types of transfer laws, the Commonwealth of Massachusetts only exercises statutory exclusion laws. Massachusetts is one of the few states in which murder is the only offense that would exclude a juvenile from being tried in juvenile court. In most states, statutory exclusion laws apply when a juvenile has committed other serious or violent felonies in addition to murder. Furthermore, these statutes also determine the minimum age that a youth must reach before being transferred to adult court. In Massachusetts, juveniles between the ages of 14 and 17 are tried as adults in cases involving murder. Across the nation, this minimum age ranges from 13 to 17 years old, but there are a few exceptions. For example, juveniles as young as 10 years old who have been accused of murder and certain violent offenses in Wisconsin can be tried and sentenced as adults, and there is no specified age limit for juveniles accused of murder in Nevada and Pennsylvania (Office of Juvenile Justice and Delinquency Prevention, 2011).

Diversion Programs

As mentioned earlier, some juvenile cases are not processed through the formal court system. Specifically, some juveniles participate in their district attorney's Juvenile Diversion Program, which provides first-time nonviolent offenders with the opportunity to receive services as an alternative to being prosecuted through the traditional system. ***Diversion programs*** are voluntary, but if the juvenile does not want to participate in the program, the case is processed through the juvenile court system (Commonwealth of Massachusetts, n.d.c).

The Juvenile Diversion Program identifies and addresses behaviors that contribute to delinquency and aims to prevent further involvement in the juvenile justice system. Consequently, juveniles in this program participate in counseling, education, and community service projects. The goal of this program is to address the root causes of juvenile delinquency and to help the juvenile make wiser life choices moving forward. Upon successful completion of the program, the district attorney does not prosecute the case, and the juvenile will not have a delinquency record. However, if the juvenile does not complete the program, the case is prosecuted in court.

Juvenile Corrections

Once a juvenile has been sentenced through the formal adjudication process, delinquent offenders receive correctional treatment. First-time offenders are usually diverted or put on probation, while repeat and serious offenders are usually placed in secure correctional facilities. We will discuss the options for juvenile corrections used throughout Massachusetts in the following sections.

Juvenile Probation

Juvenile court judges and other court officials recognize that juveniles should only be removed from their homes as a last resort. Consequently, in the majority of cases, a delinquent child is sentenced to ***probation*** and is able to complete his or her sentence within the community. Nationwide, there are approximately 400,000 juveniles on probation every year, accounting for over 60% of all juvenile dispositions (Siegel & Bartollas, 2014). Currently, there are approximately 11,000 juveniles under the supervision of a probation officer in Massachusetts (Executive Office of the Trial Court, 2018).

Similar to the adult system, juveniles sentenced to probation are required to follow certain rules, or terms, in order to remain on probation. The terms of probation are decided by the judge or determined by the probation department based on the juvenile's offense, history of substance abuse, school performance, or family issues. Examples of such terms include restitution to the victim, counseling, random drug testing, community service, school attendance, and drug or alcohol evaluation (O'Keefe, n.d.).

Also similar to the adult system, a juvenile's probation can be revoked if the juvenile does not comply with the terms of probation or commits a new crime. In the event a juvenile has violated the terms of probation, he or she must attend a revocation hearing. At this hearing, a judge determines whether to extend probation or to terminate probation and commit the juvenile to DYS.

Department of Youth Services

Although the majority of juvenile offenders are placed on probation, some offenders require more restrictive supervision. Thus, the Massachusetts DYS is the agency that serves youth who have been committed as juvenile delinquents or youthful offenders. The DYS offers a wide range of services and supervision, addressing the educational, psychological, and health needs of all juveniles in its custody. As of 2016, there were almost 1,000 youth committed to the DYS (Massachusetts Department of Youth Services, 2017).

Once a juvenile is sentenced to DYS commitment, that juvenile is assessed to determine which program would be most appropriate for his or her needs. Based on the juvenile's criminal history, need for particular counseling or treatment, family issues, and other risk factors related to offending, a DYS caseworker helps decide which program would be most suitable for that child (-O'Keefe, n.d.).

Currently, the DYS operates 63 residential programs consisting of hardware secure programs with locked doors as well as staff secure programs with unlocked doors (Commonwealth of Massachusetts, n.d.e). The focus of the secure residential programs is to rehabilitate youth by teaching them prosocial behaviors through cognitive behavioral approaches. Juveniles in these programs learn to acknowledge their criminal behaviors, understand what lead them to offend, develop a plan to avoid engaging in further criminal activity, and demonstrate patterns of prosocial behaviors while in confinement (Commonwealth of Massachusetts, n.d.a).

In addition, there are 22 district offices across the commonwealth that provide support to juveniles supervised by the DYS in nonresidential programs (Commonwealth of Massachusetts, n.d.e). Most of these youth remain at home with a parent or guardian or in foster care, and they receive services through the closest district office. There are a variety of community programs available (e.g., substance abuse, remedial education), and they primarily use a cognitive behavioral approach to emphasize accountability and prosocial skill development among juvenile offenders (Commonwealth of Massachusetts, n.d.a).

Furthermore, once the juvenile has successfully completed his or her treatment placement, the child is supervised within the community by a DYS caseworker until the child turns 18 years old. The amount of supervision ranges from weekly meetings with a caseworker to 24-hour electronic monitoring (O'Keefe, n.d.). In addition, juveniles must attend school or hold a full-time job, remain drug and alcohol free, and attend treatment or counseling. Similar to adults, juveniles need assistance readjusting to life outside of a secure institution. Therefore, it is important that they have the support they need so that they do not reoffend.

Massachusetts Department of Correction for Juveniles Transferred to Adult Court

If a juvenile between the ages of 14 and 17 is transferred to adult court and convicted of murder, he or she is sentenced to the Massachusetts Department of Correction (DOC). If convicted of murder in the first degree, the juvenile is sentenced to life in prison, with the possibility of parole after serving 20 to 30 years (St. 2014, c. 189). For murder in the second degree, the juvenile is sentenced to life in prison with the possibility of parole after 15 years of confinement (MGL c.119 §72B; MGL c.265 §1).

In the event a juvenile is required to serve time in the Massachusetts DOC for being convicted of murder or another crime under the youthful offender statute, that juvenile is held in a unit separate from the general population of adult prisoners. Additionally, these individuals cannot be held at Massachusetts Correctional Institution—Cedar Junction prior to their 18th birthday (MGL c.119 §72B).

Innovative Programs to Enhance Public Safety

Aside from traditional sentences, the Commonwealth of Massachusetts is continually thinking of innovative ways to enhance public safety and help juvenile offenders refrain from offending in the future. In this section, we will discuss youth courts, the Dual Status Youth Initiative, and Roca, which are several programs currently being used to help juveniles in Massachusetts.

South Coast Youth Courts

In 2002, the New Bedford Youth Court (NBYC) became the first youth court in Massachusetts, followed by the Fall River Youth Court, which was established in 2009. The South Coast Youth Courts are overseen by community organizations including schools, the police, court personnel, and other program providers. There are over 1,000 youth courts nationwide (National Association of Youth Courts, n.d.), and they serve as an alternative to the traditional juvenile justice system by utilizing the principles of ***restorative justice***.

With the exception of adults assisting at hearings, youth courts are operated by trained youth volunteers who serve as traditional courtroom actors. During the sentencing hearing, participants acknowledge the harm they caused as a result of their actions, and they agree to accept the sanctions imposed by a jury of their peers. Sanctions typically include community service and other service projects to help reconnect youth with their community. The goal of these sanctions is to help juveniles build pro-social skills and behaviors, so they are less apt to engage in future criminality. Juveniles who participate in youth court are usually first-time nonviolent offenders, and they tend to have lower recidivism rates than juveniles who did not participate in a youth court (South Coast Youth Courts, n.d.).

Dual Status Youth Initiative

The Dual Status Youth Initiative began in Hampden County in 2013. This initiative provides collaboration and helps to coordinate services for youth who have a history of family involvement with the DCF, in addition to having a history of delinquent charges in juvenile court (Executive Office of the Trial Court, 2018). Compared to juveniles without involvement in both the DCF and the courts, dual status youth face additional challenges, making their cases more difficult to manage.

Consequently, the Robert F. Kennedy National Resource Center for Juvenile Justice provides assistance to state and local jurisdictions to improve the outcomes for dual status youth (RFK National Resource Center for Juvenile Justice, n.d.). Because this initiative has proven to be successful in Hampden County, other counties across the commonwealth are also beginning to implement this program.

Roca and the Pay for Success Project

In 2014, Massachusetts and Roca launched the Massachusetts Juvenile Justice Pay for Success (PFS) Project. Roca is an organization that aims to disrupt the cycle of incarceration and poverty that is evident in many urban communities. Moreover, Roca has developed an intervention model for young people ages 17 to 24 who are at risk for being incarcerated. This model provides two years of services and two years of follow-up care to help transform the lives of these at-risk individuals by improving their skills and relationships.

The PFS project is designed to improve the lives of high-risk young men, reduce recidivism, save taxpayers money, and enhance community safety. Through PFS, Roca is providing its intervention model to over 900 juveniles completing their sentences through the DYS, juvenile probation, or adult probation in Boston and Springfield. As a result of this project, it is expected that approximately 250 incarcerations will be avoided because participants will be better equipped to be productive members of society (Roca, n.d.).

Juvenile Record Sealed

It is important to note that in Massachusetts juvenile court records are typically sealed and treated as though they never existed. Only select state agencies, such as the court or probation department, can be granted access to these records. Juvenile records can be sealed if the following requirements are met:

- At least three years have passed since the completion of the individual's case, including court supervision, probation, commitment, or parole.
- The individual has not been adjudicated delinquent or found guilty of a criminal offense in the Commonwealth of Massachusetts or any jurisdiction outside of Massachusetts, except for a motor vehicle offense in which the penalty is a fine of less than $50 dollars for at least three years preceding the request (MGL c.276 § 100B).

Conclusion

After reading this chapter, you should have a better understanding of the similarities and differences between the adult criminal justice system and the juvenile justice system in Massachusetts. Although the juvenile justice system was more punitive in its policies and practices in the 1990s, there has been a shift back toward rehabilitation in recent years. Because it is in the best interest of the child, the majority of juvenile delinquents are treated within the community. Currently, there are many programs and incentives in Massachusetts to keep our youth in the community and dissuade them from engaging in future criminality.

Key Terms

Arraignment: Formal proceeding in which the juvenile is charged with a crime.

Child Abuse: Physical, emotional, or sexual maltreatment of children.

Child Neglect: Form of child abuse in which the child is denied necessities, including food, shelter, care, and love.

Crime Rate: Ratio of crimes in an area to the population of that area, often expressed per 1,000 or 100,000 persons.

Discretion: Freedom to decide what should be done in a particular situation.

Diversion Program: Provides first-time nonviolent offenders the opportunity to receive services in lieu of being prosecuted through the traditional court process.

Intake: Process by which an official of the court decides whether to file a petition, release the juvenile, or place the juvenile under another form of supervision.

Judicial Waiver: Process in which the juvenile judge, based on the facts of the case, determines that the accused juvenile should be transferred to adult court.

Juvenile Court: Court with original jurisdiction over people statutorily defined as juveniles and assumed to be delinquents or status offenders.

Juvenile Delinquency: Participation in illegal behavior by minors.

***Parens Patriae*:** Latin term that means "parent of the country." Philosophy that government is responsible to look after children and to assume the role of parent when needed. It is the duty of the state to act in the best interest of children until they reach the age of majority.

Probation: Sanction in which an offender is allowed to remain in the community rather than be institutionalized.

Proof Beyond a Reasonable Doubt: Standard that must be met by the prosecution in a criminal proceeding. No other logical explanation can be derived from the facts except that the accused committed the crime.

Prosecutorial Waiver: Procedure used in circumstances when a prosecutor has discretion to decide whether a case will be heard in a juvenile court or an adult court.

Referral: Notification process through which a police officer or other concerned citizen makes the juvenile court aware of a minor's unlawful or unruly conduct.

Restorative Justice: Theory of justice that emphasizes repairing the harm caused by criminal behavior.

Status Offender: Juvenile who has engaged in behavior deemed unacceptable for persons under a statutorily defined age.

Statutory Exclusion: Process by which a juvenile is transferred to adult court as a matter of state law.

Uniform Crime Reports (UCR): Official data on crime in the United States, published by the FBI.

Victim Impact Statement: Written or oral statement made as part of the judicial process, allowing crime victims to speak during the sentencing of their offender.

Related Websites

Department of Youth Services
https://www.mass.gov/orgs/department-of-youth-services
Massachusetts Juvenile Court Department
https://www.mass.gov/orgs/juvenile-court
National Center for Juvenile Justice
http://www.ncjj.org/
Office of Juvenile Justice and Delinquency Prevention
http://www.ojjdp.gov/

Review Questions

1. What is the philosophy of *parens patriae*?
2. What is the significance of the Illinois Juvenile Court Act of 1899?
3. Explain the significance of *In re Gault*.
4. What is the difference between a status offender and a juvenile delinquent?
5. Differentiate between child abuse and neglect.
6. Why is it more important to examine crime rates rather than counts of offenses?
7. How do violent juvenile arrest rates in Massachusetts compare with national rates?
8. How do property juvenile arrest rates in Massachusetts compare with national rates?
9. What factors do police consider when deciding to detain or release a juvenile?
10. What are the options a juvenile probation officer has during the intake process?
11. What is the purpose of an arraignment?
12. What is a youthful offender?
13. How does a judge determine an appropriate sentence for an adjudicated delinquent?
14. What is the significance of a victim impact statement?

15. What are the three ways a juvenile case could be transferred to adult court?
16. Under what circumstances are juveniles transferred to adult court in Massachusetts?
17. Explain the rationale behind a juvenile diversion program.
18. What is the most common type of sentence imposed upon juveniles? Why?
19. What is the role of the DYS?
20. What is the punishment for juveniles convicted of murder in Massachusetts?
21. Explain the significance of youth courts.
22. Explain what happens to juvenile records in Massachusetts.

References

An Act Relative to Juvenile Life Sentences for First Degree Murder, St. 2014, c. 189.

Commonwealth of Massachusetts. (n.d.a). *Clinical services provided by the Department of Youth Services (DYS).* Retrieved from http://www.mass.gov/eohhs/gov/departments/dys/programs-and-services/department-of-youth-services-clinical-services.html.

Commonwealth of Massachusetts. (n.d.b). *Juvenile Court.* Retrieved from http://www.mass.gov/courts/court-info/trial-court/juv/.

Commonwealth of Massachusetts. (n.d.c). *Juvenile diversion.* Retrieved from http://www.mass.gov/essexda/prevention-and-intervention/school-safety/juvenile-diversion.html.

Commonwealth of Massachusetts. (n.d.d). *Juvenile justice legal issues.* Retrieved from http://www.mass.gov/eohhs/gov/laws-regs/dys/juvenile-justice-legal-issues.html.

Commonwealth of Massachusetts. (n.d.e). *About us: Mission statement.* Retrieved from http://www.mass.gov/eohhs/gov/departments/dys/mxission-statement.html.

Executive Office of Health and Human Services. (2014). *Department of Youth Services: Public information packet.* Boston, MA: Author.

Executive Office of the Trial Court. (2018). *State of the Massachusetts Trial Court, fiscal year 2017.* Boston, MA: Carey & Spence.

Gaines, L. K., & Miller, R. L. (2014). *Criminal justice in action: The core* (7th ed.). Belmont, CA: Cengage Learning.

In re Gault 387, U.S. 1 (1967)

Kent v. United States, 383 U.S. 541 (1966)

Lindsay, R., Warring, W., Blitzman, J., Cinquegrana, R., Coursey, S. M., DeMarco, A., Elder, J., Tewksbury, J., Witecki, M., Gottlieb, M., Keating, M., & Ward, R. (1994). *The Massachusetts juvenile justice system of the 1990s: Rethinking a national model.* Boston, MA: Boston Bar Association Task Force on the Juvenile Justice System.

Massachusetts Department of Youth Services. (2017). *Annual report 2016.* Boston, MA: Author.

MGL c.119 §21

MGL c.119 §51B

MGL c.119 §52

MGL c.119 §58

MGL c.119 §67

MGL c.119 §68

MGL c.119 §72B

MGL c.265 §1

MGL c.276 §100B

National Association of Youth Courts. (2017). *Home.* Retrieved from http://www.youthcourt.net/?page_id=3.

Office of Juvenile Justice and Delinquency Program. (n.d.a). *Case flow diagram.* Retrieved from http://www.ojjdp.gov/ojstatbb/structure_process/case.html.

Office of Juvenile Justice and Delinquency Prevention. (n.d.b). *Authorizing legislation.* Retrieved from http://www.ojjdp.gov/about/legislation.html.

Office of Juvenile Justice and Delinquency Prevention. (2011). Trying juveniles as adults: An analysis of state transfer laws and reporting. Retrieved from https://www.ncjrs.gov/pdffiles1/ojjdp/232434.pdf.

Office of Juvenile Justice and Delinquency Prevention. (2014). Jurisdictional boundaries. In *OJJDP statistical briefing book.* Retrieved from http://www.ojjdp.gov/ojstatbb/structure_process/qa04121.asp?qaDate=2013.

O'Keefe, M. (n.d.). *Juvenile proceedings.* Commonwealth of Massachusetts. Retrieved from http://www.mass.gov/capeda/docs/juvenile-justice.pdf.

Puzzanchera, C., & Kang, W. (2017). *Easy access to FBI arrest statistics 1994–2014.* Office of Juvenile Justice and Delinquency Prevention. Retrieved from http://www.ojjdp.gov/ojstatbb/ezaucr/.

RFK National Resource Center for Juvenile Justice. (n.d.). *Dual status youth reform.* Retrieved from http://www.rfknrcjj.org/our-work/dual-status-youth-reform/.

Roca. (n.d.). *Pay for success.* Retrieved from http://rocainc.org/what-we-do/pay-for-success/.

Siegel, L. J. (2011). *Essentials of criminal justice* (7th ed.). Belmont, CA: Cengage Learning.

Siegel, L.J., & Bartollas, C. (2014). *Corrections today* (2nd ed.). Belmont, CA: Cengage Learning.

South Coast Youth Courts. (n.d.). *History of New Bedford Youth Court.* Retrieved from http://www.nb-fryouthcourts.org/new_bedford_history.html.

Chapter 8

Victims' Rights in Massachusetts

Learning Objectives

- Learn about the history of victims' rights in the United States.
- Learn about victims' rights in Massachusetts.
- Recognize the significance of a victim impact statement.
- Distinguish between restitution and victim compensation.
- Become familiar with different services available to victims in Massachusetts.

Introduction

Although they are often overlooked, victims play a large role in the criminal justice system. That is, many crimes involve an individual who has been victimized by an offender. However, until the 1970s, the criminal justice system did not pay much attention to the rights of victims. Similar to many states across the country, the criminal justice system in Massachusetts has begun to pay more attention to obtaining justice for victims. In this chapter, we will discuss how legislation has impacted victims nationally and in Massachusetts. Additionally, this chapter will also cover victim compensation and various services the criminal justice system provides to victims throughout the commonwealth.

A Brief History of Victims' Rights in the United States

Starting in the 1970s, victims' rights groups, such as Mothers Against Drunk Driving and the National Center for Victims of Crime, started to surface across the country to provide support to victims and to advocate for victims' rights. The National Organization for Victim Assistance (NOVA) was established in 1975. NOVA is the oldest national victim assistance organization in the United States, and its mission is to "champion dignity and compassion for those harmed by crime and crisis" (NOVA, n.d.).

Another defining moment for victims' rights was President Ronald Reagan's establishment of the President's Task Force on Victims of Crime in 1982. The goal of this task force was to review and improve upon existing policies and programs for crime victims. As a result of the findings, the task force recognized the need for enhanced compensation and services for victims. Consequently, the Victims of Crime Act (VOCA) was established in 1984 to fund victim services through fines imposed upon federal offenders, and U.S.C. Title 42 established crime victims' rights, services, and compensation throughout the federal criminal justice system (U.S. Department of Justice, n.d.).

In 2004, President George W. Bush signed the Crime Victims' Rights Act (CVRA) into law. The CVRA gives victims a greater role in the criminal justice process and provides victims with additional rights, including the right to be protected from the accused, the right to not be excluded from public court proceedings, and the right to be heard in federal court proceedings (U.S. Department of Justice, n.d.).

Victimization Data

In addition to the initiatives discussed above, there have also been strides taken to capture data on criminal victimizations. It is important to collect this data to determine who the victims of crime are and to identify ways to help these victims. In Chapter 2, we discussed the Uniform Crime Reporting (UCR) Program, which tracks crimes reported to police. We also mentioned that there was another system of collecting data in the United States to track data on criminal victimizations and the ***dark figure of crime***, or crimes that go unreported to the police. This system, which started in the early 1970s, is called the National Crime Victimization Survey (NCVS).

The NCVS is conducted annually by the U.S. Census Bureau and the Bureau of Justice Statistics. Data is obtained from a nationally representative sample of approximately 90,000 households regarding the nature and extent of their victimizations. People who are interviewed for the NCVS self-report on victimizations that they experienced over the past six months. The NCVS collects details (e.g., sex, race, age, location of the crime, use of a weapon, etc.) about violent crimes and property crimes that people reported and did not report to the police (Bureau of Justice Statistics, n.d.). Most importantly, the NCVS has played an integral role in capturing some of the more sensitive crimes, such as rapes and sexual assaults as well as domestic violence, which people are less apt to report to the police.

While the NCVS is the most widely used system to track victimization data nationwide, it does not provide the public with victimizations at the state level. Consequently, we will now discuss the National Incident Based Reporting System (NIBRS), which allows us to examine victimization data at the state level. NIBRS, while not implemented as widely as the UCR, is administered by the FBI and is intended to improve the quality of crime data that is reported to law enforcement. Whereas the UCR was an aggregate of total crimes, NIBRS captures details on each crime incident and separate offenses within each incident. NIBRS provides information on victims, offenders, victim-offender relationships, and location of the crime, among other details related to crime incidents (Uniform Crime Reporting, n.d.).

Ideally, by improving the quality of crime data, law enforcement will have more information about crimes and will be able to allocate their resources more effectively. However, a drawback of NIBRS is that only one third of law enforcement agencies across the country participate in NIBRS. It is expensive to transition to this new system, but the UCR program is trying to increase NIBRS participation nationwide. The hope is that NIBRS will eventually become the standard for official crime statistics reported to police (Uniform Crime Reporting, n.d.).

In Massachusetts, there are 168 police agencies that report NIBRS data (Justice Research and Statistics Association, n.d.). Let's take a look at some of this data so we can get an idea of what crimes people are the victims of in Massachusetts. In 2015, NIBRS reported 65,060 violent victimizations in Massachusetts (Puzzanchera, Smith, & Kang, 2017). Less than 1% of these victimizations were homicides, 1% kidnappings, 4% rapes and sexual assaults, 6% robberies, 17% intimidation, 22% aggravated assaults, and 50% simple assaults (see Figure 8.1). Note that in addition to homicide, aggravated assault, robbery, and rape, NIBRS also reports data on incidents involving kidnappings, intimidation, and simple assaults.

Figure 8.1 Violent Victimizations Reported in NIBRS, 2015

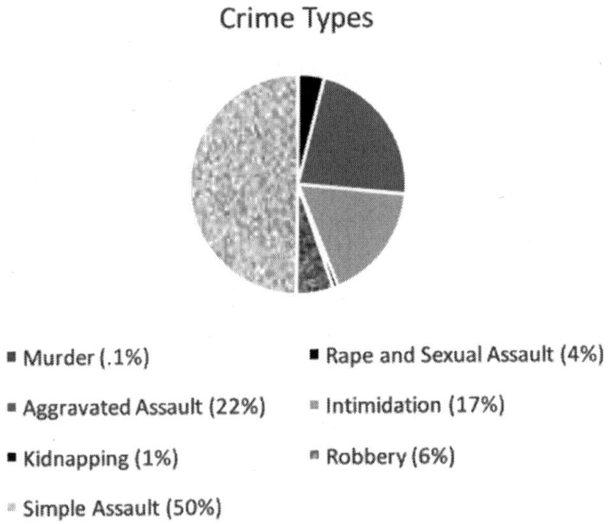

Source: Puzzanchera, Smith, & Kang, 2017. "Easy Access to NIBRS Victims, 2015: Victims Of Violence." Retrieved from http://www.ojjdp.gov/ojstatbb/ezanibrsdv/ (chart compiled by authors).

In the following sections, we will discuss some of the rights and initiatives put in place for victims of these crimes in Massachusetts.

Massachusetts Victim Bill of Rights

Given the advancement in victims' rights at the national level, the states also began establishing rights for victims. In 1983, the Victim Bill of Rights was set forth in Chapter 258B, Section 3, of the Massachusetts General Laws. The Victim Bill of Rights gives victims and their families a role in the criminal justice process, and it informs them of the resources and services available to them. Specifically, it provides for the following rights for victims of crime:

- To be informed about the victim's rights and role in the criminal process;
- To be present at court proceeding relating to their case;
- To be notified when a court proceeding to which they have been summoned has been rescheduled;
- To be notified about the level of protection available to them from law enforcement;

- To be informed of financial assistance and social services available to them;
- To a prompt sentencing of the case in which they were a victim;
- To meet with the prosecutor before the trial;
- To be informed of the right to request confidentiality in the criminal justice system to protect their privacy;
- To be provided by the court with a secure waiting area separate from that of the offender;
- To be informed of the procedures to receive victim compensation;
- To have help seeking employer cooperation to minimize loss of pay as a result of the criminal process;
- To be free from penalty by his employer due to his presence in a criminal proceeding;
- To be informed of the right to submit to or decline an interview by the defense attorney;
- To meet with a probation officer prior to the filing of the presentence investigation report;
- To request that restitution be part of the offender's sentence, and to have the prosecutor help with the documentation of the victim's losses;
- To be heard through a victim impact statement at the sentencing of the offender at a parole hearing;
- To be informed of the offender's sentence;
- To have personal property taken for evidence returned by the court;
- To be informed about the offender's eligibility for parole;
- To be informed if the offender is granted a temporary release from custody, is moved to a less secure facility, or escapes from custody; and
- To be informed of the right to pursue a civil action for damages related to the crime.

It is clear from the Victim Bill of Rights in Massachusetts that victims have a wide extent of rights, ranging from monetary compensation to being informed about each step in the criminal process related to their case. The following sections will discuss several of these rights in greater depth, including victim impact statements and compensation and restitution.

Victim Impact Statements

Victims are entitled to be heard through a written and oral ***victim impact statement*** (VIS) at the time of the offender's sentencing (MGL c.258B §3). The VIS allows the victim or the victim's representative to tell the judge and the other people in the courtroom how the crime affected his or her life. Specifically, the victim can discuss how the crime impacted him physically, emotionally, or financially. Ultimately, the extent to which the victim was negatively impacted may influence how a judge sentences an offender. More importantly, a VIS often helps the victim improve his satisfaction with the criminal justice process and helps him heal from the negative impact of the crime.

Restitution

Being the victim of a violent crime can affect many aspects of an individual's life, including the ability to work and to meet daily needs. In addition, victims often need treatment to address their physical injuries and emotional trauma caused by a violent crime. As a result, victims often incur substantial monetary expenses for medical bills and psychological treatment.

Victims can request that ***restitution*** be imposed upon an offender at sentencing (Commonwealth of Massachusetts, n.d.i). This means that the offender is responsible for reimbursing the victim for any crime-related losses. Unfortunately, it is not always viable for a victim to be reimbursed by his offender for several reasons.

First, law enforcement personnel must find and arrest a suspect to begin the criminal process (Doerner, 2012). The UCR Program indicates that only 47% of violent Part I crimes (homicide, forcible rape, robbery, and aggravated assault) and 20% of property Part I crimes (burglary, larceny-theft, motor vehicle theft, and arson) were ***cleared by arrest*** in 2014 (Uniform Crime Reporting, 2014). Stated otherwise, approximately 53% of offenders of violent crimes and 81% of offenders of property crimes were not identified or captured. Consequently, the majority of offenders will never have to pay their victims restitution because they are never apprehended by the police.

Second, even if a suspect has been arrested, he has to be convicted in order to be sentenced, and not all convicted individuals are sentenced to restitution. Research indicates that only 18% of felons sentenced in state courts receive an order to provide restitution as part of their sentence (Rosenmerkel, Durose, & Farole, 2009).

Finally, many offenders come from economically disadvantaged backgrounds (Doerner, 2012), and they are often unemployed or do not have the earning power to provide their victims with repayment. Consequently, many victims are never repaid by their offenders. There is over $50 billion in uncollected criminal debt at the federal level (House Committee on the Judiciary, 2008), and each state also has substantial amounts of uncollected restitution.

Because there are many problems associated with restitution, the Commonwealth of Massachusetts has additional means to help victims pay for costs incurred as a result of their victimization, as discussed below.

Victim Compensation

The Victim Compensation Division of the Attorney General's Office provides ***victim compensation*** to eligible victims for uninsured medical care, mental health treatment, lost wages, funeral and burial costs, and future security measures. Using funds primarily obtained from offenders, this division can provide up to $25,000 per crime or $50,000 per crime if the victim sustained serious bodily injury (Commonwealth of Massachusetts, n.d.e).

Eligible victims include individuals who were the victim of a violent crime in Massachusetts as well as the dependents or family members of homicide victims in the Commonwealth. To be eligible, victims are required to report their crime to the police within five days, and they must cooperate with law enforcement throughout the investigation and prosecution of their case. Victims are also required to apply for compensation within three years of the date the crime took place (Commonwealth of Massachusetts, n.d.e).

The One Fund Boston

In addition to compensation provided by the Victim Compensation Division, The One Fund Boston was established on April 16, 2013 by former Governor Deval Patrick and former Mayor Tom Menino (now deceased) to help the victims of the Boston Marathon bombings (Rice, 2014). This fund collected and distributed over $80 million in cash gifts, support programs, and services to victims of the bombings and their families. These efforts were made possible by donations from over 200,000 individuals, corporations, and charitable foundations from all 50 U.S. states and over 60 countries worldwide (The One Fund Boston, 2013). Among the donors were John Hancock, the president and CEO of Bank of America, the president of the Boston Foundation, and the CEO of the Boston Red Sox (City of Boston, 2013).

The One Fund Boston also provided $1.5 million to start The One Fund Center, located at Massachusetts General Hospital. This center is a collaboration between Massachusetts General Hospital, Massachusetts Eye and Ear, Spaulding Rehabilitation Hospital, and the Benson-Henry Institute for Mind Body Medicine (Rice, 2014). The center provides care and support for individuals who were injured in the Marathon bombings, aiming to maximize their life potential through innovative treatments and services (The Boston, 2013).

Nearly 300 people sustained injuries during the bombings, which primarily included shrapnel wounds, injuries to lower legs, and loss of limbs. In addition, four people were killed as a result of the bombings—Krystle Campbell, Lu Lingzi, Martin Richard, and MIT Officer Sean Collier (Boston Bombing, 2015). The families of the four victims who lost their lives in the bombings each received over $2 million in cash, services, and gifts. It is also important to note that many of the survivors chose not to be recipients of this funding. Instead, they suggested it go toward "invisible injuries," including hearing loss and mental health issues experienced by many of the spectators the day of the Boston Bombing (Rice, 2014).

While The One Fund has since closed and funds dissolved, support showed that people from not only the City of Boston, but also throughout the United States and across the globe, can unite to help others affected by tragedy. Former Governor Patrick stated that he was "humbled by the outpouring of support by the business community and individuals who are united in their desire to help.... at moments like this, we are one state, one city, and one people" (City of Boston, 2013). And former Mayor Menino said, "We are one Boston. We are one community. As always, we will come together to help those most in need. And in the end, we will be better for it" (City of Boston, 2013).

Services and Support for Victims

Not only does Massachusetts strive to provide victims with rights in the criminal process and compensation for crime-related losses, but it also has many other services for victims. In 1984, the Massachusetts Office for Victim Assistance (MOVA) was created with the enactment of the Victim Bill of Rights. MOVA advocates for and assists victims of crime and ensures that victims have consistent access to rights and services across the commonwealth (Commonwealth of Massachusetts, n.d.a).

Victims are often traumatized and do not know where to receive the help they need, and MOVA functions to provide the necessary programs and services to victims across the commonwealth. MOVA also works with community groups and the media to help educate the public about the causes and consequences of violence as well as the rights of victims. Presentations to the public focus on specific crime categories, including homicide, domestic violence, sexual assaults, and drunk driving (Commonwealth of Massachusetts, n.d.f).

MOVA also funds victims' programs across the commonwealth. The agency funds approximately 100 programs in Massachusetts that provide victims with the counseling and advocacy services they need (Commonwealth of

Massachusetts, n.d.d). Some of the specific services offered to victims in Massachusetts, including victim witness advocates, rape crisis centers, and domestic violence shelters, are discussed below.

SAFEPLAN/Victim Witness Advocates

SAFEPLAN is MOVA's court-based program that operates in over 40 district and probate courts across the commonwealth. SAFEPLAN provides victims of domestic violence, sexual assault, and stalking with trained and certified victim witness advocates to help protect them from further abuse. The advocates are employed by sexual assault and domestic violence programs across Massachusetts, and their services are free of charge to victims. They help victims obtain restraining orders and harassment prevention orders, make referrals to local support services, provide information on legal and safety options, accompany the victim to protective order hearings, and ensure that victims know their rights throughout the court process (Commonwealth of Massachusetts, n.d.h).

Rape Crisis Centers

Rape crisis centers in Massachusetts and throughout the United States began as community-based organizations to help victims of sexual violence and to change society's perceptions of rape and sexual assaults. Today's rape crisis centers are run primarily by trained professionals, but early centers were staffed by volunteers, many of whom were victims themselves. Rape crisis centers began to expand in the 1980s as they began collaborating with other agencies, such as hospitals, police departments, and service providers, to offer support to victims. Although rape crisis centers have become professional organizations over time, their focus remains the same—eliminating sexual violence and victimization (Gardiner & Mallicoat, 2012).

Currently, there are over 30 rape crisis center sites across the commonwealth that help victims of rape and sexual assault. Trained rape crisis counselors and volunteers provide hotline counseling and information, and they accompany victims to hospitals, police stations, and courts (Commonwealth of Massachusetts, n.d.g).

One such center is the Boston Area Rape Crisis Center (BARCC). BARCC was founded in 1973 and is both the largest and oldest rape crisis center in New England. It has 30 staff, over 200 volunteers, and approximately 6,000 donors every year. These individuals provide free, confidential support and services to thousands of victims of sexual violence throughout the greater Boston area each year (BARCC, n.d.).

In addition, BARCC works closely with different organizations, including public schools, colleges, law enforcement, and healthcare providers, to help them understand their role in preventing sexual violence. The center offers tools and assistance for helping these organizations create policies that prevent sexual violence. Furthermore, BARCC received the National Crime Victim Service Award from the Department of Justice in 2009. This accolade reinforced BARCC's role as a national leader in providing victims of sexual violence with appropriate services as well as educating organizations and the community about preventing sexual violence (BARCC, n.d.).

Domestic Violence Shelters

Domestic violence shelters are places where victims of domestic violence can live for several months while they receive help for their abuse. In Massachusetts, there are different types of domestic violence shelters. Some are run by nonprofit organizations, while others are funded by the Department of Children and Families (DCF). There are also "safe homes," which are provided by community members (Commonwealth of Massachusetts, n.d.c).

Domestic violence shelters are available to anyone who is in immediate danger of domestic violence in their current living situation. In order to be eligible, victims must be willing to leave their home to protect themselves and their children from further abuse. In addition, to guarantee the safety of other shelter residents, residents must have no contact with their batterer and cannot abuse substances while living at the shelter (Commonwealth of Massachusetts, n.d.c).

Jane Doe Inc.

Jane Doe Inc. (JDI) is a nonprofit, sexual and domestic violence membership organization in Massachusetts. JDI provides support and resources to its 60 community-based members, all of whom advocate for and offer support and services to victims of sexual and domestic violence (Jane Doe Inc., n.d.).

JDI also collaborates with other professionals to provide information and awareness about needed improvements in victim-related topics. Additionally, the organization collects and analyzes data to provide policy recommendations for effective changes regarding victim advocacy and services. JDI's continued efforts help to improve safety, healing, and the prevention of further abuse for victims and their families across the commonwealth (Jane Doe Inc., n.d.).

Civil Rights Victims

The Attorney General's Office in Massachusetts has the Civil Rights Division to protect citizens from discrimination based on race, age, gender, color, national origin, sexual orientation, or disability. This office investigates cases of discrimination in housing, employment, education, financial services, transportation, and healthcare, among other public accommodations (Commonwealth of Massachusetts, n.d.b). People who believe they have been the victim of a civil rights violation in Massachusetts are encouraged to file a complaint with the Civil Rights Division.

Theories of Victimization

Finally, we would like to discuss several criminological theories related to victimization. Many criminologists have noted that although the offender is the predator, the victim can often facilitate the crime by knowingly or unknowingly being the prey. In this section, we will discuss three theories that are commonly associated with criminal victimizations—victim precipitation, lifestyle theory, and routine activities theory.

Victim Precipitation

In 1958, Marvin Wolfgang, a prominent criminologist, discovered that up to one quarter of homicides were ***victim precipitated.*** That is, the victim played a role in encouraging the criminal behavior (Siegel & Worrall, 2018). For all crimes, not just homicides, there are two types of victim precipitation—active and passive. Active precipitation occurs when a victim threatens or attacks the offender first. For example, let's pretend that one person provokes another person at a bar. The second person ends up pushing the first person off of his bar stool and onto the floor. In this case, even though the second person was the offender, the first person played an active role in the victimization because he antagonized the offender.

On the other hand, passive precipitation occurs when the victim exhibits a personality, behavioral, or racial characteristic that unintentionally encourages the offender. In this case, the victim is not aware that he or she provoked the offender. For instance, many hate crimes could be the result of passive precipitation. The offender targeted the victim based solely on the victim's personal traits (i.e., race, ethnicity, sexual orientation, disability, etc.).

Lifestyle Theory

People may also become the victims of a crime because they are exposed to criminal offenders as a result of their lifestyle choices. This is often the case with gang members, prostitutes, drug users, or people who are frequently out at late hours (Siegel & Worrall, 2018). These individuals are often engaging in illegal activity themselves, making them more prone to criminal victimization.

Lifestyle theory suggests that people can reduce their risks of victimization by limiting their risk-taking behaviors and making smarter lifestyle choices. For example, by staying home and watching a movie, rather than going out and doing drugs at a club, a person would minimize their risk of becoming victimized because they are not exposed to criminal activity.

Routine Activities Theory

Routine activities refer to activities that people engage in on a day-to-day basis. Some examples are going to work, going to school, going to church, or any other activity that an individual engages in on a regular basis. According to the ***routine activities theory***, people commit crime close to where they spend most of their time as well as the major pathways in between. Similarly, individuals are victimized close to where they spend most of their time as well as the pathways in between.

According to the routine activities theory, there are three elements necessary for a crime to occur: (1) motivated offenders, (2) suitable targets, and (3) the absence of capable guardians (e.g., police, neighborhood watch groups, surveillance cameras). All three of these elements must be present for a crime to occur (Riedel & Welsh, 2015).

Let's apply this theory to gangs and crime. People who engage in gang activity often have access to drugs and illegal firearms. Many of these individuals are concentrated in certain areas. In disadvantaged areas, it is easy to have the three necessary elements for a crime to occur: (1) gang members are motivated offenders, (2) rival gang members are suitable targets, and (3) areas with high concentrations of illicit activity do not have capable guardians looking out for crime.

Conclusion

The criminal justice system in Massachusetts has taken many measures to obtain justice for its victims. The commonwealth has accomplished this through legislation as well as monetary compensation and various services for victims. Because victims play such a large role in the criminal justice system, it is important to continue to support victims' rights so that they can heal from any injustices incurred from their victimization.

Key Terms

Cleared by Arrest: Refers to crimes that are solved by law enforcement.

Dark Figure of Crime: Crimes that are not reported to police.

Domestic Violence Shelters: Places where victims of domestic violence can live for several months while they receive help for their abuse.

Lifestyle Theory: Model of victimology that posits that the likelihood an individual will be victimized depends upon the concept of lifestyle.

Rape Crisis Centers: Community-based organizations that help victims of rape, sexual abuse, and sexual violence.

Restitution: One of the penalties imposed on offenders that requires the returning of stolen goods to the victim or payment to the victim for harm caused.

Routine Activities Theory: Theory that crime is the result of three elements: motivated offenders, suitable targets, and a lack of capable guardians.

Victim Compensation: Payments or reparations made to a crime victim by the state for their crime-related losses.

Victim Impact Statement: Written or oral statement given to the sentencing judge by the victim to let the judge know how the crime impacted the victim.

Victim Precipitated: Role of the victim in provoking or encouraging criminal behavior.

Related Websites

Jane Doe Inc. (The MA Coalition Against Sexual Assault and Domestic Violence)
http://www.janedoe.org/

Massachusetts Commission Against Discrimination
https://www.mass.gov/orgs/massachusetts-commission-against-discrimination

Massachusetts Office for Victim Assistance
https://www.mass.gov/orgs/massachusetts-office-for-victim-assistance

Massachusetts Victim Bill of Rights
http://www.mass.gov/eopss/law-enforce-and-cj/prisons/dom-violence/massachusetts-victim-bill-of-rights.html

National Organization for Victim Assistance
http://www.trynova.org/

Victim Services Division, Office of Attorney General of MA
http://www.mass.gov/ago/bureaus/executive/victim-services/

Victims of Violent Crimes Resources
http://www.mass.gov/ago/public-safety/resources-for-victims/victims-of-violent-crime/resources.html

Review Questions

1. List and explain some of the rights extended to crime victims at the national level.
2. Explain the significance of NIBRS.
3. Describe some of the rights provided to victims in the Massachusetts Victim Bill of Rights.
4. What is the significance of a victim impact statement?
5. Explain the difference between restitution and victim compensation.
6. What are some of the issues associated with restitution?
7. List and describe some of the ways Massachusetts provides victims with compensation.
8. What is The One Fund Boston?
9. How does MOVA assist victims in Massachusetts?
10. Explain the role of the victim witness advocate.
11. What are rape crisis centers?
12. What are domestic violence shelters?
13. How does JDI assist victims?
14. Explain the three criminological theories associated with victimizations.

References

BARCC. (n.d.). *About the Boston Area Rape Crisis Center*. Retrieved from https://barcc.org/join/about.

The One Fund Boston. (2013). *About The One Fund*. Retrieved from https://secure.onefundboston.org/pages/about.*

Boston bombing: Dead and injured. (2015, June 24). Retrieved from https://www.cnn.com/2015/04/24/us/gallery/boston-bombing-victims/index.html.

Bureau of Justice Statistics. (n.d.). *Data collection: National Crime Victimization Survey (NCVS)*. Retrieved from https://www.bjs.gov/index.cfm?ty=dcdetail&iid=245#Methodology.

City of Boston. (2013, April 16). *Massachusetts Governor Deval Patrick and Boston Mayor Menino today announced the formation of The One Fund Boston* [Press release]. Retrieved from https://www.cityofboston.gov/news/Default.aspx?id=6081.

Commonwealth of Massachusetts. (n.d.a). *About MOVA*. Retrieved from http://www.mass.gov/mova/about-mova/.

Commonwealth of Massachusetts. (n.d.b). *Civil rights victims*. Retrieved from http://www.mass.gov/ago/public-safety/resources-for-victims/civil-rights-victims/.

Commonwealth of Massachusetts. (n.d.c). *Domestic violence programs*. Retrieved from https://www.mass.gov/service-details/domestic-violence-programs.

Commonwealth of Massachusetts. (n.d.d). *Grants*. Retrieved from http://www.mass.gov/mova/grants/.

Commonwealth of Massachusetts. (n.d.e). *Massachusetts victims of violent crime compensation*. Retrieved from http://www.mass.gov/ago/public-safety/resources-for-victims/victims-of-violent-crime/victim-compensation.html.

Commonwealth of Massachusetts. (n.d.f). *MOVA service programs*. Retrieved from http://www.mass.gov/mova/about-mova/what-we-do/mova-service--programs/.

Commonwealth of Massachusetts. (n.d.g). *Rape crisis centers*. Retrieved from http://www.mass.gov/eohhs/consumer/physical-health-treatment/health-care-facilities/rape-crisis-centers.html.

Commonwealth of Massachusetts. (n.d.h). *SAFEPLAN*. Retrieved from http://www.mass.gov/mova/safeplan/.

* Please note that The One Fund has closed down, and this website is no longer in operation.

Commonwealth of Massachusetts. (n.d.i). *The right to request restitution.* Retrieved from http://www.mass.gov/mdaa/victim-witness-info/victim-bill-of-rights/the-right-to-request-restitution.html.

Doerner, W. (2012). *Florida's criminal justice system.* Durham, NC: Carolina Academic Press.

Gardiner, C. L., & Mallicoat, S. L. (2012). *California's criminal justice system.* Durham, NC: Carolina Academic Press.

House Committee on the Judiciary. (2008). *Legislative proposals before the 110th Congress to amend federal restitution laws: Hearing before the Subcommittee on Crime, Terrorism, and Homeland Security of the Committee on the Judiciary of the House of Representatives.* U.S. Government Printing Office: Author.

Jane Doe Inc. (n.d.). *Who we are.* Retrieved from http://www.janedoe.org/who_we_are.

Justice Research and Statistics Association. (n.d.). *Statewide Crime Analysis and Mapping Program (SCAMP).* Retrieved from http://www.jrsa.org/ibrrc/references/MA_SCAMP.html.

MGL c.258B §3

NOVA. (n.d.). *Who we are.* Retrieved from http://www.trynova.org/about-us/overview/.

Puzzanchera, C., Smith, J., & Kang, W. (2017). *Easy access to NIBRS victims, 2015: Victims of violence.* Retrieved from http://www.ojjdp.gov/ojstatbb/ezanibrsdv/.

Rice, C. (2014). *One Fund Boston distributes final funds to bombing survivors.* Retrieved from https://www.boston.com/culture/health/2014/09/02/one-fund-boston-distributes-final-funds-to-bombing-survivors.

Riedel, M., & Welsh, W. (2015). *Criminal violence: Patterns, causes, and prevention* (4th ed.). New York, NY: Oxford University Press.

Rosenmerkel, S., Durose, M., & Farole, D. (2009). *Felony sentences in state courts, 2006—Statistical tables.* Washington, DC: Bureau of Justice Statistics.

Siegel, L., & Worrall, J. (2018). *Introduction to criminal justice* (16th ed.). Boston, MA: Cengage Learning.

Uniform Crime Reporting. (n.d.). *NIBRS overview.* Retrieved from https://ucr.fbi.gov/nibrs-overview.

Uniform Crime Reporting. (2014). *Offenses cleared.* Retrieved from https://ucr.fbi.gov/crime-in-the-u.s/2014/crime-in-the-u.s.-2014/offenses-known-to-law-enforcement/clearances/clearances.pdf.

U.S. Department of Justice. (n.d.). *Crime victims' rights ombudsman—Victims' rights.* Retrieved from https://www.justice.gov/usao/resources/crime-victims-rights-ombudsman/victims-rights.

Chapter 9

The Threat of Terrorism in Massachusetts

Learning Objectives

- Familiarize yourself with the legal and academic definitions of terrorism.
- Learn about the evolution of the terrorist threat in Massachusetts.
- Examine the recent targeting trends and patterns of terrorists.
- Learn about federal, state, and local responses to terrorism.
- Explore ways to improve efforts to prevent and respond to terrorist attacks.

Introduction

In this chapter, we will examine the broad spectrum of terrorist threats related to the Commonwealth of Massachusetts. After defining terrorism and terrorist ideologies, and then reviewing the contemporary nature of "***do it yourself***" terrorist attacks, the discussion will examine the kinds of targets modern terrorists might be interested in, and how the federal government and Massachusetts are responding to the threat of terrorism. The chapter will conclude with some recommendations for how authorities and communities can work together more effectively to reduce the likelihood of terrorist attacks in Massachusetts.

Defining Terrorism

It is important, at the outset, to remember that terrorism is not the existential threat that some make it out to be. Despite what some alarmists in the media would have you believe, there are not terrorists lurking around every corner or under every bed, looking for an opportunity to strike. Compared to most other kinds of violent crime in the United States, only a tiny fraction of the population is affected by any kind of terrorist activity each year. Furthermore, an overwhelming majority of terrorist groups around the world have shown little to no interest in attacking the U.S. homeland. Throughout history, most terrorist groups have attacked locally or regionally; globally oriented, anti-Western jihadist networks like ***Al-Qaeda*** or the ***Islamic State*** are an exception to the norm in the world of terrorism. This is not to suggest complacency, only that the threat of terrorism must be kept in perspective, informed by facts and reality.

Terrorism is a complex phenomenon as scores of recent events and scholarly publications have illustrated (Forest, 2016). It is therefore unsurprising that widespread consensus on a definition of terrorism has proven elusive, not only internationally but even among government agencies within the United States. However, one of the most commonly used definitions is that from the U.S. Department of State, which defines ***terrorism*** as the "premeditated, politically motivated violence perpetrated against non-combatant targets by sub-national groups or clandestine agents, usually intended to influence an audience" (22 U.S.C. §2656f (d)).

The distinction that the Department of State makes in referring to "politically motivated violence" is an important one, as terrorism is often described as a form of collective violence that is politically motivated (Forest, 2015). Scholars have explained that terrorist organizations have a political objective that they seek to obtain through violence or the threat of violence. The use of this violence is not to defeat the enemy but to send a message through violent acts of symbolic significance that gain maximum attention to a cause (Richardson, 2007; Rapoport, 2008). According to Bruce Hoffman, one of the most internationally respected scholars in this field, terrorism is defined as "the deliberate creation and exploitation of fear through violence or the threat of violence in the pursuit of political change.... [it is] designed to have far-reaching psychological effects beyond the immediate victim(s) or object of the terrorist attack ... [and] to create power where there is none or to consolidate power where there is very little" (Hoffman, 2006).

Most definitions of terrorism include some political dimension, usually a desire to bring about (or sometimes prevent) political change. Other central tenets among most descriptions and definitions of terrorism include the notion that those who engage in it intentionally target innocents (including off-duty military, law enforcement, or other government officials), and they seek to cause psychological trauma, including death and damage (Hoffman, 2006).

The Evolution of the Terrorist Threat

A review of history reveals that terrorist attacks are a rare event, yet they can have a dramatic impact on society. Three terrorist attacks in the Commonwealth of Massachusetts over the past 40 years illustrate the wide diversity of targets and perpetrators of concern to state and local law enforcement. On April 22, 1976, the United Freedom Front (an obscure Marxist group) injured 22 people in a bombing that targeted the Suffolk County Courthouse. On December 30, 1994, a lone gunman dressed all in black—later identified as John Salvi III—entered two abortion clinics on the same street in Brookline and used a rifle to kill two receptionists and wound five other clinic workers. On April 15, 2013, two bombs were detonated almost simultaneously among the crowds gathered near the finish line of the Boston Marathon, killing three people and injuring over 260 others. The perpetrators of this attack, as described below, were two brothers—Tamerlan and Dzokhar Tsarnaev—who were motivated by an extreme Islamist ideology many refer to as "global jihadism" (*USA vs. Dzhokhar A. Tsarnaev*, 2013).

Each of these incidents represents a different kind of terrorist ideology, motivation, and target. But all three have been acts of domestic terrorism, carried out by U.S. citizens or legal residents. Despite a number of news headlines devoted to protecting our country from the threat of international terrorism, the fact remains that a majority of terrorist acts throughout the United States have been of domestic origin. As a result, state and local law enforcement in Massachusetts focus a great deal of time and energy monitoring potential threats of terrorism not only from groups like al-Qaeda (AQ) or Islamic State (IS) but also from right-wing extremists, ***sovereign citizens***, and others whom the media tend to ignore.

Terrorist Ideologies

In the study of terrorism, an ***ideology*** is loosely defined as an articulation of grievances (like "this is what's wrong with the world today") and a strategy through which these issues can be addressed through violence. Terrorist group ideologies typically attempt to justify violent attacks as necessary to achieve objectives, like establishing a utopian or religiously oriented political system, changing policies (such as the right to abortion or protecting the environment), or creating an independent geopolitical entity based on ethnic identity (known as ***ethnonationalism***) (Forest, 2015).

Terrorist groups are typically organized by government agencies and researchers into categories according to their ideology. For example, groups like the Red Army Faction, Italian Red Brigades, and Weather Underground are classified as "***left wing***," while groups like the Irish Republican Army, Liberation Tigers of Tamil Eelam, or the Basque group *Euskadi Ta Askatasuna* are considered "ethnonationalist." Religiously oriented terrorist groups are also divided into subcategories. Hezbollah, a Shia Muslim terrorist group in Lebanon, is seen as significantly different from Sunni Muslim terrorist groups like Hamas, AQ, or IS. Acts of terrorism have also been committed by Jewish extremist groups like Kahane Chai, violent Christian anti-abortion groups like the Army of God, and even religious cults like Aum Shinrikyo in Japan (Forest, 2015).

Ideologically Inspired Attacks

Beyond terrorist groups, a considerable amount of research in the study of terrorism has also described individuals who have been inspired by ideologies to conceive and carry out various kinds of terrorist attacks but had no clear ties to an established organization responsible for funding, directing, or supervising their operation. This phenomenon has roots in the ***anarchist*** movement of the 19th century, as well as in the actions of late 20th-century White supremacists, and also the actions of those who organize ***anti-abortionist violence*** (Forest, 2015). As mentioned earlier, John Salvi III was inspired by a violent anti-abortion ideology promoted by the Army of God and carried out a lethal attack against two abortion clinics in Brookline.

More recently, ***right-wing extremists*** have embraced a form of ***leaderless resistance***—a concept promoted by White supremacist Louis Beam in 1983 as a method to attack the federal government (Shibuya, 2007). Beam argued that highly centralized organizations were vulnerable to infiltration and arrest by federal agents, particularly in highly technical societies where the authorities had a wide variety of means by which they could conduct surveillance (Beam, 1992). Therefore, he argued, the movement needed to abandon hierarchical arrangements and instead establish "phantom cells," tied together only by common philosophy and ideology. He and others in the right-wing extremist movement have encouraged individuals to organize and carry out attacks on their own, without relying on assistance from a group or network. Major terrorist attacks linked to right-wing extremist ideology include the 1995 bombing of the Murrah Federal Building in Oklahoma City (by Timothy McVeigh) and the 1996 bombing of the Atlanta Olympics (by Eric Rudolph). Today, law enforcement in Massachusetts are particularly concerned about the threat posed by the growing presence of right-wing extremists (Perliger, 2012) and members of the sovereign citizens movement (Berger, 2016).

AQ and IS have also adopted a similar approach to motivating individual terrorist attacks, as seen in recent plots they have inspired throughout the

United States since 2001. Terms like "lone wolf" have been increasingly used to describe attacks in places like San Bernadino and Orlando, as well as attempted terrorist attacks involving Massachusetts residents like Rezwan Ferdaus (Federal Bureau of Investigation, 2012). And of course, one of the most dramatic terrorist attacks in the United States over the past decade occurred in Boston on April 15, 2013—the Boston Marathon bombing mentioned earlier. In this attack, a young boy and two young women were killed, and over 260 other marathon spectators were injured. Some of the victims who survived will never walk again. The perpetrators of this attack were two brothers who had immigrated to the United States from Chechnya with their parents and had lived for several years in the Boston area. The younger brother exhibited various signs of normal integration into society, attending a local public university, partying with friends, and networking via social media. In contrast, the older brother appeared to have become increasingly radicalized by AQ's anti-Western ideology to a point where he was expelled from a local mosque after one of his extremist outbursts. He traveled to Dagestan, a neighboring province of Chechnya, where authorities believe he may have received some training from a local militant group. According to the investigation into the attack, the Internet played a key role in the radicalization process that led to the brothers' decision to carry out a terrorist attack on U.S. soil as well as the weapons-making instructions (particularly the online AQ magazine *Inspire,*) that culminated in the bombing (*USA vs. Dzhokhar A. Tsarnaev*, 2013).

This individualized mode of terrorism has also been embraced by others beyond the ideological categories of right-wing extremism and Islamic jihad. In fact, we see a leaderless resistance approach embraced by individuals motivated by extreme environmental, animal rights, anti-abortion, and other ideological categories. Environmental extremists, for example, have attacked timber and logging companies, SUV dealerships, pharmaceutical companies, and private homes. Animal rights extremists have attacked fur and leather companies, university research labs, and a variety of other targets. In these cases, the overall goal of the terrorist attacks has been to coerce the behavior of industries, researchers, and consumers in ways that they believe will benefit the environment (Forest, 2015).

The Modern Era of "Do It Yourself" Terrorism

Regardless of the specific type of ideology, this kind of "do it yourself" mode of terrorism involves individuals committing terrorist attacks autonomously, independent of any operational direction or support from a formal organization. They can choose their target, day, time, and mode of attack. Some researchers described these individuals as "self-starters": modestly intelligent, highly motivated, and resourceful individuals who can obtain (or fabricate) weapons and deploy them to deadly effect without any help from anyone else (Benjamin & Simon, 2005). Today's terrorists may not have attended a training camp, received funding or operational direction, or met with the principal members or leaders of an established terrorist group before carrying out their attack. Instead, many have turned to the Internet for information on what they need. There are a wide variety of training manuals and instructions for building improvised explosive devices, often translated into multiple languages. Weapons and other technologies can be ordered online and delivered in unmarked packages, particularly using deep web resources and Bitcoin payments. The Internet can also be used to gather information on potential targets and conduct surveillance. Meanwhile, Internet discussion forums and social media also serve a particularly important role as ideological incubators, connecting people around the world and legitimating their shared ideas, beliefs, and values. The online radicalization process can then meld with local socioeconomic or political conditions to produce personal grievances—and perhaps even social alienation or other issues—to produce lethal results.

This, overall, is the central nature of the terrorism threat to Massachusetts today. We are far less likely to see a sophisticated terrorist organization operating within our borders and much more likely to see individuals inspired by a terrorist ideology who then try to carry out a terrorist attack. The good news in this is that most of these individuals are amateurs with little (if any) experience with weapons, explosives, target surveillance, or other skills needed to be an effective terrorist. Many of the terrorist plots in recent years have been disrupted through investigations and sting operations linked to an individual's attempt to enlist the assistance of others. An analysis of terrorist plots and attacks can reveal some patterns among the kinds of targets these perpetrators appear most interested in.

Targeting Trends and Patterns

To begin with, Massachusetts is no different from other states when it comes to the kinds of targets a potential terrorist might choose. Aside from being home to our phenomenally successful professional sports teams (e.g., Patriots, Red Sox, Bruins, Celtics, and New England Revolution), Massachusetts is not much different than other parts of the United States in terms of offering myriad kinds of critical infrastructure and public gathering spaces that could be targeted by terrorists.

The population of Massachusetts is roughly 6.86 million, according to the most recent census count (U.S. Census Bureau, 2017). There are several densely populated urban areas (most notably metro Boston, Springfield, Worcester, and Lowell), and many more sparsely populated rural areas. Scattered across the commonwealth are many kinds of critical infrastructure, from power stations (including the Pilgrim nuclear power plant on Cape Cod) to international airports and a major seaport (in Boston Harbor). There are hundreds of corporate headquarters, industrial chemical storage facilities, biological laboratories, and defense contractors. Recent decades have seen an enormous increase in technology-oriented private sector firms, from cybercommerce to nanotechnology research and development. And of course, there are major government buildings, including the Thomas P. O'Neill Jr. Federal Building in downtown Boston. Any of these could conceivably be a terrorist target, judging from an analysis of terrorist attacks worldwide.

There are two major airports: Boston's Logan International Airport and Springfield-Branson National Airport. In 2017, over 38 million domestic and international passengers traveled through Boston's airport (Massport, 2017), from which there are direct flights to over 50 major cities outside the United States. Aviation has been of particular interest to terrorists of many kinds since the 1960s. Both airplanes and airports are popular targets for hostage taking as well as detonating explosives. Today, screening by the Transportation Security Administration is only one of several layers of security at these airports. Luggage is screened for traces of explosives, barriers have been placed in front of the terminals to prevent a car bomb from getting too close, and armed officers patrol the terminals, looking for signs of suspicious behavior.

Other transportation-related targets of terrorism have included buses (a common target of Palestinian suicide bombers in Israel), commuter railways (the target of the 2004 attack in Madrid, Spain), and subway systems (with attacks in London, Moscow, and Mumbai since 2005). Of additional concern for law enforcement and communities are the hundreds of public gathering spaces, from colleges and universities to sports arenas and stadiums, movie theaters, schools, shopping centers, and so forth. And of course, based on recent history of terrorism in Massachusetts, there continues to be a particular focus on major annual events like the St. Patrick's Day Parade, the July 4th celebration on the Esplanade, and the Boston Marathon. The bottom line from this analysis indicates that an open industrialized society like ours is a "target-rich environment" for terrorists.

Thus, preventing terrorist attacks requires more than just physically securing potential targets. Effective ***counterterrorism*** requires a sophisticated, multilayered counterterrorism effort in which everyone can play a role: state and local law enforcement, the private sector, communities, and citizens. Counterterrorism is defined as "a proactive effort to prevent, deter, and combat politically motivated violence directed at civilian and non-combatant targets, by the use of a broad spectrum of response measures" (Schmid, 2013). While these measures are predominantly formal—including lawful intelligence gathering activities and law enforcement investigations—they are supported by an array of informal relationships between the private sector, government authorities, and the communities they serve. We will discuss federal, state, and local strategies to combat terrorism in the sections below.

Homeland Security

In light of the 9/11 attacks, the U.S. government and criminal justice agencies throughout the nation began to concentrate greater efforts on combating terrorism and promoting ***homeland security***. Most notably, the Homeland Security Act of 2002 created the Department of Homeland Security (DHS) to ensure that the United States would be "safe, secure, and resilient against terrorism and other hazards" (Department of Homeland Security, 2016).

The DHS is responsible for preventing terrorist attacks in the United States, reducing the vulnerability of the United States to terrorism, and minimizing the damage in the event of a terrorist attack on U.S. soil. There are seven federal agencies responsible for counterterrorism efforts within the DHS, and together they help to manage our nation's borders and transportation systems. Below is a brief overview of their specific functions (Department of Homeland Security, 2016):

- U.S. Customs and Border Protection (CBP) helps to keep terrorists out of the United States, secures trade and travel, and enforces U.S. immigration and drug regulations.
- U.S. Citizenship and Immigration Services (USCIS) grants immigration and citizenship benefits and ensures the integrity of our immigration system.
- U.S. Coast Guard protects the maritime economy and environment, and it also defends our maritime borders.
- Federal Emergency Management Agency (FEMA) is the lead federal agency that prepares for and responds to emergencies and disasters.
- U.S. Immigration and Customs Enforcement (ICE) promotes homeland security and public safety by enforcing federal laws involving border control, customs, trade, and immigration.

- U.S. Secret Service (USSS) safeguards our financial systems and protects our nation's leaders.
- Transportation Security Administration (TSA) protects our nation's transportation systems, including airlines, railroads, buses, and ferry services.

Federal Efforts to Combat Terrorism

Although the DHS controls much of the counterterrorism efforts in the United States, other federal agencies are also involved in this battle. Because the Federal Bureau of Investigation (FBI) is the federal government's primary law enforcement agency, it had to reexamine its priorities to ensure our nation's safety against terrorist attacks after 9/11. The FBI's ***Joint Terrorism Task Forces*** (JTTFs) are a team who gathers evidence, makes arrests, collects and shares ***intelligence***, and responds to threats regarding terrorism. There are approximately 4,000 JTTFs nationwide, and they come from over 500 state and local agencies and over 50 federal agencies. By sharing intelligence, the JTTFs are able to combine their skills and knowledge to keep the nation safe from terrorism (FBI, n.d.).

In addition, the Directorate of Analysis informs policymakers and aids in homeland security efforts by tracking and analyzing information on terrorists and terrorist threats worldwide (Central Intelligence Agency, 2015). Furthermore, there is also a National Counterterrorism Center (NCTC) that was established in 2004. The NCTC is the primary federal organization that integrates and analyzes intelligence related to terrorism acquired by the U.S. government. It also serves as the central knowledge bank on terrorism information and establishes the information technology (IT) systems between NCTC and other agencies to integrate and disseminate intelligence regarding terrorism (National Counterterrorism Center, n.d.).

USA Patriot Act

The *USA Patriot Act* (an acronym for Uniting and Strengthening America by Providing Appropriate Tools Required to Intercept and Obstruct Terrorism) was passed in 2001, shortly after the 9/11 attacks. Its purpose was to increase the ability of federal law enforcement to investigate suspected terrorists, expand the definition of terrorist activities, and increase the penalties for convicted terrorists. Below is a brief summary of how this piece of legislation has improved our nation's counterterrorism strategies (U.S. Department of Justice, n.d.):

- Allowing law enforcement to use surveillance, such as wiretaps, against acts of terrorism;

- Removing legal barriers to enable information sharing between government agencies and law enforcement regarding suspected terrorists;
- Updating the law to reflect new technologies and threats;
- Allowing law enforcement to obtain search warrants in any district that terrorist-related activity has occurred;
- Increasing the penalties for individuals who commit acts of terrorism; and
- Prohibiting the harboring of a terrorist.

Security and Civil Liberties

Even though the Patriot Act has taken important counterterrorism measures, many people fear that it interferes with their ***civil liberties***, especially those found in the Bill of Rights. In one study, 42% of people thought that the Patriot Act was necessary to help the government find terrorists, while 34% feared it posed a threat to civil liberties (Pew Research Center, 2011). Many of these critics fear that the government will interfere with the rights of American citizens, especially in regards to the Fourth Amendment of the U.S. Constitution, which protects us from unreasonable searches and seizures.

Mainly, the Patriot Act has made it easier for police to conduct searches. Prior to this piece of legislation, police had to obtain a court order based on probable cause that a suspect had engaged in or was about to engage in criminal activity. However, under the Patriot Act, the FBI and other federal agents do not have to provide probable cause regarding criminal activity. Rather, they only have to assert that the warrant is needed for an ongoing terrorism investigation.

Furthermore, under the Patriot Act, the FBI can secretly conduct a wiretap to obtain evidence without showing probable cause. In 1978, the Foreign Intelligence Surveillance Act (FISA) permitted the surveillance of a suspect when the "primary" purpose was to gather foreign intelligence (50 U.S.C §1802). However, the Patriot Act has modified FISA to allow surveillance when the "significant" purpose is to gather intelligence on terrorist activity. This creates a loophole so the government can avoid the probable cause requirement of the Fourth Amendment to engage in routine law enforcement.

Responding to the Terrorism Threat in Massachusetts

In Massachusetts, state and local law enforcement agencies work closely with the FBI, DHS, and other federal agencies, as well as the private sector and community leaders, to identify and monitor potential terrorist threats. Local law enforcement plays the most critical role in preventing and responding to the threat of terrorism (as well as the criminal activities that support it). A report by the International Association of Chiefs of Police describes how, after the attacks of 9/11, law enforcement agencies in the United States were "asked to confront a new threat to their communities, perpetrated by individuals and organizations that had vastly different motivations and means of attack from traditional criminals. Accepting this challenge required law enforcement agencies to reassess their operations and reevaluate their priorities" (IACP, 2005). However, according to Chief Deputy Jose Docobo of the Hillsborough County Sheriff's Office in Tampa, Florida, it has become clear that the objectives of preventing terrorism are similar to those law enforcement use to prevent other types of crime (Docobo, 2006).

In fact, scholars across a broad spectrum of disciplines have increasingly focused on the intersections of crime and terrorism. One important study describes a "new economy of terror" in which sources of revenue include charities, profits diverted from legal and illegal businesses, kidnapping, piracy, and many other kinds of criminal activity to support the terrorists. Thus, it makes sense that those whose daily lives are focused on combating crime are also the most well positioned to combat terrorism (Docobo, 2006).

Intelligence gathering and analysis activities are also critical for successfully combating terrorism. In Massachusetts, there are several means by which multiple agencies collaborate on the analysis of intelligence on crime and terrorism. For example, the Boston Regional Intelligence Center, funded by the DHS, brings together law enforcement professionals from several agencies focused on the collection and analysis of intelligence that helps prevent and reduce violence in the City of Boston. Similarly, on a state level, the ***Commonwealth Fusion Center*** (in Maynard) is a multiagency office designed to share information about terrorism and crime.

Massachusetts also has an Anti-Terrorism Advisory Council (ATAC), composed of several hundred members from federal, state, and local law enforcement, as well as other institutions with a stake in preventing and responding to terrorism. The ATAC ensures that its members share information to coordinate their prevention and response efforts (U.S. Department of Justice, 2015). And of course, the Joint Terrorism Task Force—led by the FBI—has a Boston-based team of investigators, analysts, linguists, SWAT experts, and other specialists from U.S. law enforcement and intelligence agencies who work together on terrorism-related investigations and threat analysis.

Members of these various agencies also participate regularly in professional development workshops and conferences, school security meetings, port security vulnerability assessments, cybersecurity testing, and security collaboration for major events, including football games at Gillette Stadium. Members also participate in meetings and events hosted by InfraGard, an association with representatives from businesses, academic institutions, state and local law enforcement agencies, and other local constituents. Overall, collaboration among various government agencies is a major focus of today's counterterrorism efforts in Massachusetts (U.S. Department of Justice, 2015).

State Homeland Security Strategy

Moreover, in light of the Boston Marathon bombings of 2013, the Commonwealth of Massachusetts has incorporated additional counterterrorism measures into its State Homeland Security Strategy (SHSS). The SHSS serves as the commonwealth's guide for homeland security and state, regional, and local emergency preparedness for natural disasters, terrorist attacks, and other emergencies (Massachusetts Executive Office of Public Safety and Security, 2014).

The SHSS has several goals and objectives to address counterterrorism strategies within Massachusetts. First, the SHSS intends to protect the commonwealth by strengthening the ability to share intelligence at the federal, state, and local levels by enhancing the security of cyber systems and by improving the screening and detection of terrorist threats and hazards. Second, the SHSS plans to enhance the resilience across the commonwealth by making physical improvements to buildings, improving security, and increasing awareness. Third, the SHSS aims to improve the response to acts of terrorism by increasing the capacity to provide services to save lives and by enhancing the abilities of first responders. The final goal is to improve the commonwealth's capacity to recover from acts of terrorism by providing enhanced efforts at recovery planning (Massachusetts Executive Office of Public Safety and Security, 2014).

Emergency Preparedness in Massachusetts

The Massachusetts Emergency Management Agency (MEMA) is in charge of making sure the state is prepared to withstand, respond to, and recover from different types of emergencies and disasters. This can include natural disasters, deliberate attacks, accidents, technological failures, and problems with infrastructure. MEMA has partnerships with federal, state, and local governments, as well as private agencies, to ensure that the commonwealth is prepared to handle these types of emergencies (Commonwealth of Massachusetts, n.d.).

Historically we have had time to prepare for the majority of natural disasters and other emergencies. Unfortunately, it is much more difficult to prepare for a terrorist attack. However, MEMA offers some steps for people living in Massachusetts to take to help alleviate the fear of the unknown (Commonwealth of Massachusetts, 2015):

- Develop a family communication plan to ensure everyone's safety.
- Create a disaster kit in the event you have to survive for several days without power. This kit should include nonperishable food, water, first aid supplies, a battery-powered radio, flashlights, blankets, toiletries, and cash.
- Be familiar with your community's emergency plan, location of shelters and hospitals, evacuation routes, and emergency warning systems.

What Can You Do?

As you can see, countering terrorism is not exclusively a government responsibility—we all have a role to play. The private sector owns and operates most of the critical infrastructure and so-called "soft targets" that terrorists might seek to attack and thus have an important responsibility to be vigilant and maintain some level of security. Family members, friends, colleagues, and neighbors are most often in the best position to detect signs of an individual's radicalization or indications that an individual may be providing financial, material, or other forms of support to a terrorist network. Research on so-called lone wolf terrorists has shown that in a majority of plots or attacks, the perpetrators had produced letters or public statements outlining their beliefs, and other people were often aware of their grievances, extremist ideologies, and intent to engage in terrorist activity (Gill, 2012). Other studies have shown that a person's illicit financial activities are impossible to conceal from friends and family members. Countering terrorism should thus be viewed not as something that government agencies can or should be expected to do on their own but rather as a responsibility that is shared among the members of an entire society.

In order to answer a frequently heard question, "What can I do?" several law enforcement and other government agencies are working to provide information for the public. They are issuing regular bulletins and social media alerts and publishing brief guides to help people understand what "see something, say something" means. The following example, on behavioral indicators of radicalization for terrorism, was published recently by the DHS.

Indicators of Potential Violent Extremist Radicalization or Mobilization

- Consumption and sharing of media glorifying violent extremist acts in attempting to mobilize others to violence;
- Withholding or misrepresenting information necessary for counterterrorism efforts such as residency status or immigration history, including use of multiple questionable residence locations, Social Security numbers, or personal contacts on official DHS records or public documents;
- Communicating with known or suspected foreign- or US-based violent extremists using e-mail, social media platforms, or encrypted messaging applications;
- A subject's advocacy that their religious, cultural, or national group requires violent action against an external threat;
- Use of cover terms to mask the true meaning of events or nefarious activities combined with active advocacy of violence;
- Attempting to enlist in the US military or state and local law enforcement, or seeking employment in a correctional institution by individuals confirmed to be known or suspected terrorist matches in government counterterrorism screening databases; and
- Reports to law enforcement that a community member has initiated unexplained isolation, including broken contact with friends and family, unexplained self-initiated exit from school or work, combined with advocacy of violence.

Behaviors Associated with Pre-Operational Preparations for Attack

- Participation in weapons training, paramilitary exercises, and reconnaissance and surveillance activities in a manner that is reasonably indicative of pre-operational planning related to terrorism, particularly in conjunction with advocacy of violence;
- Use of cover terms to mask the true meaning of events or nefarious activities combined with active advocacy of violence;
- Acquisition of unusual quantities of weapons and ammunition or materials that could be used to produce explosives, such as hydrogen peroxide, acetone, gasoline, propane, or fertilizer; and
- Activities that a reasonable person would deem as suspiciously indicating a storage facility or other area is being used to construct an explosive device.

Behaviors Associated with Possible Plans for Small-Arms Attacks

- Suspicious firearms purchases such as attempted purchases by individuals providing inconsistent or suspect identification, refusal to fill out the appropriate documentation, or issuance of vague or cryptic warnings that are violent in nature during purchase;

- Suspicious training behavior, such as the targeting of effigies or mimicking of specific operational conditions at gun ranges or gun shows, or practicing assault tactics at paint ball facilities; and
- Loitering at locations frequented by government or military personnel, unusual sketching, particularly of facility layout or security measures, measuring distances, testing security through hoax emergency calls, and timing personnel ingress and egress.

Source: "Joint Intelligence Bulletin" by FBI, US, and DHS, July 2016.

In sum, there are thousands of security professionals throughout Massachusetts who are engaged in counterterrorism surveillance, investigation, interrogation, border security, interdicting financial networks, and countering online violent extremism—all within a legal framework intended to protect civil rights. Security requires collective efforts from a well-informed community working together with law enforcement and intelligence professionals.

Conclusion

After reading this chapter, you should be more familiar with the challenges of defining terrorism and how it differs from many other kinds of crime. The strategies and tactics of terrorism have been used by individuals pursuing goals of anticolonial revolution, establishing a geopolitically separate identity (often referred to as ethnonational self-determination), the cessation of animal testing or deforestation, outlawing abortion, or subjugating members of another race, ethnicity, or religion—goals that are all related to politics and power. While terrorist groups like AQ and IS will continue to pose a threat to the citizens of Massachusetts, this threat is largely manifest in the form of individuals inspired by the global jihadist ideology rather than a well-coordinated, sophisticated terror attack like we saw on September 11, 2001. Similarly, we must also continue to monitor the terrorist threat associated with other ideologies of political violence, including right-wing extremism and the sovereign citizens movement. By facilitating information sharing and collaboration between law enforcement, the private sector, and local communities, and by encouraging the general public to remain vigilant, we will be well equipped to identify and prevent an emerging terrorist threat in the future.

Key Terms

Al-Qaeda: A global network of jihadists, with a central headquarters in the Pakistan-Afghanistan region and several affiliate groups in the Middle East, North Africa, and Southeast Asia.

Anarchist: Followers of a political ideology that calls for replacing formal nation states with an informal, local collaborative decision-making process.

Anti-Abortionist Violence: Attacking an abortion clinic, or staff who work there, in order to compel other clinics to close out of fear.

Civil Liberties: Basic rights and freedoms guaranteed to American citizens that the government cannot take away.

Commonwealth Fusion Center: A statewide collaborative effort of several agencies that share resources, expertise, and information with the goal of maximizing the ability to detect, prevent, apprehend, and respond to criminal and terrorist activity.

Counterterrorism: Political or military activities designed to prevent or thwart terrorism.

Do It Yourself Terrorism: A type of terrorist attack in which the perpetrator(s) have no operational or financial ties with a known terrorist group.

Ethnonationalism: An ideology associated with terrorist groups that use violent attacks in order to create an independent geopolitical entity based on ethnic identity.

Homeland Security: National efforts to prevent terrorism within the United States and to reduce the nation's vulnerability to terrorism.

Ideology: An articulation of grievances and an argument for how those grievances should be remedied.

Intelligence: Information a government collects about an enemy or possible enemy, including criminals and terrorists.

Islamic State: A violent jihadist group that wants to establish an Islamist caliphate that would rule over all Muslims.

Joint Terrorism Task Force: A team of investigators, analysts, linguists, SWAT experts, and other specialists from dozens of U.S. law enforcement and intelligence agencies who work together on terrorism-related investigations and threat analysis.

Leaderless Resistance: A concept promoted by White supremacist Louis Beam in 1983 as a method of encouraging individuals, unaffiliated with any established organization, to attack the federal government.

Left-Wing Extremism: A category of utopian ideologies associated with Marxist communism and revolutionary activity.

Right-Wing Extremism: A category of ideologies characterized by nationalism and racism and embraced by several militia groups and others in the United States.

Sovereign Citizen: A leaderless movement in the United States whose adherents claim the government is illegitimate and has no legal jurisdiction over their actions.

Terrorism: The use or threat of violence to achieve political or social objectives.

USA Patriot Act: Legislation passed after the 9/11 terrorist attacks that increased the ability of law enforcement to investigate suspected terrorists.

Related Websites

Boston Regional Intelligence Center
http://Boston Police Departmentnews.com/bric
Directorate of Analysis
https://www.cia.gov/offices-of-cia/intelligence-analysis
Commonwealth Fusion Center
http://www.mass.gov/eopss/home-sec-emerg-resp/fusion-center
Department of Homeland Security, "See Something Say Something"
https://www.dhs.gov/see-something-say-something
Federal Emergency Management Agency
https://www.fema.gov/
Infragard
https://www.infragard.org
Joint Terrorist Task Force (FBI)
https://www.fbi.gov/investigate/terrorism/joint-terrorism-task-forces
Massachusetts Anti-Terrorism Advisory Committee (ATAC)
http://www.justice.gov/usao-ma/anti-terrorism-national-security/atac
National Counterterrorism Center
https://www.nctc.gov
National Institute of Justice website on Terrorism
http://nij.gov/topics/crime/terrorism/welcome.htm
Terrorist Organization Profiles
http://www.start.umd.edu/start/data_collections/tops

Review Questions

1. What are the most central elements to any definition of terrorism?
2. How does terrorism differ from other kinds of violent crime?
3. What are terrorists trying to achieve by using violence?
4. What are some primary types of terrorist ideologies?
5. What kinds of targets have terrorists shown the most frequent interest in?
6. Explain the significance of the USA Patriot Act.
7. How does the Patriot Act affect civil liberties?
8. What are some of the ways in which Massachusetts is combating terrorism?
9. What challenges do law enforcement face in combating terrorism?
10. How can each of us help to improve the prevention of and responses to terrorism throughout Massachusetts?

References

Beam, L. (1992). Leaderless resistance. *The Seditionist, 12.*

Benjamin, D., & Simon, S. (2005). *The next attack.* New York, NY: Times Books.

Berger, J. M. (2016). *Without prejudice: What sovereign citizens believe.* Retrieved from https://extremism.gwu.edu/sites/g/files/zaxdzs2191/f/downloads/JMB%20Sovereign%20Citizens.pdf.

Central Intelligence Agency. (2015). *Intelligence and analysis.* Retrieved from https://www.cia.gov/offices-of-cia/intelligence-analysis.

Commonwealth of Massachusetts. (n.d.). *Massachusetts Emergency Management Agency.* Retrieved from http://www.mass.gov/eopss/agencies/mema/about/.

Commonwealth of Massachusetts. (2018). *Terrorism and intentional acts.* Retrieved from https://www.mass.gov/service-details/terrorism-and-intentional-acts.

Department of Homeland Security. (2016). *Our mission.* Retrieved from http:/www.dhs.gov/our-mission.

Docobo, J. M. (2006). Protecting America's communities from terrorism: A law enforcement perspective. In J. J. F. Forest (Ed.), *Homeland security: Protecting America's targets.* Westport, CT: Praeger.

Federal Bureau of Investigation. (n.d.). *Joint terrorism task forces.* Retrieved from https://www.fbi.gov/investigate/terrorism/joint-terrorism-task-forces.

Federal Bureau of Investigation. (2012). *Man sentenced in Boston for plotting attack on Pentagon and U.S. Capitol and attempting to provide detonation devices to terrorists* [Press release]. Retrieved from https://archives.fbi.gov/archives/boston/press-releases/2012/man-sentenced-in-boston-for-plotting-attack-on-pentagon-and-u.s.-capitol-and-attempting-to-provide-detonation-devices-to-terrorists.

Foreign Intelligence Surveillance Act, 50 U.S.C. §1802 (2011)

Forest, J. (2015). *The terrorism lectures (*2nd Ed). Orange County, CA: Nortia Press.

Forest, J. (2016). *Essentials of counterterrorism.* Westport, CT: Praeger.

Gill, P. (2012). Bombing alone: Tracing the motivations and antecedent behaviors of lone-actor terrorism. *Journal of Forensic Sciences 59*(2), 425–435.

Hoffman, B. (2006). *Inside terrorism.* New York, NY: Columbia University Press.

Homeland Security Act of 2002, 22 U.S.C. §2656f (d) (2010)

International Association of Chiefs of Police. (2005). *From hometown security to homeland security: IACP's principles for a locally designed and nationally coordinated homeland security strategy.* Retrieved from http://www.theiacp.org/portals/0/pdfs/HomelandSecurityWP.pdf.

Massachusetts Executive Office of Public Safety and Security. (2014). *The Commonwealth of Massachusetts State Homeland Security strategy.* Boston, MA: Author.

Massport. (2017). *Monthly airport traffic summary—December 2017.* Retrieved from http://www.massport.com/media/2685/1217-avstats-airport-traffic--summary.pdf.

National Counterterrorism Center. (n.d.). *Who we are.* Retrieved from http://www.nctc.gov/whoweare.html.

Perliger, A. (2015). *Challenges from the sidelines: Understanding America's violent far-right.* New York, NY: Combating Terrrism Center at West Point.

Pew Research Center. (2011, February 11). Retrieved from http://www.pewresearch.org/2011/02/15/public-remains-divided-over-the-patriot-act/.

Rapoport, D. C. (2008). Before the bombs there were the mobs: American experiences with terror. *Terrorism and Political Violence, 20*, 167–194.

Richardson, L. (2007). *What terrorists want.* New York, NY: Random House.

Schmid, A. (2013). *The Routledge handbook of terrorism research.* New York, NY: Taylor and Francis.

Shibuya, E. Y. (2007). The struggle with violent right-wing extremist groups in the United States. In J. J. F. Forest (Ed.) *Countering terrorism and insurgency in the 21st century* (pp. 574–575). Westport, CT: Praeger.

USA vs. Dzhokhar A. Tsarnaev (2013)

U.S. Census Bureau. (2017). *Population and housing unit estimates*. Retrieved from https://www.census.gov/programs-surveys/popest.html.

U.S. Department of Justice. (n.d.). The USA Patriot Act: Preserving life and liberty. Retrieved from http://www.justice.gov/archive/ll/what_is_the_patriot_act.pdf.

U.S. Department of Justice. (2015). *Massachusetts Anti-Terrorism Advisory Committee (ATAC)*. Retrieved from http://www.justice.gov/usao-ma/anti-terrorism-national-security/atac.

Chapter 10

Employment Trends for the Criminal Justice System in Massachusetts

Learning Objectives

- Familiarize yourself with different occupations in the criminal justice field.
- Learn about salaries for criminal justice positions in Massachusetts.
- Recognize how these salaries compare to positions nationwide.
- Understand projected growth patterns for criminal justice jobs.
- Learn about requirements for criminal justice jobs in Massachusetts.

Introduction

The criminal justice system provides a variety of opportunities for employment. Employment in this field offers stable growth opportunities to work in law enforcement, the courts, or corrections. Throughout this chapter, you will learn about some opportunities to work in the criminal justice system within the Commonwealth of Massachusetts.

Careers in Law Enforcement

The first thing that comes to many peoples' minds when they think of careers within the criminal justice system is law enforcement. This is because there are more people employed in law enforcement than in any other part of the criminal justice system. You learned about law enforcement in Chapter 3, but we will go into further detail about several job opportunities in the following sections.

Police Officer

Massachusetts General Law (MGL c.31 §58-58A, 61A) requires that police officers in the Commonwealth of Massachusetts meet the following requirements:

- Possess a high school diploma or GED equivalent;
- Minimum age of 21 years old on the date of the civil service examination for appointment to the position of police officer;
- Maximum age of 32 years old on the date of the civil service examination for appointment to the position of police officer;
- Move within 10 miles of the perimeter of the city or town she or he is employed within nine months of appointment; and
- Meet health and physical fitness standards.

The Municipal Police Training Committee (MPTC) is responsible for establishing training standards for municipal, University of Massachusetts, and environmental police officers within the Commonwealth of Massachusetts (Commonwealth of Massachusetts, n.d.j). The MPTC provides professional development training programs to veteran police officers as well as the 800-hour/20-week basic training to the five regional police academies throughout Massachusetts. The MPTC has an oversight board comprised of chiefs of police representing Western, Central, Northeastern, and Southeastern Massachusetts. This board guides the MPTC and establishes training standards for police officers within the commonwealth.

In addition, the Division of Standards and Training (DST) is responsible for setting the standards for the Massachusetts State Police (Commonwealth of Massachusetts, n.d.i). The DST provides the most up-to-date training, conducts regular inspections of the department, and investigates and prosecutes police misconduct. The DST is divided into two sections—*Standards* and *Training*. Officers in the Standards section conduct background investigations on state employees, investigate allegations of discrimination or harassment, conduct inspections, and investigate citizen complaints. Officers in the Training section provide training to recruits and Massachusetts State Police officers.

In 2017, the Bureau of Labor Statistics (BLS) estimated that police officers in the United States earned an average* salary of $62,960, while police officers in Massachusetts earned an average of $68,190 (see Table 10.1). In addition to

* Throughout this chapter, the "average" annual salary will refer to the median annual salary, which is the salary in the middle. So 50% will fall below the median annual salary, while 50% will be above it.

Table 10.1 Massachusetts Law Enforcement: Employment and Salary Statistics, 2017

Job Title	National Average Salary[1]	Massachusetts Average Salary[1]	Estimated MA Employment[1]	Annual Average Openings in MA[2]
Correctional Officers	$43,510	$66,060	6,080	160
Fish and Game Wardens	$58,570	$47,090	90	4
Forensic Science Technicians	$57,850	$68,990	40	N/A
Emergency Dispatchers	$39,640	$48,500	2,510	70
Police and Sheriffs Officers	$62,960	$68,190	17,750	567
Private Investigators	$50,700	N/A	760	48
Security Guards	$30,730	$33,690	21,580	364

Sources:

[1] "Massachusetts law enforcement employment and salary statistics, 2017" by Bureau of Labor Statistics, 2018a.

[2] "Labor market information" by Executive Office of Labor and Workforce Development, n.d. Retrieved from http://lmi2.detma.org/lmi/Occupation_projection_a.asp.

salary, police departments often have attractive benefits packages, including medical and dental insurance, vacation, long-term disability, educational incentives, and retirement prior to age 55.

In 2008, state and local law enforcement agencies employed approximately 810,000 sworn officers (Reaves, 2011). Local police departments employed the majority of sworn police officers, accounting for 60% of the total. The BLS projected employment of police officers to grow 4% from 2014 to 2024, which is slower than the average growth for all occupations (Bureau of Labor Statistics, 2018b). However, there is always a desire for public safety, so demand for employment will vary by location and state budget. Applicants with a bachelor's degree, military experience, or those who speak more than one language are expected to have higher chances of obtaining a job in policing. In addition, there are over 550 openings per year for this position in Massachusetts.

Private Investigator

In Massachusetts, a private investigator is someone who is paid to 1) use a lie detector to gain information related to the conduct, integrity, or activities of someone, or 2) conduct investigations related to a criminal act, association of a person, or damage or loss of property (MGL c.147 §22). Individuals who work as private investigators in Massachusetts must be licensed with the State

Police. Additionally, the individual must have been employed for at least three years as a detective, as a member of a federal investigative service, as a police officer of a rank higher than patrol, or as a police officer for at least 10 years (Commonwealth of Massachusetts, n.d.f). In 2017, private investigators in the Boston area earned an average salary of $70,380, although the average salary for the state was not available.

Security Guard

While private investigators primarily investigate past crimes, security guards spend the majority of their time guarding a particular space to prevent crime. Security guards can be armed or unarmed, and they are employed by a range of companies, including department stores, schools, restaurants, hospitals, and bars. There is no certification required to become an unarmed security guard in Massachusetts, but the basic requirements for this position include being at least 18 years old and passing a drug test and background check. In addition, armed guards require a firearm license in Massachusetts. The average annual salary for a security guard in Massachusetts is $33,690.

Environmental Police (Fish and Game Warden)

In Massachusetts, the environmental police work within the Executive Office of Energy and Environmental Affairs Department. Environmental police enforce laws in the commonwealth that focus on protecting waterways as well as overseeing commercial and recreational outdoor activities. Candidates for this position are required to take a civil service examination, be at least 21 years old, and have a high school diploma or GED equivalent. They must also have at least two years of full-time professional experience in wildlife or fisheries conservation, natural resources conservation, biological or environmental science, forestry, ecology, marine science, or conservation law enforcement (Commonwealth of Massachusetts, n.d.b). Environmental police in Massachusetts earned an average of $47,090 in 2017.

Forensic Science Technician

Forensic science is a field that has advanced since the turn of the century, and technicians in this field analyze and process evidence from crime scenes. Many employers require forensic science technicians to have a bachelor's degree with concentrations in biology and chemistry. In Massachusetts, many forensic science technicians work for the State Police Crime Laboratory. This lab provides forensic services for the commonwealth, including fingerprint identification, DNA analysis, and chemical analysis for different types of evidence. The crime lab has eight locations across Massachusetts, and it is accredited by the American Society of Crime Laboratory Directors (Commonwealth of Massachusetts, n.d.g).

Forensic science technicians average $68,990 per year in Massachusetts. The BLS reports that the job outlook for forensic science technicians is growing much faster than the average for all occupations. However, it is a small occupation, so even though there is increased growth, there will be few new positions available in Massachusetts each year.

Emergency Dispatcher

Emergency dispatchers receive and prioritize incoming calls, and they dispatch police officers and other first responders to areas in which people need assistance. Emergency dispatchers must be able to multitask and make important decisions quickly. The State 911 Department establishes certification requirements for 911 telecommunicators, including emergency medical dispatch programs in Massachusetts (Commonwealth of Massachusetts, n.d.a).

Emergency dispatchers earned an average of $48,500 in Massachusetts in 2017. The BLS reports that there is an expected decline in the job outlook for this position due to the consolidation of emergency communication centers and advances in technology. However, job prospects should remain positive, given that the stressful nature of this work results in high turnover.

Profile: Scott Dranka, Police Dispatcher, Ludlow Police Department

The best part of my job is that I am able to provide assistance to individuals in need during every shift I work. While caller's needs vary call by call, I always take pride in realizing that I, and fellow dispatchers, are historically the first people being informed of the nature of the call, and I am proud to be able to render professional assistance during the caller's time of need. As the department receives calls of varying intensity and call reason, that, in and of itself, allows dispatchers the ability to regather themselves after more intense calls and to also be able to handle other responsibilities during the shift.

Some of the areas of the job that I find particularly rewarding are the thankful callers who reconnect with dispatch after their matter has been taken care of where they either call or respond to the station in person to express thanks to the dispatchers and to the officers for the assistance that was rendered. I have always commented that it is great that we have a close department where the officers, dispatchers, and administrative assistants work very well together. Being in a mid-sized town, you also get to know many of the workers or business owners representing various agencies throughout the community.

I feel that the hardest part of this job revolves around time allowance and timing. When dealing with high priority calls you don't have an abundance of time; therefore, you must ascertain all of the relevant information in a timely and efficient manner while advising the caller about what they need to do prior to police, fire, or EMS arriving on scene. While managing the current call, many times you have preexisting calls or you will receive additional calls of varying nature and you need to handle those calls as well. Additionally, besides handling all calls, we are monitoring radio transmissions and utilizing radio equipment to dispatch accordingly.

One of the policies within our department that has worked out well is having dispatchers partake in professional development opportunities, including continuing education classes. Besides staying current with the required annual refresher courses, the sergeants and other supervisors encourage dispatchers to undertake additional professional development opportunities throughout the year. By being a proactive department who values training, dispatchers are able to stay up-to-date, knowledgeable about technology changes, and are able to connect with fellow dispatchers in the field where they can interact, share experiences, and learn from one another.

I feel that a problem facing any agency nowadays is the life stressors that people are facing along with the associated coping mechanisms resulting in an increase in the type of calls and volume of calls that are received, compared to what I remember receiving when I began this job in the 1990s. As far as the stressors that some callers face, trained dispatchers and trained responding officers are able to de-escalate difficult situations and render assistance needed in order to help rectify the matter, sometimes with the assistance of additional resources when needed.

Some advice that I would give people entering this position is that they need to be able to stay calm, composed, and handle stress well. People entering this profession must be confident in their decisions and must be able to clearly convey information in a relatively timely turn around period. Dispatchers must also be able to collaborate with fellow dispatchers and police supervisors. People entering this profession must be able to multitask, prioritize, and realize that they will be dealing with critical matters in this type of employment. During employment interviews, people need to be able to articulate why they are interested in a police dispatcher position.

As this field is utilizing more and more advanced technology, I would recommend that one should feel comfortable utilizing technology. As "overtime" in this profession is usually available in any agency, dispatchers sometimes find themselves working double shifts or working on one or sometimes both of their scheduled days off. While I totally support helping the department, in an environment that can be stressful at times, I would recommend that both new and longstanding dispatchers properly balance work and time off and also maintain great nutrition and fitness.

Table 10.2 Massachusetts Court and Legal Careers: Employment and Salary Statistics, 2017

Job Title	National Average Salary[1]	Massachusetts Average Salary[1]	Estimated MA Employment[1]	Annual Average Openings in MA[2]
Court Reporter	$55,120	$76,700	270	3
Judges	$115,520	$140,690	411	N/A
Lawyers	$119,250	$157,450	17,820	363
Paralegals and Legal Assistants	$50,410	$56,970	7,720	177
Probation Officer	$51,410	N/A	356	7

Sources:

[1] "Massachusetts law enforcement employment and salary statistics, 2017" by Bureau of Labor Statistics, 2018a.
[2] "Labor market information" by Executive Office of Labor and Workforce Development, n.d.

Careers in the Court System

You learned in Chapter 5 that there are many people involved in the court system. For the courtroom to run smoothly, different actors have to work together, including judges, lawyers, court officers, court reporters, and other support staff. In this section, we will discuss the job outlooks for some of these positions.

Judge

You learned about judges in Chapter 5. Recall that their primary function is to oversee the trial process, but some judges serve an appellate role. There are 411 judicial positions in Massachusetts: 7 justices in the Supreme Judicial Court (SJC), 25 in the Appeals Court, and 379 in the Trial Court (Healy, 2012).

All judges in Massachusetts are appointed by the governor. Individuals seeking appointment as a judge must be members of the Massachusetts Bar Association, have graduated from an accredited law school, and have a minimum of 10 years legal experience for the Trial Court and 13 years for the Appeals Court (Healy, 2012).

According to the BLS, the average salary for a judge in Massachusetts in 2017 was $140,690 (see Table 10.2). Given the competitive nature of this work and that individuals remain in judicial positions for extended periods of time, job growth is projected to be slower than in other legal fields.

Profile: Francis X. Spina, Retired Judge, MA SJC, Appeals Court and Superior Court

The best part of the job of a judge is the inherent satisfaction of public service. The work is particularly meaningful. Judges play a significant role in the peaceful resolution of disputes. They work to dispense justice—righting and preventing wrongs. Their work involves seeing that government does what it is supposed to do and not do what it should not be doing, per the demands of the applicable constitution and laws of the United States or the states.

One of the most rewarding parts of judging is "getting it right." The law is not always settled, or even clear, and working to attain a principled interpretation or application of the law in a given case is a challenge, and it is its own reward.

Some of the most difficult aspects of judging involve entering what seems to be a harsh judgment against someone. This may occur during the imposition of a sentence against a criminal defendant after a jury returned a verdict of guilty in a case where the judge thought the defendant was not guilty. It also may occur after a jury decided that a seriously injured plaintiff was entitled to little or no damages, and the judge thought the plaintiff was entitled to an award of substantial damages. In each case, the losing party seeks an order setting aside the jury verdict.

Another difficult aspect of judging involves the maintenance of an authentic attitude of fairness and impartiality. This is a mentally draining exercise. Paying close attention to what lawyers and witnesses are saying requires a constantly high level of concentration, care, and patience that is hard work. A judge must, within reason, treat what some might describe as a trivial case with the same level of dignity and attention that is accorded the most high profile cases. The parties, the witnesses, the lawyers, and the jury are entitled to nothing less. A judge must avoid outbursts of displeasure and invitations to make light of something or someone and present with calm concern throughout the trial.

Generally, the application of time standards, or case flow management techniques, has improved the public's perception of the judicial branch of government. Most people understand that judges work hard to be fair and that they try to resolve cases in a timely and fair manner.

Two related problems present great challenges to the judicial system. The first problem is the access to justice. The cost of litigation has risen with the increased complexity of the law, and fewer people (partly due to the demise of the middle class) have the financial resources needed to seek a judicial resolution to their problems or just to hire a lawyer. One potential solution calls for simpler, more streamlined procedures, especially for the most common cases.

The second problem is the increasing lack of civility on the part of lawyers and litigants in dealings with opponents. The growing reluctance to understand the position of the other side and to compromise fairly has unreasonably protracted the life of cases involving litigants having the financial resources to fight to the bitter end. Conversely, where one party lacks adequate financial resources to litigate, settlements often are forced prematurely and for inadequate amounts. More face-to-face contact (where a demand on the use of social skills is required) between the parties and a judge, such as discovery conferences and settlement conferences, can help expedite the litigation and improve the chances of compromise, but not always.

I tell young people entering the legal profession that they will pay more for a law school education today and earn less than their counterparts 50 years ago, but they can still make an adequate living and reap great satisfaction in the work of what remains a noble profession that has myriad opportunities for public service at many levels.

Attorney/Lawyer

Recall from Chapter 5 that there are different types of attorneys—district attorneys and defense attorneys. District attorneys represent the government, and it is their job to prosecute criminal cases. There are 11 district attorneys throughout the commonwealth, and they typically represent a district at the county level. District attorneys hire assistant district attorneys who are responsible for the management of activities in the office as well as prosecutorial duties. These attorneys appear in courts throughout Massachusetts, and they represent the interest of the commonwealth.

On the other hand, defense attorneys represent the defendant. Recall from Chapter 5 that there are two types of defense attorneys—private defense attorneys and public defenders. If a defendant can afford to do so, he hires a private defense attorney. If not, he is assigned to a public defender.

To become an attorney in Massachusetts, candidates must earn a degree from an accredited law school and pass the bar exam in Massachusetts. There are nearly 18,000 attorneys in Massachusetts, and the average salary in 2017 was $157,450. This is considerably higher than the national average salary of $119,250 for an attorney. Furthermore, there are over 350 openings per year for this position in Massachusetts.

Court Officer

Court officers, or bailiffs, are officers who maintain order and provide safety and security for everyone in the courtroom. They screen people entering the courthouse for weapons and contraband, operate metal detectors, manage emergencies, enforce the laws of the courtroom, and keep records of disturbances, among other duties.

In Massachusetts, court officers are required to complete an application, take the *Court Officer Entry Exam*, and go through an extensive screening process that involves a criminal background investigation and drug screening.

Furthermore, candidates are also required to attend an eight-week court officer academy in which they must successfully pass physical fitness, educational, and defensive tactics components prior to becoming a court officer. Court officers must also have at least four years of experience working in a security-related job (Commonwealth of Massachusetts, n.d.c).

The average annual salary for a court officer nationwide in 2017 was $43,510. However, there was no salary information for this position that was specific to Massachusetts. The BLS projects that job growth for court officers will be slower than the average for all occupations. However, there is high job turnover in this field, and the rate of growth will vary by location and state budget.

Paralegal/Legal Assistant

Paralegals and legal assistants assist lawyers with a variety of tasks such as conducting legal research, drafting documents, and maintaining files. Although they support lawyers, paralegals are not lawyers themselves. There are no specific educational requirements for paralegals, but many have an associate's degree or a certificate in paralegal studies, and others have a bachelor's degree and are trained on the job. In Massachusetts, the average yearly salary for this position was $56,970 in 2017.

Court Reporter

Court reporters are responsible for creating transcripts for trials and other legal proceedings. The Commonwealth of Massachusetts does not require a certification to work as a court reporter, but many community colleges and technical institutes offer certificate programs for this line of work. The average salary for a court reporter in Massachusetts was $76,700 in 2017. The BLS projects that the job outlook for this occupation is slower than the average for all occupations. However, people with experience working with deaf populations are expected to have the best job prospects.

Careers in Corrections

You learned about the correctional system in Massachusetts in Chapter 6 of this book. Recall that corrections refers to the institutions and methods used to punish, control, and change the behavior of convicted offenders. Some offenders serve their sentence within a correctional institution, such as a jail or a prison; others serve their sentence in the community under the supervision of a probation officer. In this section, we will discuss jobs within the field of corrections.

Correctional Officer

In Chapter 6, you learned that correctional officers are responsible for maintaining the safety and security of inmates and staff within jails and prisons. In Massachusetts, correctional officers are required to take a civil service exam and undergo 400 hours of training at the Basic Correction Officer Academy before becoming an officer. Applicants must also meet the following requirements (Plymouth County Sheriff's Department, n.d.):

- Be at least 21 years old at the time of appointment;
- Be a U.S. citizen;
- Pass psychological, medical, and physical abilities examinations;
- Complete a training program for corrections officers;
- Cease smoking tobacco products; and
- Not have a felony conviction.

In 2017, the average salary for a correctional officer in Massachusetts was $66,060, which is considerably higher than the national average of $43,510 for a correctional officer. Moreover, correctional officers also have an attractive benefits package, including a retirement pension, life insurance, medical insurance, tuition remission, up to five weeks of vacation, sick leave, and paid holidays (Commonwealth of Massachusetts, n.d.h). The BLS projects the employment of correctional officers to be slower than average, but prison populations and state budgets vary. Furthermore, there is high turnover in this profession due to the stress associated with the job.

Community Supervision

You learned in Chapter 6 that some offenders are supervised within the community as an alternative to being incarcerated. This allows them to live and work in the community, receive rehabilitative services, and support their families. These offenders are usually supervised by a probation officer or a parole officer. Probationers and parolees are different populations of offenders, but the premise behind community supervision is similar. Probationers are often first-time nonviolent offenders who have been given an opportunity to serve their sentence within the community as an alternative to incarceration, whereas parolees are offenders who have been incarcerated but are granted an early release from a correctional facility to spend the remainder of their sentence in the community. In both cases, however, offenders must abide by certain conditions or they will be sent to jail or prison.

Profile: Ron Corbett, Former Commissioner of Probation, Commonwealth of MA

The best part of the job is the constant variety of (good and exciting) challenges in trying to develop a more effective system for supervising offenders. Offenders come in a variety of different "shapes and sizes" with some unique problems that present a constant diet of intellectual challenges. Also, if you are even moderately interested in the human drama, the case examples are fascinating and never lose interest.

Introducing new programs—even on a pilot or experimental basis—is the most rewarding part of the job. Trying something new—constantly working the edges in hopes of improving effectiveness—keeps the agency vitalized and freely is fun!

Furthermore, initiatives that come from the staff (particularly line staff) often bring the best ideas. Innovations in street work and in assessing offenders are two areas where line staff had great input, and those initiatives seemed to have staying power as a result.

In regards to the hardest part of the job, for any executive, the fairly constant stream of insoluble personnel issues is a drag. In a big agency, there are always employees who are getting in trouble or falling down on the job. Responding to those problems keeps you away from the real work.

The biggest problem is almost always the same—keeping staffing levels at an appropriate level. Budget fluctuations play havoc with continuity of operations. Personally, I would favor having the legislature go to a biennial, rather than an annual, budget. In that way, we would have a budget crisis only half as often!

I would tell young people that probation can be an immensely rewarding career IF you are sure you are interested in the causes and prevention of criminal behavior and can imagine yourself working closely with offenders who have sometimes committed abhorrent acts. Separating the acts from the person and having a keen interest in fellow human beings, their troubles, and their hopes for improvement are the keys to a successful and enjoyable career in probation.

Probation Officer/Parole Officer

There are more than 80,000 offenders under probation supervision in Massachusetts, and probation officers work under the Office of the Commissioner of Probation, the Office of Community Corrections, the Trial Court Community Service Program, or the Electronic Monitoring Center (Commonwealth of Massachusetts, n.d.e). To be considered for this position in the commonwealth, candidates are required to take a civil service exam and have a bachelor's degree from an accredited college or university. It is preferred that candidates have experience working in human or allied services, including social welfare, criminal justice, or the behavioral sciences.

The Massachusetts Parole Board, which is under the Executive Office of Public Safety, is authorized to grant and supervise parole, and it currently supervises over 8,000 parolees (Commonwealth of Massachusetts, n.d.d). Parole officers are required to take a civil service examination in Massachusetts. They must also satisfy the parole board's qualifications of at least five years of experience working in human or allied services or a combination of education and experience.

According to the BLS, probation and parole officers earned an average of $51,410 nationwide in 2017, but salary information was not available for these occupations in Massachusetts. The BLS projects that employment in these positions will be slower than the average for all occupations due to limited state and local government funding for corrections.

Conclusion

After reading this chapter, you can see that there are many opportunities to work in the criminal justice system in Massachusetts. Even though some positions currently have lower than average expected growth, the criminal justice system provides a variety of stable jobs for individuals who desire to work in this field. There will always be a demand for protecting the public, defending individuals' rights, and providing administrative support to various sectors within the criminal justice system.

Related Websites

Bureau of Labor Statistics
http://www.bls.gov/
Executive Office of Labor and Workforce Development (EOLWD)
http://lmi2.detma.org/lmi/Occupation_projection_a.asp

References

Bureau of Labor Statistics. (2018a). *Massachusetts law enforcement employment and salary statistics, 2017*. Retrieved from https://www.bls.gov/oes/current/oes_ma.htm.

Bureau of Labor Statistics. (2018b). *Police and detectives*. Retrieved from http://www.bls.gov/ooh/protective-service/police-and-detectives.htm#tab-6.

Commonwealth of Massachusetts. (n.d.a). *Information for Emergency Medical Dispatch (EMD)*. Retrieved from http://www.mass.gov/eopss/agencies/state-911/emergency-medical-dispatch-emd-regulations.html.

Commonwealth of Massachusetts. (n.d.b). *Environmental police officer duties and entrance requirements*. Retrieved from https://www.mass.gov/service-details/environmental-police-officer-duties-and-entrance-requirements.

Commonwealth of Massachusetts. (n.d.c). *How to become a Massachusetts Trial Court Officer*. Retrieved from http://www.mass.gov/courts/court-info/trial-court/exec-office/ocm/how-to-become-a-court-officer.html.

Commonwealth of Massachusetts. (n.d.d). *Massachusetts Parole Board*. Retrieved from http://www.mass.gov/eopss/agencies/parole-board/.

Commonwealth of Massachusetts. (n.d.e). *Massachusetts probation service*. Retrieved from http://www.mass.gov/courts/court-info/probation/.

Commonwealth of Massachusetts. (n.d.f). *Requirements for a private investigator license*. Retrieved from http://www.mass.gov/eopss/agencies/msp/prof-stds/cert-unit/pi-license-requirements.html.

Commonwealth of Massachusetts. (n.d.g). *Massachusetts State Police Crime Laboratory*. Retrieved from https://www.mass.gov/orgs/massachusetts-state-police-crime-laboratory.

Commonwealth of Massachusetts. (n.d.h). *Summary of employee benefits*. Retrieved from http://www.mass.gov/eopss/law-enforce-and-cj/prisons/recruitment/employee-benefits.html.

Commonwealth of Massachusetts. (n.d.i). *Massachusetts State Police*. Retrieved from http://www.mass.gov/eopss/agencies/msp/standards-and-training.html.

Commonwealth of Massachusetts. (n.d.j). *Municipal Police Training Committee*. Retrieved from http://www.mass.gov/eopss/law-enforce-and-cj/law-enforce/mptc/our-organization/the-municipal-police-training-committee.html.

Executive Office of Labor and Workforce Development. (n.d.). *Labor market information*. Retrieved from http://lmi2.detma.org/lmi/Occupation_projection_a.asp.

Healy, M. W. (2012). *A guide to the Massachusetts judicial selection process: The making of a judge*. (2nd ed.). Boston, MA: Massachusetts Bar Association.

MGL c.31 §58A

MGL c.31 §58

MGL c.31 §61A

MGL c.147 §22

Plymouth County Sheriff's Department. (n.d.). *Training: Basic Correction Officer Academy*. Retrieved from http://www.pcsdma.org/co.html.

Reaves, B. A. (2011). *Census of state and local law enforcement agencies*. Retrieved from http://www.bjs.gov/content/pub/pdf/csllea08.pdf.

Chapter 11

The Future of the Criminal Justice System in Massachusetts

Learning Objectives

- Learn about cybercrime and the penalties associated with it in Massachusetts.
- Recognize how criminal justice practitioners respond to cybercrimes in Massachusetts.
- Learn about the significance of forensic evidence.
- Understand the importance of DNA analysis.
- Become familiar with the concept of environmental justice.
- Discover ways that Massachusetts promotes environmental justice.
- Learn about recent legislation legalizing marijuana in Massachusetts.

Introduction

Throughout this book, we have focused on traditional crimes and how the criminal justice system has responded to them. However, it is important to recognize that the criminal justice system is always evolving. Societal, political, economic, and technological changes create new types of crime, and members of the criminal justice system must adapt accordingly. In this chapter, we will focus on several of the challenges that are shaping the future of our criminal justice system—cybercrimes, forensic evidence, environmental justice, and the legalization of marijuana.

Cybercrime

Aside from terrorism, another recent challenge facing the criminal justice system is *cybercrime*. Cybercrime includes a wide range of offenses that involve the Internet, computer systems, or computer technology. The majority of cybercrimes are not new crimes but are existing crimes in which the Internet is used in the commission of these crimes.

This type of crime is particularly challenging for law enforcement for several reasons. First, technology advances quickly, so members of the criminal justice system must acquire the technical skills to catch perpetrators of cybercrimes. Second, the Internet provides a great deal of anonymity, making it even more challenging to catch perpetrators of cybercrimes. Finally, large amounts of information can be deleted or transferred quickly in cyberspace, making it difficult to track individuals engaging in cybercrime (Gaines & Miller, 2014).

In this section, we will address several forms of cybercrime, including cyberstalking, hate crimes, cyberbullying, illegal downloads, and identity theft. We will also discuss some of the measures law enforcement is taking to control these types of crimes in Massachusetts.

Cyberstalking

Cyberstalking is a criminal practice in which a person uses the Internet to harass or threaten someone else. It can be perpetrated through social media, chat rooms, instant messaging, email, or any other type of online means. Historically, perpetrators of traditional stalking had to be in close physical proximity to their victims. Cyberstalkers, on the other hand, can live next door to their victims, or they can be across the state, country, or world. This type of stalker hides behind a username, and it is often difficult for law enforcement to identify these perpetrators because they are constantly changing their accounts and usernames (Commonwealth of Massachusetts, n.d.b).

Usually, cyberstalkers and victims have had a prior relationship in real life or online, and the stalking begins after the relationship ends. However, strangers can also engage in cyberstalking. These perpetrators obtain the victim's personal information online from social networking sites, and they are able to find additional information about the victims online (Commonwealth of Massachusetts, n.d.b).

Regardless if the stalking takes place in real life or online, or if the stalker is known to the victim or is a stranger, stalking can cause a great deal of stress for the victim. Massachusetts's law defines a stalker as someone who

> Willfully and maliciously engages in a knowing pattern of conduct or series of acts over a period of time directed at a specific person which seriously alarms or annoys that person and would cause a reasonable person to suffer substantial emotional distress, and makes a threat with the intent to place the person in imminent fear of death or bodily injury (MGL c.265 §43).

This conduct can include, but is not limited to, acts or threats through mail, the telephone, email, fax machines, and Internet communication. Because the Commonwealth of Massachusetts recognizes stalking as a serious crime, it is punishable by up to five years imprisonment in a state prison, a fine up to $1,000, imprisonment in a county house of correction for up to two-and-a-half years, or a combination of imprisonment and a fine (MGL c.265 §43).

Hate Crimes

A ***hate crime*** is a traditional crime, but it is motivated by bias. Specifically, Congress considers crimes motivated by an offender's bias against race, religion, disability, ethnic origin or sexual orientation to be hate crimes (Federal Bureau of Investigation, n.d.).

It is important to note that the First Amendment protects our right to free speech. Unfortunately, the Internet has provided people with a new way to communicate hate through hate websites. Although hateful expression can be hurtful and offensive, this alone is not a crime. Consequently, when websites express hatred toward protected groups of people, the authors of these websites are protected by the First Amendment. However, once this hateful expression becomes a direct and credible threat, it is no longer protected by the First Amendment (Commonwealth of Massachusetts, n.d.f).

Perpetrators of hateful threats in Massachusetts can be punished by criminal and civil laws addressing hate crimes. Particularly, anyone who commits assault or battery with the intent to intimidate the victim based on their race, religion, national origin, sexual orientation, gender identity, or disability can be punished by a fine up to $5,000, imprisonment in a house of correction for up to two-and-a-half years, or both a fine and imprisonment (MGL c.265 §39).

In addition, the Attorney General's Office enforces the Massachusetts Civil Rights Act (MCRA). The MCRA protects the rights of residents and visitors of Massachusetts against interference with their civil rights, including the right to be free from bias-motivated threats, coercion, or violence. Under the MCRA, the attorney general can obtain an injunction if someone is the victim of threats, intimidation, or coercion based on a protected category. An ***injunction*** is a civil order issued by the court prohibiting a perpetrator from committing certain actions. Correspondingly, a civil rights injunction protects the victim and others in the victim's protected category from further intimidation or violence and prohibits perpetrators from future acts of intimidation or violence. Violation of a civil rights injunction is a crime punishable with fines up to $10,000, up to two-and-a-half years in a house of correction, or up to ten years in state prison in cases involving severe bodily injury (Commonwealth of Massachusetts, n.d.f).

Cyberbullying

Bullying occurs when one or more students or staff repeatedly engage in written, verbal, or physical acts or behavior toward a victim that

> causes physical or emotional harm to the victim or damage to the victim's property; places the victim in reasonable fear of harm to himself or of damage to his property; creates a hostile environment at school for the victim; infringes on the rights of the victim at school; or materially and substantially disrupts the education process or the orderly operation of a school (MGL c.71 §370).

A form of bullying that has become more widespread in recent years is ***cyberbullying***, or bullying through technology or electronic communication. Perpetrators of this type of bullying may send hurtful, derogatory, or threatening messages to victims through technology. Perpetrators may also spread rumors or send pictures through electronic means to intimidate or ridicule the victim (Commonwealth of Massachusetts, n.d.c).

Similar to the other states across the nation, Massachusetts has anti-bullying legislation in place, which also encompasses cyberbullying. Bullying is prohibited on school grounds, at school-related events or programs, and through technology leased by a school in Massachusetts. Furthermore, all schools, both public and private, must provide evidence-based instruction on bullying prevention. Each school must have a plan that includes procedures for collecting data on bullying, reporting incidents of bullying, procedures to respond to bullying, and disciplinary actions for perpetrators of bullying, among other provisions. Finally, all schools are required to report the nature and extent of bullying incidents to the department annually. This way, the data can be analyzed, and steps can be taken to improve upon existing policies (MGL c.71 §370).

Illegal Downloads

A *copyright* is a form of protection granting individuals who have created original work, including literature, music, and art, exclusive rights to its use and distribution. However, the Internet has created new challenges for existing copyright laws. Specifically, people have been obtaining materials illegally, cracking the copyright protections, and sharing the files with other users. This most often occurs when people illegally download and share music, computer software, videos, and other materials.

Unfortunately, there are risks that come with illegally downloading files and online material. First, file sharing sites invite the threat of viruses and other harmful code located in illegal files. Second, and more importantly, it is against the law to download copyrighted work without permission to do so (Commonwealth of Massachusetts, n.d.g). Anyone in Massachusetts who transfers sound recordings without the owner's consent, records live performances for financial gain without the owner's consent, or manufactures, rents, sells, or transports recorded devices in packaging not bearing the name and address of the transferor, can face imprisonment up to five years, a fine up to $250,000, or both imprisonment and a fine (MGL c.266 § 143E).

Cyber Identity Theft

Identity theft is another type of crime that can take place in cyberspace. In this type of crime, an offender steals the personal identity of a victim from the Internet. This information can include the victim's name, social security number, credit card numbers, account numbers, passwords, or other personal information. Perpetrators of cyber identity theft can obtain victims' personal information through unsecured websites, fraudulent emails, computer viruses, or by using computer software found on public access computers. Once the perpetrator has access to the victim's information, he or she is able to commit a variety of crimes, including accessing the victim's financial resources or opening new credit cards.

According to Massachusetts law, a defendant can be found guilty of identity fraud if he or she posed as another person without their permission and used that person's personal information to obtain money, goods, services, or credit. Someone can also be convicted of this crime by obtaining someone else's personal identifying information with the intent to pose as that person or assisting someone in posing as the victim to obtain money, goods, services, credit, or anything of value (MGL c.266 § 37E).

This crime is punishable by a fine up to $5,000, two-and-a-half years in a county jail, or a combination of a fine and imprisonment. In addition, a person found guilty of identity theft may also have to pay restitution for any costs incurred by the victim as a result of the crime (MGL c.266 §37E). Note that victims of identity theft not only lose the money stolen from their accounts, but their credit scores may also decrease. This can hurt their chances of obtaining loans or approval for other items requiring credit.

Cybercrime Initiative

The Attorney General's Office in Massachusetts is being funded through the U.S. Department of Justice to develop a cybercrime information sharing program. Law enforcement across the state have access to the most up-to-date information to help them investigate and prevent cybercrimes (Commonwealth of Massachusetts, n.d.a).

The Cyber Crime Division of the Attorney General's Office investigates and prosecutes criminal cases involving digital evidence, and it works to enhance the cybercrime initiative. This division has helped develop and deliver training to over 11,000 police officers and prosecutors across the Commonwealth of Massachusetts on subjects related to cybercrime (Commonwealth of Massachusetts, n.d.i).

Cybercrime Strategic Plan

Established in 2007 by the Attorney General's Office, the Cybercrime Strategic Plan is a statewide plan that prevents, investigates, and prosecutes all types of cybercrimes. This plan has improved training for law enforcement investigating cybercrimes, enhanced cybercrime prevention and information sharing, examined statewide digital forensic evidence processing requirements, secured funding for cybercrime programs, and amended jurisdictional and substantive law (Office of Attorney General Martha Coakley, 2007). As a result of this plan, law enforcement and other members of the criminal justice system in Massachusetts are better equipped to confront the challenges posed by cybercrimes.

Forensic Evidence

After reading the last section, you are aware of how important it is for members of the criminal justice system to keep up with technology. Technology has also played a pivotal role in assisting detectives in crime scene investigations. Specifically, ***forensics*** is the practice of using science and technology for these investigations. Forensics can be helpful for a number of reasons, including determining the cause and time of death or injury, type of weapon used, and the identity of the victim and offender (Gaines & Miller, 2014).

Police departments are often associated with crime laboratories and forensic science facilities. In Massachusetts, the State Police Forensic Services Group provides forensic services to criminal justice practitioners such as fingerprint identification and DNA analysis. The Forensic Services Group has a variety of specialties and units throughout its 11 locations in the state (Commonwealth of Massachusetts, n.d.h).

Fingerprint Identification and DNA Analysis

For over a century, the human fingerprint had been the most important piece of trace evidence used to assist detectives at a crime scene. No two fingerprints are identical, so forensic scientists can match fingerprints found at crime scenes with suspects' fingerprints. Unfortunately, this method of identifying suspects is not always dependable because it is often hard to find suitable fingerprints at the scene of a crime. Consequently, there have been many cases in which innocent people have been convicted as a result of lifting flawed fingerprints, which we will discuss in further depth shortly.

However, beginning in the 1990s, the technique of ***DNA analysis*** began to replace fingerprint identification. DNA is the genetic material found in cells, and it provides a unique code for each person. In this type of analysis, forensic scientists obtain sources of DNA, such as blood, skin, saliva, hair, or semen, from the crime scene. They can then use a suspect's DNA to match a sample of DNA found at a crime scene. If the characteristics of the DNA samples match, the odds are extremely low that the match could have come from a source other than the suspect. Because of this accuracy, police have greater chances of solving crimes.

DNA analysis can also be useful for solving cold cases, or unsolved investigations. The FBI operates the Combined DNA Index System (CODIS), which provides state and local law enforcement agencies access to DNA profiles of people who have been convicted of different crimes. Forensic scientists can then determine whether or not the DNA samples of suspects match DNA found at a crime scene. In Massachusetts, the DNA Unit of the State Police Forensic Services Group enters DNA samples into CODIS, contributing to this important database and increasing the likelihood of solving cold cases (Commonwealth of Massachusetts, n.d.d).

Exoneration through DNA

Over the years, many people have been wrongfully convicted of crimes they did not commit, most often due to eyewitness misidentification or improper forensics. However, with the increasing use of DNA evidence, many of these cases have been overturned. According to the Innocence Project (n.d.a), approximately 330 people in the United States have been ***exonerated***, or freed of blame, as a result of DNA testing. Although this is good news for the exonerated individuals, only a small percentage of cases have biological evidence that can be exposed to DNA testing. Consequently, the majority of people who have been wrongfully convicted are unable to prove their innocence.

DNA Exonerees in Massachusetts

Of the 330 DNA exonerations in the United States, the Innocence Project reports that there have been ten cases in Massachusetts (refer to Table 11.1). These 10 individuals served an average of 13 years in prison before being exonerated and released. As a result of their wrongful convictions, each of these people encountered a variety of hardships. For example, they suffered the agony of being in prison, the loss of many freedoms, and the deprivation of time with family and friends. In addition, they suffered problems upon release, including trouble finding housing and employment. As a result of these hardships, the state has a responsibility to compensate individuals affected by this miscarriage of justice. Consequently, the Commonwealth of Massachusetts compensates individuals who have been wrongfully convicted with up to $500,000. In addition, the state will also pay for physical and emotional services as well as educational services at any state or community college within the commonwealth (Innocence Project, 2009).

Environmental Justice

Throughout this book, we have examined many aspects of the criminal justice system and acts that we consider traditional crimes. However, some criminologists have also taken an interest in examining issues related to social justice, rather than studying only criminal justice. Therefore, in this section, we will be discussing ***environmental justice*** (EJ). EJ is based on the notion that everyone is entitled to a clean and healthy environment. Furthermore, advocates of EJ maintain that everyone deserves equal protection from environmental

Table 11.1 DNA Exonerees in Massachusetts

Name	Conviction Date	Exoneration Date	Causes	Real Offender Found
Ronjon Cameron	2003	2015	Eyewitness Misidentification; Inadequate Defense; Improper Forensic Science	No
Ulysses Rodriguez Charles	1984	2001	Eyewitness Misidentification; Improper Forensic Science	No
Stephan Cowans	1998	2004	Eyewitness Misidentification; Government Misconduct; Improper Forensic Science	No
Dennis Maher	1984	2003	Eyewitness Misidentification	No
Neil Miller	1990	2000	Eyewitness Misidentification; Improper Forensic Science	Yes
Marvin Mitchell	1990	1997	Eyewitness Misidentification; Improper Forensic Science	No
Anthony Powell	1992	2004	Eyewitness Misidentification; Improper Forensic Science	Yes
Eric Sarsfield	1987	2000	Eyewitness Misidentification	No
Eduardo Velasquez	1988	2001	Eyewitness Misidentification; Improper Forensic Science	No
Kenny Waters	1983	2001	Informants	No

Source: "The Cases: DNA Exoneree Profiles" by Innocence Project, n.d.b. Available at https://www.innocenceproject.org/all-cases/#massachusetts,exonerated-by-dna.

harms, such as air pollution, water contamination, or exposure to hazardous waste, irrespective of their race, income level, or any other category.

The Environmental Protection Agency (EPA) defines EJ as the

> fair treatment and meaningful involvement of all people regardless of race, color, national origin, or income with respect to the development, implementation, and enforcement of environmental laws, regulations, and policies. EPA has this goal for all communities and persons across this nation. It will be achieved when everyone enjoys the same degree of protection from environmental and health hazards and equal access to the decision-making process to have a healthy environment in which to live, learn, and work (Environmental Protection Agency, 2018).

Background of the Environmental Justice Movement

Public awareness about environmental protection heightened in the United States in the late 1960s, prompting the need for more stringent environmental legislation. Because industries were not responding to their social obligations to protect the environment, grievances gave rise to public policy through environmental legislation and regulations. The EPA was created in 1970, and it is the primary governmental agency that recommends policies for environmental protection and enforces environmental laws and regulations (Cheek, Crow, & Hartman, 1995).

The environmental movement of the 1960s and 1970s focused on resource conservation, pollution abatement, and water standards, and it was largely a concern of middle- and upper-class Whites (Bullard, 1994). During this time, low-income and minority members had minimal involvement in the environmental movement. As a result, there was less attention paid to these communities regarding environmental issues. With time, these residents began to notice that their communities contained a disproportionate share of environmental burdens such as hazardous waste facilities or excessive air pollution.

The EJ movement unofficially began in 1982 when hundreds of people were arrested for protesting a landfill in Warren County, a predominantly African American region of North Carolina. Warren County was chosen as a site for PCB-contaminated soil that had been illegally dumped along the highway of 14 different North Carolina counties in 1978. Over 30,000 gallons of PCB-contaminated oil had been left on a stretch of highway spanning over 200 miles, constituting one of the largest PCB spills in U.S. history. It took the federal EPA and the state of North Carolina four years to clean up this spill, and the remains were deposited in Warren County (Bullard, 1994).

During the Warren County protests, civil rights leaders, elected officials, and environmental activists joined grassroots groups and local residents to oppose the landfill. Although these protests did not stop the siting of the landfill, they raised national awareness that certain communities were facing excessive environmental burdens, and they helped put EJ on the map. They also led countless scholars to conduct studies on EJ issues, most of which found disparities based on race or income.

Federal Response to Environmental Justice Concerns

As support for the EJ movement continued to grow and research continued to suggest environmental disparities, the government responded with initiatives to remedy these inequities. In 1992, the EPA published *Environmental Equity: Reducing Risks for All Communities*, recognizing that certain communities faced greater amounts of environmental burdens than others. Specifically, this report found that minority and lower-income populations exhibited greater exposure to hazardous waste facilities, air pollution, and other toxins (U.S. EPA, 1992). This report was noteworthy because it was the first time the EPA publicly acknowledged there were environmental disparities in certain communities.

As a result of this report, the EPA created the Office of Environmental Equity in 1992, later renamed the Office of Environmental Justice. This office takes EJ issues into consideration in the implementation of the EPA's policies and programs. Additionally, President Bill Clinton signed Executive Order No. 12,898 (1994), "Federal Actions to Address Environmental Justice in Minority Populations and Low-Income Populations," which focused attention on achieving environmental protection for all communities. This order required federal agencies to develop strategies to remedy any class-based or race-based inequities in their programs or policies (Executive Order No. 12898, 1994).

Furthermore, Executive Order No. 12898 (1994) reinforced Title VI of the Civil Rights Act of 1964, which states that "no person in the United States shall, on the ground of race, color, or national origin, be excluded from participation in, be denied the benefits of, or be subjected to discrimination under any program or activity receiving federal financial assistance" (Civil Rights Act of 1964). Consequently, the EPA has adopted regulations to inhibit discriminatory practices in violation of Title VI.

Environmental Justice Policies in Massachusetts

Article 97 of the Constitution of the Commonwealth of Massachusetts states that

> The people shall have the right to clean air and water, freedom from excessive and unnecessary noise, and the natural, scenic, historic, and esthetic qualities of their environment; and the protection of the people in their right to the conservation, development and utilization of the agricultural, mineral, forest, water, air and other natural resources is hereby declared to be a public purpose.

As a result of the heightened awareness of EJ issues nationwide and the fact that the right to a healthy environment is stated in the Constitution of the Commonwealth of Massachusetts, there was a need to create a statewide EJ Policy. In 2002, the Executive Office of Energy and Environmental Affairs (EEA) created such a policy to help address environmental disparities existing in lower-income and minority communities. Because many of these communities lack the resources to foster a healthy environment, this policy helps ensure they are protected from environmental harms. Furthermore, this policy also enhances the environmental quality of these neighborhoods by investing in additional urban parks and green spaces (Commonwealth of Massachusetts, n.d.e).

The EEA's policy considers EJ populations as neighborhoods that meet at least one of the following criteria (Executive Office of Environmental Affairs, 2002):

- Median household income is at or below 65% of the statewide median income,
- 25% of the residents are minority,
- 25% of the residents are foreign born, and
- 25% of the residents lack English language proficiency.

It is important to identify EJ populations because the residents of these communities often face barriers to participating in environmental decision-making, including lack of financial resources, unfamiliarity with issues, and language barriers. To help these communities, the EEA has taken a number of steps, including EJ training, developing EJ outreach teams, creating EJ maps, increasing public participation programs, targeting inspection and enforcement efforts, increasing funding, and continuing brownfield revitalization. All of these steps have been helpful in ensuring that everyone has access to a clean environment (Executive Office of Environmental Affairs, 2002).

Finally, there have been some recent efforts to enhance EJ in Massachusetts. In 2014, former Governor Deval Patrick issued Executive Order No. 552 (2014), "Executive Order on Environmental Justice," expanding upon the requirements of the EJ policy of 2002. As a result of this order, the entire executive branch in Massachusetts, not just environmental agencies, is now required to promote EJ in their policies and practices. Consequently, the secretariats of each agency in the executive office are obliged to develop strategies to advance environmental justice and to work closely with the director of EJ within the EEA.

In addition, this order established an EJ advisory council to advise the governor and EEA secretary on environmental justice policies and practices. Furthermore, EEA was required to update its EJ policy from 2002, guaranteeing equal enforcement for facilities in EJ communities, ensuring brownfield remediation in EJ communities, and creating an online EJ repository with the commonwealth's initiatives so that the public can be informed.

Legalization of Marijuana in Massachusetts

Massachusetts is one of eight states and the District of Columbia to have legalized the use of recreational marijuana. Voters in Massachusetts had previously decriminalized marijuana in 2008 and had voted to legalize it for medicinal purposes in 2012 (Miller, 2016a). But in November 2016, the results of Ballot Question 4 indicated that 53.6% of the voters chose to legalize the use of recreational marijuana for adults 21 and older in Massachusetts (The Boston Globe, 2016).

The Governor's Council certified the results of a ballot question in December of 2016 and the state treasurer appointed a Cannabis Control Commission to regulate the marijuana industry within the state (Miller, 2016a). This commission began issuing provisional retail licenses to marijuana dispensaries across Massachusetts beginning in July of 2018. However, the regulators must still inspect the dispensaries before they can begin sales (DeCosta-Klipa, 2018, August 15).

Moreover, while it is now legal to buy up to one ounce of marijuana in Massachusetts from a dealer, the dealer is still breaking the law. Selling marijuana outside of the regulated market remains a crime punishable by up to two years of incarceration and a $5,000 fine (Miller, 2016b).

There are also other provisions related to the new marijuana legislation. Adults 21 and over can now legally purchase accessories for marijuana. According to the ballot measure, this includes equipment for growing, storing, ingesting, and inhaling marijuana (The Boston Globe, 2016). Furthermore, adults 21 and over can grow up to 6 plants in their home, with a maximum of 12 plants per household (Miller, 2016a).

Although it has now been legalized, people still cannot use marijuana in public, and it is still illegal to drive under the influence of marijuana (Miller, 2016a). Furthermore, colleges have the right to ban the use of recreational marijuana, even for students 21 and older (The Boston Globe, 2016). Finally, it is still illegal to possess marijuana under federal law, and individuals could still be prosecuted under federal law (Miller, 2016a). Consequently, it is important for individuals in states that have legalized the use of recreational marijuana to abide by the regulations set forth by their state.

Conclusion

After reading this chapter, you should be more familiar with some of the challenges facing the criminal justice system in the new millennium. Although law enforcement, the courts, and corrections will always be the backbone of the criminal justice system, our world is continually evolving. As a result, members of the criminal justice system must respond to these changes by keeping up-to-date with technology and being prepared for the latest challenges. By keeping up-to-date with these challenges, we will be better equipped to prevent crimes from happening in the first place.

Key Terms

Copyright: Form of protection granting individuals who have created original work, including literature, music, and art, exclusive rights, to its use and distribution.

Cyberbullying: Bullying through technology or electronic means.

Cybercrime: Criminal activity involving the Internet, a computer system, or computer technology.

Cyberstalking: Criminal practice in which a person uses the Internet to harass or threaten someone. Cyberstalking can be perpetrated through social media, chat rooms, instant messaging, email, or any other type of online medium.

DNA Analysis: Identification of a person based on a sample of his or her DNA.

Environmental Justice: Fair treatment and involvement of all people regardless of race, color, national origin, or income with respect to the development, implementation, and enforcement of environmental laws, regulations, and policies.

Exonerate: To free from blame.

Forensics: Application of science to help in investigating crimes.

Hate Crime: Traditional crime motivated by bias.

Identity Theft: Theft of personal information such as name, date of birth, social security number, or driver's license number.

Injunction: Legally enforceable civil order issued by the court prohibiting a perpetrator from committing specified actions.

Related Websites

Innocence Project
http://www.innocenceproject.org/

Massachusetts Environmental Justice Policy
https://www.mass.gov/environmental-justice

Massachusetts State Police Crime Laboratory
http://www.mass.gov/eopss/law-enforce-and-cj/criminal-investig/crime-lab/

Review Questions

1. What challenges do cybercrimes pose for law enforcement?

2. What is the significance of the Massachusetts Civil Rights Act regarding cybercrimes?

3. What is cyberbullying?

4. What is the importance of the Cybercrime Strategic Plan?

5. How do forensics aid law enforcement?

6. Why is DNA analysis superior to fingerprint identification for helping to solve crimes?

7. Why is it important to compensate people who have been wrongfully convicted?

8. Explain the concept of environmental justice.

9. What steps did the federal government take to incorporate environmental justice into its policies?

10. How does the EEA define an environmental justice population?

11. What is the significance of Executive Order 552?

References

The Boston Globe. (2016, December 12). *Here's what you can—ad cannot—do when pot becomes legal Thursday*. Retrieved from https://www.bostonglobe.com/metro/2016/12/12/here-what-you-can-and-cannot-when-pot-becomes-legal-thursday/zXhyt6uDx365NPRaNCJjCL/story.html?p1=Article_Inline_Bottom.

Bullard, R. D. (1994). *Dumping in Dixie: Race, class, and environmental quality*. Boulder, CO: Westview Press.

Cheek, R., Crow, S., & Hartman, S. (1995). Environmental apocalypse now: Environmental Protection Agency policies as threats to the environment. *Industrial Management, 37*(3), 6–11.

Civil Rights Act of 1964 §6, 42 U.S.C §2000d (1964)

Commonwealth of Massachusetts. (n.d.a). *Cyber crime initiative*. Retrieved from http://www.mass.gov/ago/public-safety/cybercrime-and-internet-safety/cybercrime-initiative/.

Commonwealth of Massachusetts. (n.d.b). *Cyber stalking*. Retrieved from http://www.mass.gov/ago/public-safety/cybercrime-and-internet-safety/cybercrimes/cyberstalking.html.

Commonwealth of Massachusetts. (n.d.c). *Bullying and cyberbullying*. Retrieved from http://www.mass.gov/berkshireda/crime-awareness-and-prevention/bullying-and-cyberbullying/bullying.html.

Commonwealth of Massachusetts. (n.d.d). *Forensic biology sections*. Retrieved from https://www.mass.gov/service-details/forensic-biology-sections.

Commonwealth of Massachusetts. (n.d.e). *Environmental justice policy*. Retrieved from https://www.mass.gov/service-details/environmental-justice-policy.

Commonwealth of Massachusetts. (n.d.f). *Hate crimes, racism, and hate websites*. Retrieved from http://www.mass.gov/ago/public-safety/cyber-crime-and-internet-safety/cyber-crimes/hate-crimes-racism-and-hate-websites.html.

Commonwealth of Massachusetts. (n.d.g). *Illegal downloads, copyright, file sharing, and piracy*. Retrieved from http://www.mass.gov/ago/public-safety/

cybercrime-and-internet-safety/cybercrimes/illegal-downloads-copyright-file-sharing-and-.html.

Commonwealth of Massachusetts. (n.d.h). *Massachusetts State Police Crime Laboratory*. Retrieved from https://www.mass.gov/orgs/massachusetts-state-police-crime-laboratory.

Commonwealth of Massachusetts. (n.d.i). *The Cyber Crime Division*. Retrieved from http://www.mass.gov/ago/bureaus/criminal/emcc/the-cyber-crime-division/.

DeCosta-Klipa, N. (2018, August 15). What we know about the marijuana dispensaries poised to open in Massachusetts. Retrieved from https://www.boston.com/news/local-news/2018/08/15/recreational-marijuana-dispensaries-massachusetts.

Environmental Protection Agency. (2018). *Environmental justice*. Retrieved from http://www.epa.gov/environmentaljustice/.

Executive Office of Environmental Affairs. (2002). *Environmental justice policy*. Boston, MA: Author.

Exec. Order No. 552 (2014)

Exec. Order No. 12898, 3 C.F.R. (1994)

Federal Bureau of Investigation. (n.d.). *Hate crimes*. Retrieved from https://www.fbi.gov/investigate/civil-rights/hate-crimes.

Foreign Intelligence Surveillance Act, 50 U.S.C. 1802 (1978)

Gaines, L. K., & Miller, R. L. (2014). *Criminal justice in action: The core* (7th ed.). Boston, MA: Cengage Learning.

Innocence Project. (n.d.a). *Our work*. Retrieved from http://www.bls.gov/oes/current/oes339021.htm#st.

Innocence Project. (n.d.b). *The cases: DNA exoneree profiles*. Retrieved from http://www.innocenceproject.org/cases-false-imprisonment/front-page#c10=published&b_start=0&c4=Exonerated+by+DNA&c5=MA.

Innocence Project. (2009, December 2). *Making up for lost time: What the wrongfully convicted endure and how to provide fair compensation*. Retrieved from https://www.innocenceproject.org/executive-summary-making-up-for-lost-time-what-the-wrongfully-convicted-endure-and-how-to-provide-fair-compensation/.

Massachusetts Constitution (Article 97). (2018). Retrieved from https://malegislature.gov/Laws/Constitution.

MGL c.71 §370

MGL c.265 §39

MGL c.265 §43

MGL c.266 §37E

MGL c.266 §143E

Miller, J. (2016a, December 14). *It's official: Marijuana is legal in Massachusetts. The Boston Globe*. Retrieved from https://www.bostonglobe.com/metro/2016/12/14/official-marijuana-legal-midnight-massachusetts/10Rl2inZQMj-SPrNAMSBkCJ/story.html.

Miller, J. (2016b, December 13). With pot law, Mass. enters legal gray zone. *The Boston Globe*. Retrieved from https://www.bostonglobe.com/metro/2016/12/13/with-legal-marijuana-massachusetts-state-enters-hazy-legal-gray-zone/jLjYVpIvgevl28jidQQWtO/story.html?p1=Article_Inline_Bottom.

Office of Attorney General Martha Coakley. (2007). *The Massachusetts Strategic Plan for Cyber Crime*. Boston, MA: Author.

The Boston Globe. (2016, November 16). Massachusetts ballot questions, 4—Legalize marijuana. Retrieved from https://www.bostonglobe.com/elections/2016/MA/Question/4%20-%20Legalize%20Marijuana?p1=BG_election_full_results.

U.S. Environmental Protection Agency. (1992). *Environmental equity: Reducing risk for all communities*. Washington, DC: Author.

Glossary

Actus Reus: "Wrongful act."

Aggravated Assault: Unlawful attack by one person upon another for the purpose of inflicting severe or aggravated bodily injury.

Aggravated Assault and Battery: Assault and battery in which the victim sustains a serious bodily injury.

Aggravating Circumstance: Circumstance that increases the seriousness of a given crime, increasing the offender's punishment.

Al-Qaeda: A global network of jihadists, with a central headquarters in the Pakistan-Afghanistan region and several affiliate groups in the Middle East, North Africa, and Southeast Asia.

Anarchist: Followers of a political ideology that calls for replacing formal nation states with an informal, local collaborative decision-making process.

Anthony Burns: A fugitive slave from Virginia whose Boston trial attracted national attention and ignited riots and protests in Boston. Burns was the last escaped slave in the United States to be returned to the South under the Fugitive Slave Act.

Anti-Abortionist Violence: Attacking an abortion clinic, or staff who work there, in order to compel other clinics to close out of fear.

Appellate Jurisdiction: Authority of a court to review decisions and change outcomes that were decided in a lower court.

Armed Robbery: The crime of taking money or property from a person by means of force and the use of a deadly weapon.

Arraignment: Criminal proceeding in which a judge informs the defendant of the charges against him, and the defendant enters a plea of guilty, not guilty, or no contest.

Arson: The criminal act of deliberately setting fire to a building or property.

Assault and Battery: Combination of assault (threat of violence) and battery (physical violence).

Bail: Monetary amount set as a condition of pretrial release to ensure the return of the accused at subsequent proceedings.

Bellino and Gertson: Philip Bellino and Edward Gertson were the last people to be executed in Massachusetts. They were executed in the electric chair at the Charlestown State Prison on May 9, 1947.

Bench Trial: Trial in which a judge determines the guilt or innocence of a defendant without a jury.

Black Lives Matter: Chapter-based national organization working for the validity of Black lives.

Body Camera: Video recording system used by law enforcement to record their interactions with the public.

Booking: Procedure by which law enforcement record details of an arrest and charges against a suspect, including the crime for which the arrest was made, information used to identify the suspect, and other pertinent facts related to the arrest.

Boston Police Strike: A work stoppage conducted by the police in an attempt to improve wages and working conditions for patrolmen and recognition for its trade union.

Breach of Contract: Violation of a provision in a legally enforceable contract, allowing the injured party the right to remedy the matter in a court of law.

Brief: Written legal argument, stating the legal reasons in support of a party's position or appeal based on statutes, case precedents, and reasoning applied to the facts in the particular situation.

Burglary: Breaking and entering of a home at night with the intent of committing another felony.

Challenge for Cause: Request that a potential juror be dismissed because there is reason to believe he cannot serve as a fair and impartial juror.

Charles Street Jail: also known as the *Suffolk County Jail*, located at 215 Charles Street in the old West End of Boston, operated from 1851–1990.

Charlestown State Prison: A state-run correctional facility in the Charlestown section of Boston from 1805 to 1955 and was the location of the last execution in the state.

Child Abuse: Physical, emotional, or sexual maltreatment of children.

Child Neglect: Form of child abuse in which the child is denied necessities, including food, shelter, care, and love.

Circumstantial Evidence: Evidence presented in a criminal trial that permits conclusions indirectly establishing the existence or nonexistence of a fact.

Civil Commitment: Legal process through which an individual is deemed to have symptoms of psychiatric disease and is court ordered into treatment in a mental institution, correctional facility, or the community.

Civil Law: Branch of law pertaining to suits outside of criminal practice; pertains to rights or people in contract, tort, or real estate law.

Civil Liberties: Basic rights and freedoms guaranteed to American citizens that the government cannot take away.

Civil Process: The handling and serving of legal and court documents, including summons, subpoenas, and restraining orders.

Cleared by Arrest: Refers to crimes that are solved by law enforcement.

Commonwealth Fusion Center: *A statewide collaborative effort of several agencies who share resources, expertise, and information with the goal of maximizing the ability to detect, prevent, apprehend, and respond to criminal and terrorist activity.*

Community Corrections: Correctional supervision of offenders within the community as an alternative to incarceration.

Copyright: Form of protection granting individuals who have created original work, including literature, music, and art, exclusive rights to its use and distribution.

Correctional Officer: Individual responsible for overseeing people who have been sentenced to serve time in jail or prison.

Correctional System: Institutions and methods used to punish, control, and change the behavior of convicted offenders.

Counterterrorism: Political or military activities designed to prevent or thwart terrorism.

Crime Control Model: Criminal justice model that emphasizes the right of society to be protected from crime and criminals.

Crime Rate: Ratio of crimes in an area to the population of that area; often expressed per 1,000 or 100,000 persons.

Crime Trend: Change in the nature of selected crime types within a specified geographical area and time period.

Criminal Justice System: set of agencies and processes that the government establishes to control crime and penalize people who have violated the law.

Criminal Law: Statutes that define conduct prohibited by government because the conduct threatens or harms public safety and welfare; also establishes punishment to be imposed for commission of such acts.

Cross-Examination: Process whereby an attorney interrogates witnesses of the opposing side during a criminal trial.

Cyberbullying: Bullying through technology or electronic means.

Cybercrime: Criminal activity involving the Internet, a computer system, or computer technology.

Cyberstalking: Criminal practice in which a person uses the Internet to harass or threaten someone. Cyberstalking can be perpetrated through social media, chat rooms, instant messaging, email, or any other type of online medium.

Dark Figure of Crime: Crimes that are not reported to police.

Deadly Force: Force applied by a police officer that is likely to cause death.

Defendant: Person or entity accused of a crime in a criminal prosecution.

Defense Attorney: Attorney who represents the defendant in a criminal trial.

Deliberation: Phase of a criminal trial at which the jury meets in private to discuss the evidence presented in court to decide whether a defendant is guilty or innocent.

Deterrence: Use of punishment as a threat to deter people from offending.

Direct Examination: Questioning of one's own witness during a trial.

Directed Verdict: Right of a judge to direct a jury to acquit a defendant because the state did not prove the elements of the crime or has not established guilt according to law.

Discretion: Ability of people in the criminal justice system to make decisions based on personal judgment instead of formal rules.

District Attorney: Attorney who represents the Commonwealth of Massachusetts in a criminal trial.

Diversion Program: Provides first-time nonviolent offenders the opportunity to receive services in lieu of being prosecuted through the traditional court process.

DNA Analysis: Identification of a person based on a sample of his or her DNA.

Do It Yourself Terrorism: A type of terrorist attack in which the perpetrator(s) have no operational or financial ties with a known terrorist group.

Domestic Violence Shelters: Places where victims of domestic violence can live for several months while they receive help for their abuse.

Dual Court System: Administratively separate court systems in the United States, consisting of the federal courts and the state courts.

Due Process Model: Criminal justice model that emphasizes the right of the individual to be protected from the power of the government.

Enact: To establish by law.

Environmental Justice: Fair treatment and involvement of all people regardless of race, color, national origin, or income with respect to the development, implementation, and enforcement of environmental laws, regulations, and policies.

Ethnonationalism: An ideology associated with terrorist groups that use violent attacks in order to create an independent geopolitical entity based on ethnic identity.

Exonerate: To free from blame.

Federalism: Division of power between federal and regional governments.

Felony: Serious crime for which a person may be imprisoned for over one year.

Forcible Rape: Natural or unnatural sexual intercourse by force and against the will of the victim.

Forensics: Application of science to help in investigating crimes.

Fugitive Slave Act of 1850: A law that compelled Northern citizens to cooperate with Southern masters in reclaiming their runaway slaves.

General Deterrence: Theory of punishment in which the law seeks to deter the public from engaging in criminal acts.

General Jurisdiction: Power of a court to hear any type of case that arises within its geographical area.

Grand Larceny: Theft of property with a value exceeding $250.

Hate Crime: Traditional crime motivated by bias.

Hierarchy Rule: The Uniform Crime Reports (UCR) requires counting only the highest offense and ignoring the others.

Homeland Security: National efforts to prevent terrorism within the United States and to reduce the nation's vulnerability to terrorism.

Homicide: Killing of a human being.

House Arrest: State of being confined to one's home as a sentence as an alternative to incarceration.

House of Correction: A term that is synonymous for a jail in Massachusetts.

Hung Jury: Trial jury selected to make a decision in a criminal case regarding a defendant's guilt or innocence, which cannot reach a verdict due to divisions in opinion.

Identity Theft: Theft of personal information such as name, date of birth, social security number, or driver's license number.

Ideology: An articulation of grievances and an argument for how those grievances should be remedied.

Incapacitation: Philosophy that crime can be prevented by detaining criminals in prison to physically separate them from the community, reducing criminal opportunities.

Indigent Defendant: A defendant who cannot afford a private defense attorney.

Injunction: Legally enforceable civil order issued by the court prohibiting a perpetrator from committing specified actions.

Intake: Process by which an official of the court decides whether to file a petition, release the juvenile, or place the juvenile under another form of supervision.

Intelligence: Information a government collects about an enemy or possible enemy, including criminals and terrorists.

Intermediate Sanctions: Sanctions that are more restrictive than probation and less restrictive than imprisonment.

Involuntary Manslaughter: Unintentional killing of another person as the result of wanton or reckless conduct.

Islamic State: A violent jihadist group that wants to establish an Islamist caliphate that would rule over all Muslims.

Jail: Facility operated at the county level, used to hold people awaiting trial or those who have been found guilty of misdemeanors.

John Augustus: A Boston area bootmaker who was the first person to supervise a probationer and is credited with being the father of probation.

Joint Terrorism Task Force: A team of investigators, analysts, linguists, SWAT experts, and other specialists from dozens of U.S. law enforcement and intelligence agencies who work together on terrorism-related investigations and threat analysis.

Judicial Waiver: Process in which the juvenile judge, based on the facts of the case, determines that the accused juvenile should be transferred to adult court.

Jurisdiction: Power to govern an area.

Jury Trial: Judicial proceeding to determine a defendant's guilt or innocence by a body of persons sworn to render a verdict based on law and evidence.

Just Deserts: Punishment that is deserved.

Juvenile Court: Court with original jurisdiction over people statutorily defined as juveniles and assumed to be delinquents or status offenders.

Juvenile Delinquency: Participation in illegal behavior by minors.

Larceny-Theft: Unlawful taking of property from the possession of another person.

Leaderless Resistance: A concept promoted by White supremacist Louis Beam in 1983 as a method of encouraging individuals, unaffiliated with any established organization, to attack the federal government.

Left-Wing Extremism: A category of utopian ideologies associated with Marxist communism and revolutionary activity.

Lex Talionis (the law of talion): A retaliation authorized by law in which the punishment corresponds in kind and degree to the injury.

Lifestyle Theory: Model of victimology that posits that the likelihood an individual will be victimized depends upon the concept of lifestyle.

Malcolm X (Malcolm Little): an outspoken leader of the Nation of Islam and an influential Black leader who served a 7-year sentence in the Charlestown State Prison for burglary.

Malice Aforethought: Intention of killing or harming another human being.

Manslaughter: Unlawful killing of another person without malice.

Massachusetts General Laws: Statutes of the Commonwealth of Massachusetts that have been codified.

Massachusetts Trial Court Probation Service: More commonly referred to as the **Massachusetts Probation Service** is the commonwealth's primary supervisory law enforcement agency.

Maximum Security Prison: A correctional facility designed to control dangerous felons and prevent escapes.

Medium Security Prison: A correctional facility that houses less dangerous inmates and uses less restrictive measures to prevent violence and escapes.

Mens Rea: "Guilty mind" or criminal intent.

Metropolitan Police Act: An 1829 law that stablishing the first organized police force in London.

Minimum Security Prison: A correctional facility designed to allow inmates who pose a low security threat to have contact with the outside world.

Misdemeanor: Less serious offense, punishable by a fine or imprisonment up to one year.

Mitigating Circumstance: Information about the defendant that does not justify or excuse a criminal act but which may lessen the defendant's degree of culpability.

Motor Vehicle Homicide: Homicide resulting from the negligent operation of a motor vehicle.

Motor Vehicle Theft: Criminal act of stealing a motor vehicle.

Municipal: Relating to a city or town or its governing body.

Murder/Nonnegligent Manslaughter: Willful killing of one human being by another.

Nonstate Actors: Entity that plays a role in international affairs but does not represent an established state or nation.

Opinion: Legal document stating the reasons for a judicial decision.

Original Jurisdiction: Authority of a court to hear a case for the first time.

***Parens Patriae*:** Latin term that means "parent of the country." Philosophy that government is responsible to look after children and to assume the role of parent when needed. It is the duty of the state to act in the best interest of children until they reach the age of majority.

Parole: Conditional release of an inmate before his sentence has expired.

Parolee: An individual released on parole.

Part I Index Crimes: Eight crimes (murder/nonnegligent homicide, rape, robbery, aggravated assault, burglary, motor vehicle theft, larceny-theft, and arson) that are reported to the UCR program.

Peremptory Challenge: The dismissal of a potential juror by the prosecution or defense for unexplained reasons.

Petty Larceny: Theft of property valued at less than $250.

Plea Bargain: Agreement between the prosecution and defense in which the accused agrees to plead guilty to a lesser charge or to a particular sentencing recommendation.

Premeditation: Deliberate plan to commit a crime.

Prerelease Facility: A type of correctional facility that provides a gradual transition from prison life to the community by means of reintegration through releases to work or educational programs.

Prison: A place of confinement for persons convicted of serious crimes.

Private Investigator: Person hired by individuals or corporations to undertake investigatory law services.

Probable Cause: Evidence discovered through logical inquiry that would lead a reasonably prudent person to believe an accused person has committed a crime warranting prosecution.

Probation: Criminal sanction in which a convicted offender is allowed to remain in the community as an alternative to incarceration.

Probation Officer: Individual who supervises offenders who are on probation.

Probationer: A convicted offender on probation.

Prosecutorial Waiver: Procedure used in circumstances when a prosecutor has discretion to decide whether a case will be heard in a juvenile court or an adult court.

Procedural Law: Law regulating governmental procedure.

Proof Beyond a Reasonable Doubt: Standard that must be met by the prosecution in a criminal proceeding. No other logical explanation can be derived from the facts except that the accused committed the crime.

Property Crimes: In the UCR, property crimes include burglary, larceny-theft, motor vehicle theft, and arson. The object of these offenses is taking money or property, but there is no threat of force against the victims.

Prosecutorial Waiver: Procedure used in circumstances when a prosecutor has discretion to decide whether a case will be heard in a juvenile court or an adult court.

Rape: Penetration of the vagina or anus with any body part or object, or oral penetration by a sex organ of another person, without the consent of the victim.

Rape Crisis Centers: Community-based organizations that help victims of rape, sexual abuse, and sexual violence.

Real Evidence: Evidence that is tangible and can physically be brought into the courtroom for the judge and jury to see.

Reasonable Force: Degree of force appropriate to protect a police officer or other citizens.

Recidivism: Refers to a person's relapse into criminal behavior after receiving a sanction or undergoing an intervention for a previous crime.

Referral: Notification process through which a police officer or other concerned citizen makes the juvenile court aware of a minor's unlawful or unruly conduct.

Rehabilitation: The process of improving a criminal's character so he will become a productive member of society.

Reintegration: Goal of corrections that focuses on preparing the offender for a successful return to the community without reoffending.

Restitution: One of the penalties imposed on offenders that requires the returning of stolen goods to the victim or payment to the victim for harm caused.

Restorative Justice: Theory of justice that emphasizes repairing the harm caused by criminal behavior.

Retribution: Punishment inflicted on someone as vengeance for a criminal act.

Right-Wing Extremism: A category of ideologies characterized by nationalism and racism, and embraced by several militia groups and others in the United States.

Robbery: Taking or attempting to take anything of value from another person with the use of force or the threat of force and putting the victim in fear.

Routine Activities Theory: Theory that crime is the result of three elements: motivated offenders, suitable targets, and a lack of capable guardians.

Sacco and Vanzetti: In a widely celebrated and controversial case, Nicola Sacco and Bartolomeo Vanzetti were convicted of murder in 1921, sentenced to death, and executed in a case in which many believe they were wrongly convicted.

Sanction: Penalty for disobeying a law or rule.

Sir Robert Peel: Known as the father of modern policing, introduced the Metropolitan police act in 1829, establishing a modern police force in London.

Social Control: Enforcement of conformity by society upon its members, by law or social pressure.

Sovereign Citizen: A leaderless movement in the United States whose adherents claim the government is illegitimate and has no legal jurisdiction over their actions.

Special Police Officer: A specially trained, licensed security officer, hired by private companies or public agencies, who underwent special training under the supervision of the Massachusetts State Police or Boston Police Department.

Specific Deterrence: Method of punishment intended to discourage criminal behavior in a specific individual charged with a crime.

Status Offender: Juvenile who has engaged in behavior deemed unacceptable for persons under a statutorily define age.

Statutory Exclusion: Process by which a juvenile is transferred to adult court as a matter of state law.

Statutory Rape: The unlawful sexual intercourse or unnatural sexual intercourse and abuse of a child under 16 years of age.

Subject Matter Jurisdiction: Power of a court over the nature of a case and the type of remedy sought.

Substantive Law: Law that defines criminal offenses and specifies punishments.

Sworn Police Officer: Police officer who has been sworn in under oath and has the authority to arrest citizens and carry a firearm.

Terrorism: Use or threat of violence to achieve political or social objectives.

Testimonial Evidence: Evidence obtained from a witness who makes a sworn statement or declaration of fact about a criminal case.

Tort: A wrong other than a breach of contract, whereby the remedy is a civil suit for damages.

Troop: Assignment areas for police in the Massachusetts State Police.

Unarmed Robbery: The crime of taking money or property from a person by means of force but without the use of a deadly weapon.

Uniform Crime Reporting (UCR) Program: Official data on crime in the United States, published by the Federal Bureau of Investigation (FBI).

USA Patriot Act: Legislation passed after the 9/11 terrorist attacks that increased the ability of law enforcement to investigate suspected terrorists.

Use of Force: Amount of effort required by police to compel compliance by an unwilling subject.

Venire: The panel of prospective jurors from which a jury is selected.

Verdict: Formal decision made by a jury concerning the questions submitted to it during a trial.

Victim: An individual who suffers physical, emotional, or financial harm as the result of a crime.

Victim Compensation: Payments or reparations made to a crime victim by the state for their crime-related losses.

Victim Impact Statement: Written or oral statement made as part of the judicial process, allowing crime victims to speak during the sentencing of their offender.

Victim Precipitation: Role of the victim in provoking or encouraging criminal behavior.

Violent Crimes: The FBI's UCR considers four offenses to be violent crimes—murder/nonnegligent manslaughter, rape, robbery, and aggravated assault. Violent crimes involve force or the threat of force.

***Voir Dire*:** The process by which prospective jurors are questioned by counsel and the court before being selected to serve on a jury.

Voluntary Manslaughter: Intentional killing of a human being without malice and usually happening during the heat of passion.

William Cloran Training Academy: A training academy for special police officers in Boston.

Index